The Media and the Law

edited by
Howard Simons
Joseph A. Califano, Jr.

Published in cooperation with
the Washington Post Company

The Praeger Special Studies program —
utilizing the most modern and efficient book
production techniques and a selective
worldwide distribution network—makes
available to the academic, government, and
business communities significant, timely
research in U.S. and international economic, social, and political development.

✓ KF4770.A75 F7   Free Speech + Assoc.
JC591 US M83   Meaning free speech
KF2750.A7F73   1st Amend 4th Estate
KE4714 A98 — Can (Canad) + 1st Amend
KF4300.D43   Banned films

The Media and the Law

edited and with
an introduction by
Howard Simons
Joseph A. Califano, Jr.

Praeger Publishers   New York   London

Praeger Special Studies in U.S. Economic, Social, and Political Issues

Library of Congress Cataloging in Publication Data
Main entry under title:

The Media and the law.

(Praeger special studies in U.S. economic, social, and
political issues)
Under the sponsorship of the Washington Post and the Ford
Foundation, representatives of the media and the law hold discus-
sions with government officials on three hypothetical cases.
Includes index.
1. Press law—United States.   2. Confidential communications—
Press—United States.   3. Journalistic ethics—United States.
I. Simons, Howard.   II. Califano, Joseph A., 1931-
III. Washington Post.   IV. Ford Foundation.
KF2750. M4   343'. 73'0998   75-19822
ISBN 0-275-55820-7
ISBN 0-275-89530-0 (student ed.)

PRAEGER PUBLISHERS
200 Park Avenue, New York, N.Y., 10017

Published in the United States of America in 1976
by Praeger Publishers
A Division of Holt, Rinehart and Winston, CBS, Inc.

89   038   98765432

Printed in the United States of America

For Tod and For Trudy

Because some deeply concerned and influential reporters, editors, government officials, and attorneys recognized that the sound and the fury of their dialogue surrounding the law and the media had reached alarming and discordant crescendos, a remarkable and unprecedented event took place over the weekend of March 7-9, 1975. Top journalists, jurists, lawyers, and government appointees joined together at the Homestead in Virginia to participate in the Washington Conference on the Media and the Law sponsored by the Washington *Post* and the Ford Foundation. They struggled with the most troublesome First Amendment problems, argued, tested the high ground of principle against the erosive force of real world legal and journalistic practice, agreed to disagree, sometimes even agreed, and learned more about each other than most had ever known before.

Unlike most conferences, there were no long speeches. No papers were issued for comment. Participants were presented with the three hypothetical cases, published for the first time in this book. Each case is designed to raise the issues that currently confront the judiciary, the government, and the journalists.

Case I raises issues relating to national security, the methods by which the press gathers information, and the role of the courts in assessing the competing claims of national security and the public's right to know.

Case II raises issues relating to rights of privacy, libel, the public's access to the media, and, again, the methods by which information to be published is gathered.

Case III raises the issues surrounding the judicially sanctified nature of grand jury proceedings, gag orders, and whether it is appropriate for the media to put cash on the line for news stories.

The cases were presented by two professors from the Harvard Law School: Charles Nesson and Arthur Miller. Professor Nesson presented Cases I and III; Professor Miller, Case II.

The conferees—both participants and observers—were not academicians. Listed on pages xiii-xvi of this book, they are men and women whose daily

---

*Professor Albert Sachs, Dean of the Harvard Law School, prepared Case III, but was unable to present it at the Conference.

work brings them in intimate contact with the intractable issues these cases raise. Among the conferees were a Supreme Court Justice, the Chief Judge of the Court of Appeals for the Fourth Circuit, several federal appellate and district judges, the Solicitor General of the United States, the Director of the Central Intelligence Agency, the Deputy Assistant Secretary of Defense for International Security Affairs, the United States Attorney for the State of Maryland, a former Assistant Attorney General in charge of the Criminal Division (who in private practice has been one of Richard Nixon's attorneys), a former Attorney General and Undersecretary of State, and a former FBI Director, as well as attorneys who represent media clients.

From the journalism side, the executive editors of the Washington *Post* and *U.S. News and World Report*, the editor of the Chicago *Tribune*, the Washington Bureau Chief of *Newsweek*, columnists for the *Wall Street Journal* and the New York *Times*, the White House correspondent for the Baltimore *Sun*, and several other editors and reporters were present. Television news experience was provided by Daniel Schorr and Fred Graham of CBS, Frank Reynolds of ABC, and Jim Lehrer of the National Public Affairs Center for Television.

The conference was not designed to achieve agreement or recommend sweeping proposals for the future. Its purpose was to make judges, executive branch officials, and lawyers more aware of the problems of editors and reporters, and journalists more sensitive to the views of the judges, lawyers, and bureaucrats. During the course of the conference—as this book dramatically reveals—it became clear that there was not only a difference in the way in which issues were characterized, but a disturbing and dangerous lack of understanding of the day-to-day processes by which each profession attempts to exercise its rights and fulfill its responsibilities.

On the whole, the journalists were essentially insensitive to rights of privacy, the rights of the accused in criminal cases, and the right of the government to preserve national security secrets. The jurists invoked their responsibility to sit in judgment on individual rights as a source of omniscient power that entitled their activities in courtrooms to immunity from public scrutiny not available to any other segments of American society, and vested their orders with an absolutism they denied journalists under the First Amendment. Government executives, while skeptical of the fairness, accuracy, and First Amendment claims of the press, were for the most part more sensitive to free-press values in practice than their colleagues in the judicial branch.

The level of discussion during the consideration of these three cases was sophisticated, generally well informed, and highly articulate. At times the discussion was emotional, but the emotions were founded in strongly held and often thoughtful principle. The atmosphere was electric, not because of occasional outbursts, but because issues were joined by the best and the brightest of each profession. That, unfortunately, is not the way these issues are considered in most courtrooms and newsrooms in America.

The editors of this book have a natural bias. One of us is the Managing Editor of the Washington *Post*, a provocative newspaper pressing the frontier on many of these issues. The other is an attorney, a large part of whose private practice in recent years has been spent representing the Washington *Post* and other media clients on the types of issues discussed at the Homestead Conference. We reveal these prejudices so that there can be no question about the empirical footing of the introductory essay that follows. In that essay we attempt to set forth issues of consuming interest in the clash between the jurists and the journalists, and the numerous questions that must be faced by reporters, jurists, attorneys, and, in the last analysis, the American people, who must judge, as they read their daily newspapers and watch their evening television news shows, why—indeed, whether—the special rights that the framers of the First Amendment granted to the press in these United States are essential to the conduct of the affairs of the nation as it enters its third century.

Some procedural notes are in order. A list of participants and observers at the Homestead Conference precedes the transcript of the discussion of the three cases. But in the text of the dialogue, participants in the discussion are identified only as "judge," "editor," "reporter," "lawyer," etc. Prior to the conference, all participants and observers agreed that the views expressed would not be attributed to specific individuals. This was considered essential to a candid discussion, particularly with respect to judges who must decide so many of these issues. The objective was achieved. There were no holds barred in the discussion of the three cases. As conference observer and Washington *Post* ombudsman Charles Seib wrote (Washington *Post*, March 29, 1975):

> The press and the law confronted each other in the Virginia mountains a few weeks ago. It was eyeball to eyeball and sometimes claw to claw. Both sides survived with convictions and prejudices intact for the most part, but with sensitivities raised.

The transcripts of the dialogue are substantially accurate reflections of what was said and argued at the Homestead. There has been some editing to make points clearer, to explain references so that the reader can easily follow the discussion, to disguise the identities of the speakers, and to eliminate redundancy.

Only the professors are named on the transcript pages. Their questions and comments do not necessarily express their personal views. They are expert in the use of the Socratic method as a discussion and teaching device. Their questions, their short jabs, and their gasping reactions are designed to sharpen issues, to force the judges, journalists, lawyers, and bureaucrats to think through to logical conclusion and full ramification the positions they take during the conference. That the professors succeeded is apparent in a reading of the discussions. As Charles Seib also wrote (Washington *Post*, March 29, 1975):

> At the end, there was a sense of exhaustion; the Socratic method is draining for those who participate and even for those who watch. There was also evident a sense of mutual understanding and respect among the participants—perhaps partly the camaraderie of people who have gone through a difficult experience together. As they departed the Homestead, a neutral observer might have observed that the press was waving the First Amendment just a bit less defiantly and that the judges had lowered slightly, but not furled, their restraining orders. But the lawyers who attended had no reason to fear a drying up of First Amendment litigation in the months and years ahead. The Homestead conference . . . [was] only the beginning in what must be a long dialogue before there is any broad understanding between the judiciary and the press.

ACKNOWLEDGMENTS

We are indebted to the Washington *Post* and the Ford Foundation for the opportunity to edit this extraordinary dialogue among editors, reporters, judges, high government officials, and lawyers.

A special measure of our appreciation goes to John B. Kuhns, an unusually brilliant and energetic young attorney, who provided research and editorial assistance in the preparation of the essay and the editing of the three case discussions. Mr. Kuhns' legal expertise and wise counsel were invaluable.

Finally, we are grateful for the good-natured secretarial help of Evelyn Furgerson, Virginia Johnson, and Pamela Whitehead.

Of course, we alone bear responsibility for the contents of the introductory essay and for the editing of the conference transcript.

CONTENTS

034997

THE WASHINGTON CONFERENCE
ON THE MEDIA AND THE LAW:
PARTICIPANTS AND OBSERVERS

PARTICIPANTS

George Beall, Esq.
U.S. Attorney for the
   District of Maryland

Robert H. Bork
The Solicitor General

Benjamin C. Bradlee
Executive Editor
Washington *Post*

Adam Clymer
White House Correspondent
Baltimore *Sun*

William E. Colby
Director
Central Intelligence Agency

Lyle W. Denniston
Supreme Court Reporter
Washington *Star*

Mel Elfin
Washington Bureau Chief
Newsweek

Margaret Gentry
Reporter
Washington Bureau
Associated Press

Seymour Glanzer, Esq.
Dickstein, Shapiro & Morin
Former Assistant U.S. Attorney

Fred Graham
News Correspondent
Columbia Broadcasting System

Meg Greenfield
Deputy Editorial Page Editor
Washington *Post*

Barry Hager
Reporter
Washington Bureau
Time Magazine

Clement F. Haynsworth, Jr.
Chief Judge
U.S. Court of Appeals
   for the Fourth Circuit

Amos Jordan
Deputy Assistant Secretary of
   Defense (International
   Security Affairs)

Nicholas de B. Katzenbach, Esq.
IBM Corporation
Formerly Attorney General of
   the United States and
   Undersecretary of State

Clayton Kirkpatrick
Editor
Chicago *Tribune*

James C. Lehrer
Senior Correspondent
National Public Affairs
    Center for Television

Harold Leventhal
Judge
U.S. Court of Appeals for the
    District of Columbia Circuit

Robert R. Merhige, Jr.
Judge
U.S. District Court for the
    Eastern District of Virginia

Herbert J. Miller, Jr., Esq.
Miller, Cassidy, Larroca & Lewin
Formerly Assistant Attorney
    General (Criminal Division)

Charlotte Moulton
Supreme Court Reporter
United Press International

Ronald J. Ostrow
Reporter
Washington Bureau
Los Angeles *Times*

Alan Otten
Columnist
Wall Street Journal

Frank Reynolds
News Correspondent
American Broadcasting Company

Harry M. Rosenfeld
National Editor
Washington *Post*

William Ruckelshaus, Esq.
Ruckelshaus, Beveridge
    & Fairbanks
Formerly Director,
    Federal Bureau of Investigation
    and Deputy Attorney General

Daniel Schorr
News Correspondent
Columbia Broadcasting System

Marvin Stone
Executive Editor
U.S. News & World Report

Malcolm R. Wilkey
Judge
U.S. Court of Appeals for the
    District of Columbia Circuit

OBSERVERS

Floyd Abrams, Esq.
Cahill, Gordon & Rendel

Robert E. L. Baker
Deputy Managing Editor
Washington *Post*

Joseph A. Califano, Jr., Esq.
Williams, Connolly & Califano
Formerly Special Assistant
    for Domestic Affairs to
    President Lyndon B. Johnson

James Clayton
Editorial Writer
Washington *Post*

Norman Davis
Deputy General Manager
Post-Newsweek Stations
    Florida, Inc.

Leonard Downie
Assistant Managing Editor/
    Metropolitan News
Washington *Post*

Alan R. Finberg, Esq.
General Counsel
Washington Post Company

Fred W. Friendly
Professor of Journalism
Columbia School of Journalism
    and Vice-President, the
    Ford Foundation

David Ginsburg, Esq.
Ginsburg, Feldman & Bress

Katharine Graham
Publisher
Washington *Post*

Henry Goldberg, Esq.
General Counsel
Office of Telecommunications
    Policy

James C. Goodale
General Counsel
New York *Times*

John Kuhns, Esq.
Williams, Connolly & Califano

Jack Landau
Supreme Court Correspondent
Newhouse News Service, and
    Trustee, Reporters Committee
    for Freedom of the Press

Anthony Lewis
Columnist
New York *Times*

Linda Mathews
Reporter
Washington Bureau
Los Angeles *Times*

Robert Maynard
Editorial Writer
Washington *Post*

Lesley Oelsner
Supreme Court Reporter
New York *Times*

Dan Paul, Esq.
Paul and Thomson
Miami, Florida

John H. Pickering, Esq.
Wilmer, Cutler & Pickering

Richard M. Schmidt, Jr., Esq.
Counsel, American Society
    of Newspaper Editors

Charles Seib
Ombudsman
Washington *Post*

Howard Simons
Managing Editor
Washington *Post*

The Media and the Law

INTRODUCTORY ESSAY:
THE JURISTS AND
THE JOURNALISTS

The judiciary and the press are institutions pedestaled in fragile loneliness by the Constitution. Neither has the power to execute or legislate. Neither has an army, police force, or extensive bureaucracy to enforce its rulings or its editorials. The judiciary gains vitality from individual jurists; the press from individual journalists.

The judiciary is constitutionally established as a separate branch of government. Nevertheless, it is dependent upon the executive for enforcement of its rulings and orders and on the legislature for funds to carry out its work and for a definition of the jurisdictional limits of its power.

The press is enshrined as independent of all branches—and levels—of government. The First Amendment is sparsely straightforward: "Congress shall make no law . . . abridging . . . the freedom of the press. . . ." Most journalists interpolate "the government" for "Congress" and read the prohibition absolutely; most judges are intellectually tortured by perceived ambiguity. Journalists prefer to read the First Amendment in vacuumed isolation; judges weigh its forbidding mandate against other rights and duties set forth in the Constitution. Journalists believe the First Amendment places them in a constitutionally elite class; judges tend to remind journalists that they are citizens just like every other American.

Washington *Post* Executive Editor Benjamin C. Bradlee and Supreme Court Justice Potter Stewart provide the point-counterpoint. Bradlee put it this way in a commencement address at Franklin and Marshall College on June 2, 1974:

Journalists like to believe that it is no accident that the First Amendment comes first, that all constitutional rights depend on the right to know, and that the right to know depends on a free press.

1

Justice Stewart preferred this characterization in a 1974 address to the Yale Law School:

> So far as the Constitution goes, the autonomous press may publish what it knows and may seek to learn what it can.
>
> But this autonomy cuts both ways. The press is free to do battle against secrecy and deception in government. But the press cannot expect from the Constitution any guarantee that it will succeed.

For the Supreme Court Justice, "The Constitution . . . establishes the contest, not its resolution." For the newspaper editor, the First Amendment declares the press the winner. The journalist may reluctantly admit that the Supreme Court Justice has the better of this argument. But not without pointedly, sometimes caustically, noting that the judges have arrogated to themselves the roles of both participant and umpire.

The dispute is not without irony. The central foundation of support for the rulings of the judiciary is the people. That support can be most effectively achieved through the media, in contemporary times particularly television. Such a condition might be thought to lead to a level of cooperation between those in the courtroom who interpret the laws and those in the newsroom who write about the conduct of the public business.

More than any branch of government or private institution (with the possible exception of the church), the judges and the journalists depend on moral suasion for effective institutional survival. During the early 1970s these were the constitutional pillars of American society. They remained independent and strong in the face of a national executive paralyzed by corruption and paranoid suspicion, and a national legislature fragmented by special interests, frustrated by inordinate delay, and abused by individual political ambition. If any segments of society deserve accolades for the demise of Richard M. Nixon and the cleansing of a corrupt executive, they are the judiciary and the journalists. Judge John Sirica and publisher Katharine Graham are heroic figures in the national drama of Watergate—and neither could have played the part alone.

Despite such convincing recent historical evidence, the clash between jurist and journalist is more serious than at any time in recent memory. Its persistent escalation threatens our society. What should be a coherent dialogue more nearly resembles a Tower of Babel in which judges and journalists do not even seem to be speaking the same language. The ancient dispute between the First Amendment right to publish and the Sixth Amendment right to a fair trial—the so-called free press-fair trial debate—has recently been conducted with a vengeance. The press calls the current symptom of this constitutional collision "gag" orders; the word "gag" is pithy, highly descriptive, threatening, and pejorative. The judges call such orders "protective" or "restraining"; the words are dignified, just, somber, and paternalistic. The judges inveigh against invasions of privacy; the journalists charge "cover-up" in their headlines about Wilbur Mills at the Tidal Basin and Edward Kennedy at Chappaquiddick. The judges weigh the justification for secrecy in terms of national security; the press, skeptical as always, talks about the right of the public to know. Judges often characterize confidential sources in the national security area as criminals; journalists tend to think of them as heroes.

Judges and journalists do not believe each other's rhetoric. The words one speaks are not the sounds the other hears. Judges declare that the right to publish news also includes the right to gather news; journalists dismiss such judicial pronouncements as rhetorical hypocrisy each time a reporter is held in contempt of court for failure to disclose a confidential source. Judicial opinions condemn prior restraints as unconstitutional under the First Amendment; but journalists tremble with rage—and fear—as "gag" orders clatter like hobnailed boots across newspaper rooms in New Orleans, Washington, and New York and echo through the halls of book publishing houses. Investigative reporters and editorial writers expose and condemn violations of law and white-collar crime; but judges are appalled at their defiance of court orders and their vicarious theft of documents. Major newspapers vehemently attack virtually any judicial approval of presidential assertions of executive privilege; but they demand the untrammeled right of a newsman's privilege to protect their confidential sources.

The First Amendment has become a hair shirt for a large segment of American society, including not only public officials but also private individuals who feel that the press violates their privacy and who confuse the messenger with the maker of bad news. It is probably true, as Chief Justice Earl Warren remarked about the Bill of Rights in St. Louis, Missouri, on February 19, 1955, that the First Amendment would never be adopted in Bicentennial America. That attitude may provide a significant insight as to why First Amendment decisions of the Supreme Court of the United States are so little understood and so parsimoniously applied in the lower federal, state, and county courts across our nation.

For example, in a county court case involving a libel suit about a school board official, the judge remarked from the bench when counsel cited *New York Times v. Sullivan,* 376 U.S. 254 (1964), "the New York *Times* is not printed in this county." In the Southwest, a federal district judge refused to dismiss a libel suit allegation that did not even plead fault, as required by the Supreme Court in *Gertz v. Welch,* 418 U.S. 323 (1974). The judge was not sure what *Gertz* held, and his comments from the bench revealed that he probably had not read and certainly did not understand the case before entering his courtroom.

This disparity between the lofty pronouncements of the highest court of the nation and the actions and rulings of lower federal, state, county, and city courts is even wider than the gap between the encyclicals of the Pope and the activities of millions of Roman Catholics throughout the world. Perhaps such disparities are endemic to the conduct of human affairs. Perhaps a sophisticated analysis of treasured rights of free speech, free press, and free association cannot be translated into everyday actions by hundreds of judges across our nation, some able, others inept; some honest, a few corrupt.

But surely, judges can try harder. For the implications are profound for American democracy. If a man's judgment is only as good as the facts before him, then in a representative democracy it is essential that the people be informed. What information is of public importance? What price is too high to pay to provide such information to the people? Who decides—and how—what information is of such critical national security importance that the people have no right to know it, because there is no way to inform the citizenry of an open society, without informing the enemies of that society? Do journalists have any special status in society that permits them to "steal" public documents, or harass individuals who become inadvertently and involuntarily swept up in public events? The question could be put: "What price freedom?" But that question would be understood in two different contexts by most journalists and most judges in this nation. Where the public's right to know confronts the individual's right to privacy or the state's right to security, even the questions may not be subject to general agreement.

Yet these questions arise in a context of First Amendment principles that have long been enunciated. The Supreme Court has consistently recognized that the basic concern underlying the First Amendment's protection of freedom of the press is society's interest in preserving the free flow of information to the public, so that the people in a democratic, one-man, one-vote society may have the opportunity to be well informed and therefore able to participate intelligently in the political process. In *Associated Press v. United States*, 326 U.S. 1, 20 (1944), the Court observed, "[The First] Amendment rests on the assumption that the widest possible dissemination of information from diverse and antagonistic sources is essential to the welfare of the public, that a free press is a condition of a free society." And in *Garrison v. Louisiana*, 379 U.S. 64, 74-75 (1964), the Court declared that "speech concerning public affairs is more than self-expression; it is the essence of self-government."

Journalists are important; but their special status derives from the right of the people. For the journalists hold the public's right-to-know hat in their right-to-print hand. As James Madison wrote, "A popular government without popular information or the means of acquiring it is but a prologue to a farce or tragedy or perhaps both." 6 *Writings of James Madison* 298 (Hunt ed. 1906).

Journalists and jurists often intone these kinds of quotes when they speak about a free press. But do they mean the same thing? Most reporters take an essentially absolutist view. They believe that any publication in this nation—from a mimeographed one-pager to a pornographic magazine to a metropolitan daily to a television network—is free to publish whatever it learns, so long as the writers and editors honestly believe that what they have learned is true. There

are, of course, self-imposed limitations. Most publications have their own standards of taste and fairness. They will not knowingly publish false information or
material that will endanger human life. They recognize that there can be and are
legitimate national secrets.

But self-imposed standards can be lowered in self-interest. Most journalists
point out that the metropolitan dailies and suburban weeklies where they work
will not publish information that would endanger a human life, but they defend
the right to publish such information without going to jail for violating espionage
laws. Most journalists argue that it is the function of the government to keep its
national secrets, but they believe that a reporter with the milk to lure a national
secret cat out of the government bag and into his newsroom has the right to
publish what he discovers. In effect, the journalists say, *we and we alone* should
make the decisions as to what and when to publish.

The judges give the journalists plenty of ammunition with which to support
their view. Here is one jurist:

> In the First Amendment the Founding Fathers gave the free press
> the protection it must have to fulfill its essential role in our democ-
> racy. The press was to serve the governed, not the governors. The
> government's power to censor the press was abolished so that the
> press would ever remain free to censure the government and inform
> the people. Only a free and unrestrained press can effectively expose
> deception in government. . . .

Here is another:

> Security also lies in the value of our free institutions, a cantankerous
> press, an obstinate press, a ubiquitous press must be suffered by
> those in authority in order to preserve the even greater values of
> freedom of expression and the right of the people to know. . . .

The first quote is from Supreme Court Justice Hugo Black, perhaps the
most eloquent exponent of the absolutist view of the First Amendment ever to
sit on or off the bench. The second is from Judge Murray Gurfein of the U.S.
District Court for the Southern District of New York. Both are excerpts from
opinions rendered during the Pentagon Papers case, in which the first government-
requested and judicially sanctioned prior restraint was imposed on American
newspapers.

Despite the restraints imposed on the Washington *Post* and New York
Times during the collision between the government and the press over the
Pentagon Papers, journalists tend to read such judicial language through their
absolutist First Amendment glasses. This, of course, is a source of friction
between the courtroom and the newsroom.

But the absolutist view of the First Amendment is not the only gasoline poured on the fire that rages between journalists and jurists. News stories are often incomplete. Sometimes they are inaccurate. Reporters and editors can be captives of pseudo-events staged for their benefit. Too frequently daily journalism is practiced the way the State Department conducts too many diplomatic relations, with a crisis mentality and a crisis response. Some of these problems attend the human condition: People who know do not speak, at least not soon enough; people who think they know tell only part of the story; some lie, others obfuscate, all try to protect their own interest. Other problems stem from institutional limitations of newspapering: the daily component of daily journalism; the pressure of space limitations in increasingly expensive newsprint; the different metabolisms, skills, sources, and perceptions of individual editors and reporters.

Particularly daily journalism, but weekly journalism and television specials as well, is at best a quick glance of history on the run. Nevertheless, without such journalism, the citizen would not be sufficiently informed to intervene, on a timely basis, in the processes that determine his or her life, or his or her livelihood. Without such journalism, deception—call it Watergate, Vietnam, or Central Intelligence Agency excesses—would succeed and democracy indeed would be short-lived.

Judges have their own special problems. They treasure their own privacy, particularly during deliberations. Steeped in the concept that they only decide the cases and controversies to come before them, they tend to prefer individual rights over the rights of institutions like the press. They are particularly concerned when reporters begin investigating the judicial and criminal justice process, especially as it affects grand and petit jury deliberations. Judges tend to distrust the imprecise way in which newspapers write about facts, and they contrast the care with which facts are proven in a courtroom or pleadings are drafted in a lawsuit. Most importantly for this discussion, rare is the judge who in his constitutional heart considers the First Amendment preeminent. Much more than journalists, jurists are conscious of the other amendments to the Constitution—the Sixth Amendment right to a fair trial, the Fifth Amendment right to be protected against self-incrimination, and the Ninth Amendment from which the embryonic constitutional right of privacy springs.

GAG ORDERS

Like two heavyweight boxers with glass jaws, the courts and the media for a good part of our history finessed most direct confrontations on First Amendment issues. In recent years, however, they seem almost to have sought opportunities to take each other's measure in the constitutional ring. The gloves come off most often in the series of bouts over gag orders.

Highly publicized criminal cases have always raised fair-trial questions in the minds of defense counsel seeking an acquittal, prosecutors seeking a conviction, and judges who are often deeply concerned about the rights of the accused, particularly with sensitive appellate courts looking over their shoulders. Until the early 1970s the consequences of contemporaneous and pretrial publicity were for the most part balanced against the right of a fair trial for the defendant on an informal scale gingerly held by judges and journalists. Except in the most egregious cases—like the sensational 1954 trial of Dr. Sam Shephard in Cleveland where the courthouse took on a "carnival atmosphere" or the Billie Sol Estes trial where television cameras were permitted in the courtroom—jurists and journalists warily relied on each other's discretion and good judgment to resolve the issue of free press versus fair trial. By and large newspapers were careful as to what they printed about the prior record of an accused defendant du..ng a trial. Judges kept their admonitions to the press low-key and informal. Studies—dominated by judges and lawyers like the Reardon and Kaufman reports—proposed rules designed to strike a balance between the competing interests.

Then came Watergate. Prior to the trial of the Watergate burglars, Judge John Sirica issued a sweeping gag order which, on its face, applied even to presidential candidate George McGovern during his 1972 campaign. Within 48 hours, however, Judge Sirica limited his gag order to parties, witnesses, and attorneys before the court and called in the press informally to urge them to exercise restraint.

Then came the case of *United States v. Dickinson,* 465 F.2d 496 (5th Cir. 1972). In Baton Rouge, Louisiana in 1971 a state grand jury indicted Frank Stewart, a black VISTA worker, for conspiring to murder a state official. Stewart asked the federal court in New Orleans to enjoin state prosecution, claiming that Louisiana officials were interfering with the VISTA program. During the federal hearing on his request for an injunction, U.S. District Judge E. Gordon West pronounced from the bench:

> At this time, I do want to enter an order in the case, and that is in accordance with this court's rule in connection with Fair Trial-Free Press provisions, the Rules of this court.
>
> It is ordered that no report of the testimony taken in this case today shall be made in any newspaper or by radio or television, or by any other news media. . . .

Larry Dickinson, an experienced court reporter of the Baton Rouge *State Times,* consulted with his publisher, editors, and lawyers. Together, they decided that he should defy the order. In a routine and restrained manner, Dickinson reported what happened in the open courtroom, including Judge West's gag order. It was a single-column story, placed on the inside pages of the afternoon newspaper. The next morning, the same story was reported by Gibbs Adams of the *Morning Advocate*.

On the following day, Judge West closed the courtroom, but continued the hearing. He also issued an order to show cause why newspapermen Dickinson and Adams should not be held in contempt of court. A week later, Judge West found both reporters in criminal contempt for writing their news stories in violation of the original order he had issued. He fined them $300 each.

Dickinson and Adams appealed the decision to the Fifth Circuit Court of Appeals. *Nine* months later, that court declared the order of Judge West to be an unconstitutional prior restraint on freedom of the press. In the appellate court's words, Judge West's order could not "withstand the mildest breeze from the First Amendment." But in the ruling that shocked journalists across the nation, the Fifth Circuit also held that the reporters were obliged to obey the order until it was reversed, despite its patent unconstitutionality. The case was returned so Judge West could determine whether to hold the reporters in contempt. Judge West reaffirmed the original fine of $300.

Reporters Dickinson and Adams promptly appealed. The Fifth Circuit affirmed the imposition of the penalty, despite the unconstitutionality of the order entered by Judge West. This occurred on April 9, 1973, a full 17 months after Judge West originally prohibited reporting what had occurred in an open courtroom. During this interim, all the charges against the original defendant, Frank Stewart, were quietly dropped.

Dickinson has set a chilling tone. Former CIA agent Victor Marchetti's book on the CIA fought its way through the Northern Virginia Federal District Court which held that almost all of what the CIA proposed deleting could be published. The district court stayed its order pending appeal, and the Fourth Circuit left this prior restraint in effect for over ten months before announcing its decision to place the burden of proving the right to publish on the author. *Alfred A. Knopf, Inc. v. Colby*, 509 F.2d 1362 (4th Cir. 1975). The Supreme Court implicitly approved this unprecedented ruling by refusing to review the case in late May 1975.

During early 1975, another book on the CIA was banned; a two-year ban was placed on a psychiatric book and broad orders barring news media access to or coverage of public court trials were issued in New Orleans, Louisiana; Providence, Rhode Island; Boston and New Bedford, Massachusetts; Tucson, Arizona; Macon, Georgia; San Bernardino, Fresno, and Los Angeles, California; Fort Lauderdale, Florida; Boise, Idaho; Greenville, Mississippi; New York City; Harrisburg, Pennsylvania; Prince George's County, Maryland; and the District of Columbia.

Judges have great difficulty trying to explain why court orders subsequently held to be unconstitutional have to be obeyed under pain of punishment in the form of fine and/or imprisonment. What, journalists ask, is the distinction between a court order and a legislative act? Martin Luther King and black and white Americans across the South sat-in at lunch counters in violation of segregated accommodations laws to force the issue of their constitutionality. As those laws fell before the Equal Protection Clause of the Constitution, the courts made it abundantly clear that no punishment could be imposed on those who defied the unconstitutional statutes. Why then, ask journalists, are patently invalid court orders so precious that their violation justifies punishment?

For their part, journalists tend to stammer in responding to the repeated queries of judges as to what is so important about time. Why must a news story be printed on the following day? Why cannot the news media wait until after the trial is over before reporting on its most salient aspects?

The journalists counter: If a judge feels that an unusual case cannot be fairly tried with contemporaneous newspaper publicity, then he should sequester the jurors. After all, it is the jurors who must make the objective judgments.

Sequestration is a difficult and troublesome tool, respond the judges. It is expensive, but most important, sequestration can put the jurors in a frame of mind that can make a fair trial difficult to achieve.

Journalists have yet to convince judges of the overriding constitutional significance of time. Nevertheless, recent First Amendment cases should give judges some sense of how deeply reporters and editors feel about time, of the competitive aspects of daily journalism, and of why, on the whole, the rhetoric of the Supreme Court abhors prior restraints. Journalists jousting with jurists on these issues should get some appreciation of the need some courts have for adequate time to assess the issues before them. From the beginning of the Pentagon Papers litigation, for example, New York *Times* lawyers recognized that one of their greatest difficulties in convincing the courts to act promptly was that *Times* reporters and editors had worked secretly for months in preparing the stories that raised issues they then asked the courts to resolve in hours. The other side of the judicial coin is the *Marchetti* case, where the Fourth Circuit lingered for more than ten months, secure in its prior restraint.

Recognizing the reality that judges are likely to face situations in which they consider restraining orders necessary, we submit that the following suggestion deserves consideration by the bench:

No gag orders should be issued against the press. In the unusual circumstances in which such orders are necessary, they should be limited to the parties before the court, attorneys representing those parties and court officials, and all other individuals subject by tradition, law, and their profession to the core power of the court. As the Sixth Circuit has recently recognized, the press should have the right to challenge such gag orders.* Under no circumstances should the press be subjected to contempt for publishing information obtained from someone subject to such judicial restraints. Where the press does challenge gag orders, the courts should be required to act within days to resolve the issues raised.

This latter suggestion places a heavy burden on the judiciary to act promptly. This will not be easy, for judges tend to operate in an environment of deliberate—sometimes tedious—care; they hold in high regard those values, like precision and thoughtfulness, that encourage delay. Nevertheless, First Amendment considerations appear of sufficiently signal importance for the judiciary to devise special and expedited procedures in those cases in which a judge considers the use of gag orders essential to the constitutional security of the criminal justice system.

Our proposal is consistent with the warning of the Federal Judiciary Committee report that precipitated the guidelines of most federal courts in this area. That report recognized the pernicious nature of the contempt power in these circumstances. The Committee chairman, Second Circuit Chief Judge Irving Kaufman, warned that the use of such power in First Amendment situations "is both unwise as a matter of policy and poses serious constitutional problems."

The continuing dialogue on the gag order issue has been inconclusive. But it has revealed that judges tend to proffer unsatisfactory answers to the journalists' question: What makes jurists so special, so royal, so sovereign that they can sit as both judge and jury over violations of their own orders, and that even when those orders are patently unconstitutional, journalists can be required to obey them under penalty of fine or imprisonment. At the same time, the journalists have left much to be desired in their attempt to enshrine the urgency and immediacy of daily journalism as a preeminent constitutional value. On the whole, however, judges and journalists can come much closer to agreement in dealing with this issue. We hope both will at least experiment with our proposal.

CONFIDENTIAL SOURCES

Remember Marie Torre?

In the late 1950s, superstar Judy Garland sued CBS for libel based on a gossip column comment Marie Torre reported and attributed to an anonymous

---

*In *Columbia Broadcasting System v. Young*, No. 75-1646 (6th Cir. July 2, 1975), the court held that CBS had standing to challenge a gag order addressed to court personnel, counsel, parties, and their relatives, close friends, and associates. The court determined that the gag order was unconstitutional because it was not supported by evidence indicating that publicity would cause a clear and imminent danger to the fair administration of justice.

Columbia Broadcasting System executive. The identity of the source was crucial to Judy Garland's case. Only if the source were a CBS executive would Ms. Garland have had an action against the network and its deep pocket. After lengthy consideration and analysis, the court ordered New York *Herald Tribune* reporter Torre to disclose her source.

The Court of Appeals for the Second Circuit noted that the identity of the source "went to the heart of the plaintiff's claim" since that would determine whether CBS could be held liable. The court's holding was in a context where disclosure was considered essential to establishing or dismissing a cause of action. *Garland v. Torre,* 259 F.2d 545 (2d Cir.), *cert. denied,* 358 U.S. 910 (1958). As the result of that decision Marie Torre went to jail. But she never revealed the source.*

Remember who wrote the opinion in the Torre case?

Then Judge—now Mr. Justice—Potter Stewart.

The same Potter Stewart who wrote what journalists regard as a brilliant dissent in the decision that ignited the confidential source issue for a new generation of journalists—the Supreme Court case of *Branzburg v. Hayes,* 408 U.S. 665 (1972). *Branzburg* was in reality three cases:

Branzburg. A staff reporter for the *Courier Journal* in Louisville, Kentucky, wrote two articles on drug usage in which he described in detail his observations of individuals smoking marijuana and making hashish. When called before a county grand jury, Branzburg refused to reveal the names of the individuals he had witnessed violating federal and state drug laws.

Pappas. A Massachusetts television newsman gained entrance to the local Black Panther party headquarters during a time of serious civil disturbances in New Bedford, Massachusetts. When called before a county grand jury investigating the disturbances, Pappas refused to appear and answer any questions about the actions and statements of individuals he had observed while inside the party headquarters.

Caldwell. The New York *Times* reporter assigned to cover the Black Panther party and other black militant groups refused to appear before the federal grand jury investigating possible criminal conduct of Black Panther party members, including threats of presidential assassination, interstate travel to incite riot, and mail fraud, all federal crimes.

The Supreme Court held that the First Amendment did not protect Branzburg from testifying about "criminal conduct which he had observed." Pappas and Caldwell could not refuse to appear before the grand jury, the Court said, specifying the issue of appearance in those two cases as "the only question presented at the present time." None of the three reporters has to this day appeared before the grand juries that precipitated the landmark decision; two were not even sought by those grand juries after the decision.

---

*As of this writing, Ms. Torre is a popular TV personality in Pittsburgh.

The majority opinion had the verbatim support of four Justices (White who authored it, Burger, Blackmun, and Rehnquist); four Justices dissented (Douglas, Stewart, Brennan, and Marshall), and Mr. Justice Powell wrote such a decidedly narrow concurring opinion essential for the majority of five that the *Branzburg* decision has been characterized as 4½ to 4½.

The majority was deeply troubled about leveling testimonial requirements upon reporters. The source of the trouble for the majority was their unequivocal conviction that "without some protection for seeking out the news, freedom of the press could be eviscerated." All nine justices stood behind this proposition. The minority four believed that under the First Amendment news gathering is such an essential corollary to the right of the press to publish and of the public to be informed that reporters should not have to testify even before grand juries under the limited circumstances of *Branzburg, Pappas,* and *Caldwell.* Justice Powell's separate opinion emphasized that only in severely restricted situations could reporters be required to testify before grand juries. He stressed that competing interests must be evaluated on a case-by-case basis, and that the courts will always be available to protect the First Amendment interest in news gathering in other factual contexts.

The nine justices, so obviously troubled about the application of First Amendment dogma in the *Branzburg* cases, might well have shared another concern—whether orders to disclose confidential sources are enforceable, or whether they will amount to little more than a series of judicial, antipress Volstead acts.

The often unspoken, but nonetheless sacred, pledge of every journalist is this: "I will go to jail before revealing the identity of anyone who tells me something confidentially." This moral code is in the heart, mind, and blood of every good journalist. Indeed, the very fact that people have this impression of journalists—that they will go to jail to protect their sources—has brought a wealth of news tips to newspapers and television stations across this nation and profoundly affected the course of story telling and news reporting. Unless their need to protect confidential sources is given the sacrosanct status accorded the rights of priests to withhold what penitents tell them in the confessional, of doctors to honor their patient privileges, of lawyers to honor their client privileges, reporters and editors are convinced that the free flow of information to them will slowly diminish and eventually newspapers will be printing public relations handouts and press releases. As far as the journalist is concerned, without this protection lives and livelihoods of news sources would be jeopardized. Put bluntly, only the very dumb or the eternally secure would come forward to offer material to the press that, by its nature, will upset those in power or those who have power over them.

Any number of reporters have attested, in a variety of lawsuits, to the importance of confidential sources:

● Jack Anderson, the syndicated columnist and Pulitzer Prize winner, stated that he would not have been able to break the International Telephone &

Telegraph corporate financing scandal without the benefit of confidential sources; that such sources were critical in his stories concerning the top hard-drug trafficker in the Western Hemisphere who was eventually returned to the United States for criminal prosecution; and that such sources were essential in his series of columns on the new wave of payola—drugs and prostitution—in the broadcast industry.

• Clark R. Mollenhoff, former White House counsel and Washington Bureau Chief of the Des Moines *Register and Tribune,* noted that confidential sources were essential for various books that he has written on government and corruption, as well as numerous stories involving county welfare frauds, organized crime, corruption in state government, James Hoffa, Senate aide Bobby Baker, and the Pentagon TFX investigation.

• Haynes Johnson, a national reporter for the Washington *Post* and a Pulitzer Prize winner for the Washington *Evening Star,* has stated that his reporting during the 1960s on civil rights activities at Selma and elsewhere in the South would not have been possible without assurances of confidentiality to his frightened sources.

• Michael Causey, who writes "The Federal Diary" column for the Washington *Post,* relies critically on confidential sources for his daily column reporting on the activities of the federal bureaucracy. Most of his sources demand the promise of confidentiality and this assurance was essential in stories he broke on payroll errors, corruption in the Postal Department, improper hiring procedures, and Blue Cross overcharges.

• Frances Barnard, the Washington correspondent for the Fort Worth *Telegram,* considers information obtained through confidential sources essential to her stories about discriminatory hiring practices in the U.S. Congress. Those articles prompted a change in the House rules to prohibit discrimination in hiring.

Such sources are also critical for stories on local corruption.

• Robert Dudney, a star reporter for the Dallas *Times Herald,* has attested that without information obtained from confidential sources, he would never have been able to write articles about irregularities in the Dallas County Sheriff's bail bond system, nor about stock kickback schemes involving the City of Dallas employees retirement fund which prompted a full-scale investigation by the U.S. Securities and Exchange Commission.

• Charles Kilpatrick, editor and publisher of the San Antonio *Express and News,* has stated that information obtained from confidential sources was essential to his articles exposing hidden funds in the San Antonio budget, corrupt practices by the South-Western Bell Telephone Company, and a fake portion of a CBS documentary, "Hunger in America."

Nor is it only reporters that have this sense of the critical importance of confidential sources in the flow of information to the public. In an affidavit filed in connection with Vice President Spiro Agnew's attempt to subpoena reporters to identify their confidential sources, Richard Neustadt, Professor of

Government at Harvard University, has noted that sources are critical in the explanation of public policy by governmental officials and to the flow of information to the public from government individuals:

> The class of confidential communications commonly called "leaks" play, in my opinion, a vital role in the functioning of our democracy. A leak is, in essence, an appeal to public opinion. Leaks generally do not occur in dictatorships, where public opinion is not a force that those in power must take into account. In our country, leaks commonly occur when significant questions of public policy are being decided in secret. A leak opens the decision to public scrutiny and evaluation, and brings into play the forces that act in the public forum—congressional and other agencies of government, political party organizations, interest groups and other segments of society that have a stake in the decision. If the confidentiality of communications to newsmen could not be assured, I am convinced that the number of leaks would be greatly diminished, and that our political institutions would be less subject than they are to public monitoring and public control.

Despite this eloquent historical and expert testimony, attempts by attorneys and courts to subpoena reporters to reveal confidential sources has become one of the most serious immediate problems facing the press. In the first year after the *Branzburg* decision, the Los Angeles *Times* alone spent some $200,000 in legal fees to resist such subpoenas. The Reporter's Committee for Freedom of the Press revealed that in the first three months of 1975, more than 50 subpoenas—an unprecedented high—had been issued to compel news reporters to reveal confidential news sources. By then the problem had become national in scope. During that quarter, subpoenas were served on reporters in Alabama, California, New Hampshire, New York, the District of Columbia, Ohio, Louisiana, Oklahoma, Missouri, and Washington, as well as on the three television networks.

Initially, in the wake of *Branzburg*, the subpoena problem was thought by some to be a temporary phenomenon of developing law. Now, however, it appears to be a significant part of the journalistic landscape—and will continue to be a central problem until the pernicious implications of the *Branzburg* decision are fully appreciated by the courts and a decisive Supreme Court ruling is issued. Lawyers, who are either too lazy, besieged by client complaints about skyrocketing legal fees, or tempted by the publicity given to any subpoenaed reporter by his colleagues, increasingly look to journalists to testify. They see reporters as cheap or often expert witnesses; frequently reporters can be called about an event in which they are professionally involved, sometimes as eyewitnesses.

The *Bridge* and *Farr* cases are celebrated examples of how the State courts in New Jersey and California read *Branzburg* as a license to compel disclosure of confidential sources.* Most other courts have read the Supreme Court decision narrowly. Aside from the *Bridge* and *Farr* cases, most federal and state courts that have addressed the issue whether newsmen may be ordered to disclose the identity of confidential sources have decided against compulsory disclosure.

In addition to recognizing that *Branzburg* established some First Amendment protection for seeking out the news, some federal courts have indicated that when a reporter obtains news by communicating with a person who has information to impart, that is, a source, the case involves not just freedom of the press, but also First Amendment freedom of association. See, for example, *Bursey v. United States*, 466 F.2d 1059 (9th Cir. 1972). With such an analysis, they have buttressed their inclination to protect confidential sources with the long line of cases holding that the First Amendment protects such association against unduly burdensome investigation. Recognizing that forced public revelation of the source of information or ideas can stifle speech on public affairs because of fear of retaliation or punishment, the Supreme Court has expressly held that rights of speech and association, if they are to have meaning, must often be exercised anonymously. As the Court said in *NAACP v. Alabama*, 357 U.S. 449 (1958), "Inviolability of privacy in group association may in many circumstances be indispensable to preservation of freedom of association. . . ." In deference to human nature, the court has also recognized that the mere threat of sanctions may deter the exercise of First Amendment freedoms as much as their actual application. *NAACP v. Button*, 371 U.S. 415, 433 (1963).

In *Baker v. F & F Investment Co.*, 470 F.2d 778 (2d Cir. 1972), *cert. denied*, 411 U.S. 966 (1973), Judge Irving Kaufman, writing for a unanimous three-judge panel, concluded that a writer for the *Saturday Evening Post* did not have to reveal his source, even though that source had direct knowledge of facts central to the issues of an antiblockbusting suit before the court. Neither the writer nor the publication was a party to the litigation.

In *Bursey v. United States, supra,* the Ninth Circuit held that two staff members of a Black Panther party newspaper did not have to disclose identities of persons associated with the publication to a federal grand jury investigating threats of presidential assassination and other possible criminal conduct by Black Panter party members.

In *Democratic National Committee v. McCord*, 356 F.Supp. 1394 (D.D.C. 1973), the court quashed, on First Amendment grounds, subpoenas directed to

---

*Both the *Bridge* and *Farr* courts ordered newsmen to disclose sources without applying the balancing test set forth in *Branzburg. In re Bridge*, 120 N.J. Super 460, 295 A.2d 3 (1972); *Farr v. Superior Court*, 22 Cal. App. 3d 60, 99 Cal. Rptr. 342 (1971). The Ninth Circuit recently affirmed the *Farr* decision. *Farr v. Pitchess*, No. 72-3171 (9th Cir. 1975).

members of the press, including Washington *Post* reporters Bob Woodward and Carl Bernstein. The court concluded that the plaintiff had not made the requisite "positive showing of the materiality of the documents and other materials sought by the subpoenas." 356 F.Supp. at 1398.

Similarly, in *Apicella v. McNeil Laboratories, Inc.*, Civil No. 74-635 (E.D.N.Y. Feb. 24, 1975), the court refused to order a medical newsletter to disclose its confidential sources, even though those sources possessed information relevant to plaintiff's allegations of adverse drug effects. The court reasoned that "the information sought here is relevant, but not essential to the resolution of the judiciary controversy."

In libel suits, courts have also refused on First Amendment grounds to order disclosure of a defendant's confidential news sources except in the unusual circumstances in which (a) the plaintiff has demonstrated a substantial likelihood that disclosure will lead to persuasive evidence on the issue of liability, and (b) alternative sources have been exhausted.

In *Cervantes v. Time, Inc.*, 464 F.2d 986 (8th Cir. 1972), *cert. denied*, 409 U.S. 1125 (1973), the Eighth Circuit held that a *Life Magazine* reporter did not have to reveal the confidential source of allegedly libelous statements about the organized crime connections of St. Louis Mayor Alfonso J. Cervantes. Cervantes was suing *Life* for libel. The Supreme Court declined to review this case and let the decision stand.

As this is written, only one federal appellate court has ordered a libel defendant to disclose the identity of a confidential news source. That case arose out of a Jack Anderson column reporting on the United Mine Workers and its general counsel, Edward Carey. *Carey v. Hume*, 492 F.2d 631 (D. C. Cir. 1974), *cert. dismissed*, 417 U.S. 938 (1974). The court emphasized that it was not establishing a general rule applicable to all libel defendants, but rather was limiting its decision to order disclosure to the extraordinary circumstances before it. The court ordered disclosure because the allegedly libelous statement was based *entirely* on confidential sources and the plaintiff had no way of proving either falsity or recklessness without knowledge of the identity of those sources. The court stressed its agreement with the rule applied by the Eighth Circuit in the *Cervantes* case, that a libel defendant may not be constitutionally required to disclose the identity of confidential news sources except when the information obtained from the source is the sole basis for the allegedly libelous statements. The Supreme Court never had to consider this case because the source released Anderson aide Brit Hume from his pledge of confidentiality.

Most journalists consider the subpoena issue to go far beyond confidential sources. They are concerned about revealing their notes, their methods of gathering news, and indeed any information—written material, photographs, or film—that is not actually printed in the newspaper or shown on television. A federal district court in Florida refused to allow the discovery of any materials developed in the preparation of a newspaper article, even though no confidential sources were involved. *Loadholtz v. Fields,* Civil No. 74-587 (N.D. Fla., Feb. 7, 1975). The court reasoned "that the paramount interest served by the unrestricted flow of public information protected by the First Amendment outweighs the subordinate interest served by the liberal discovery provisions embodied in the Federal Rules of Civil Procedure." Few courts have gone this far and most judges are not likely to join in the journalistic applause for this Florida federal court.

In 1971 the Justice Department under Attorney General John Mitchell issued guidelines which, if followed, sharply restrict the power of U.S. attorneys to subpoena reporters, whether or not confidential sources are involved. 28 C.F.R., 50.10 (1974). Under these guidelines, no U.S. attorney may subpoena a reporter unless he has exhausted all other possible sources of the testimony he seeks. Even in such circumstances, the U.S. attorney must first obtain the explicit permission of the Attorney General before he subpoenas the reporter. Experience with these guidelines has been mixed. As recently as late 1974, we have had experiences with some government attorneys who were not even aware of the guidelines. Nevertheless, they do stand as a formal Justice Department statement of principle and policy, initiated by an Attorney General singularly insensitive to First Amendment rights.

The problem for the press in protecting the confidentiality of its editorial processes is complicated by the special treatment it has been accorded in the libel arena since the Supreme Court decision of *New York Times v. Sullivan,* 376 U.S. 254 (1964). In that case, the Court required public officials to prove constitutional malice to prevail in a libel action, to show that the libelous material was published with knowledge that it was false or in reckless disregard of the truth. Reckless disregard of truth is defined in the *Times-Sullivan* decision to mean knowledge on the part of the writer or editor that the material published was likely false. In *Curtis Publishing Co. v. Butts,* 388 U.S. 130 (1967), the public official libel standard was extended to public figures, that is, individuals with some degree of celebrity.

More recently, the Supreme Court decided *Gertz v. Welch,* 418 U.S. 323 (1974), a libel suit brought by an attorney who was not a public official or a celebrity. He had been labeled "a communist-fronter" in *American Opinion* magazine in part because of his involvement as an attorney in a suit against Chicago police. The Court held that the constitutional malice standard of knowing falsity or reckless disregard of truth was inapplicable, since the plaintiff was neither a public official nor a public figure, even though the article discussed an issue of public interest. Nevertheless, in such cases, the court held that a private person instituting a libel action must show fault—presumably negligence—on the part of the publisher before he can obtain a judgment. The court further held in *Gertz* that private individual libel plaintiffs are limited to recovery of actual damages. Courts may not permit recovery of presumed or punitive damages, at least when liability is not based on knowledge of falsity or reckless disregard of the truth. The court broadly defined actual injury to include "impairment of reputation and standing in the community, personal humiliation, and mental anguish and suffering."

The *Times-Sullivan* and *Gertz* opinions leave much uncertain in the law of libel. Who is a public official? Who is a public figure? Is the extent to which a person becomes voluntarily, as distinguished from involuntarily, involved in an issue or event of public interest relevant in determining whether he or she is a public figure? How should corporations be characterized?

But one thing now is clear: The level of care exercised by a newspaper, magazine, or television station in preparing, writing, and presenting a story is the critical factor in determining whether it can be held liable for defamatory statements it publishes. Once that is recognized, the conflict is obvious: On the one side, reporters and editors want to protect confidential sources, to withhold notes and methods of operation, and to maintain the privacy of the editorial process; on the other, judges perceive a need to examine the editorial process to determine the level of care used in working on a particular story. How else can judges determine whether the *Times-Sullivan* standard of constitutional malice or the *Gertz* standard of negligence has been satisfied? For these standards, the judges point out, have nothing to do with the intent of editors, reporters, or publishers; they have everything to do with the state of the journalists' knowledge about the truth or falsity of the statement written about a particular plaintiff. Thus, the argument continues, judges must examine in depth the editorial processes of newspapers in order to assess their potential liability.

The Supreme Court, in easing the libel situation for the media, has created yet another problem. Journalists are likely to be extremely reluctant to permit courts and libel plaintiffs to rummage through their editorial offices and second-guess their news processes. Most editors argue that what they do and do not print are their decisions; to allow anyone to examine how they make such decisions is an invasion of their First Amendment rights. "Editing is what editors are for," said Chief Justice Warren Burger in *Columbia Broadcasting System v. Democratic National Committee*, 412 U.S. 94 (1973). If so, argue the journalists, the courts should not examine editorial processes, or review unpublished notes in the reporter's desk or television film on the cutting room floor. This arena—with the courts trying to obtain enough information to render intelligent judgments on standards of constitutional malice and fault, and the press increasingly suspicious of any intrusion into its news and film editing rooms—is certain to provide major conflict in the years ahead.

NEWS GATHERING

Most information reported in a daily newspaper or on a television news show is relatively straightforward. The sources of information are on-the-record statements by individuals, government officials, people trying to obtain good publicity, companies issuing financial statements, etc. Every good reporter recognizes his professional duty to obtain as much information as possible on the record. But at the same time, the journalist knows that he is not simply an amplifier for the press releases of institutions and individuals that believe they have something newsworthy to say.

In pursuit of the news behind such handouts—or deliberately obfuscated in their careful texts—the professional reporter seeks out many sources of information. The various journalistic devices—background, deep background, off-the-record, nonattribution—that such sources often seek to impose upon reporters are, in effect, a series of last-resort steps for the professional reporter. Experience has repeatedly demonstrated the importance of such devices, for some of the most significant stories come through their use.

Sometimes even these devices are not sufficient to elicit newsworthy information, particularly for the aggressive investigative reporter hot on the trail of official wrongdoing. What are the limits on such a journalist's right to obtain information? In his quest for facts, we believe the journalist should be free to ask any individual for information—whether he be the CIA director or a grand or petit juror during a court proceeding. The individual queried does not have to respond to the reporter's questions. Reporters should, of course, be guided not only by a sense of legality, but also by a sense of decency and ethics. Reporters should not steal information. Reporters should not commit crimes—for example, threaten blackmail—in the course of obtaining information. But like all moral codes, the statement of these general principles is far simpler than their application in the complex, harassed, and competitive life of a journalist. What is elegant in theory can be elusive in practice.

The extent to which a grand jury is subject to penetrating investigative reporting has become a fashionable subject for the lawyer and the journalist, especially since Watergate. At one time, no editor in the nation would have seriously considered violating the sanctity of the grand jury. Each grand juror wore a journalistic chastity belt. The sanctity accorded a grand jury was not a capricious act. The grand jury was originally designed to protect the innocent against the excesses of their fellow men and women, and to provide a secret forum to determine whether a criminal indictment—and hence a public trial—was warranted. Even during Watergate, the Washington *Post* and other newspapers were edgily cautious about contacting grand jurors.

But like the times, the institution of the grand jury has changed. Watergate demonstrated that grand juries can be manipulated by participants and others. Some individuals did not have to appear before the grand jury; rather, like Maurice Stans, financial factotum of Richard Nixon's reelection campaign, they were accorded special treatment, private questioning in the offices of the Justice Department. Assistant U.S. Attorney Earl Silbert was presenting one case in the courtroom prosecution of the Watergate burglars, while another was unfolding on the pages of the Washington *Post.* Assistant Attorney General Henry Peterson and Silbert were so deferential to presidential power that they lost their perspective on the significance of equally administered justice in a democratic society. A special prosecutor was eventually appointed.

If Watergate is an aberrational experience, there are more pervasive problems with the grand jury system. Grand juries are increasingly tools of prosecutors. They are inclined to do whatever U.S. attorneys presenting cases ask of them. The Watergate grand jury, for example, desired to indict President Richard M. Nixon. Special Prosecutor Leon Jaworski urged them not to do so, suggesting that they merely cite the president as an unindicted coconspirator. That is exactly what the Watergate grand jury did.

That particular incident worked in favor of a potential defendant. In most cases, however, prosecutors urge grand jurors to indict individuals who are targets of their investigations and are afforded supine compliance with their requests. Too often the grand jury functions not as a judicious finder of facts, but as a prosecutorial tool in the preparation of a case, subjecting defendants to debilitating financial expenses, and inducing plea bargaining by witnesses who will agree to testify against prosecutorial targets.

Something else has recently become commonplace at the grand jury stage of the criminal justice process. U.S. attorneys and defense lawyers have begun to leak material to reporters, where it serves their own or their client's purposes. They attempt to induce newspapers to write stories at a time and in a manner they consider advantageous. John Dean's defense attorneys played such a brilliant game in the press they never had to try a case in the courtroom. Through their clever and shrewd use of national newspapers and magazines, as well as television, they put enormous pressure on the special prosecutor's office to handle John Dean favorably. On the other hand, U.S. attorneys have not hesitated to use the press by leaking certain elements of cases to reporters to increase the pressure on potential witnesses and target defendants. And the media readily and often knowingly lets itself be used, not out of recklessness or malice, but because the information they receive is so newsworthy.

During the exposure of Watergate by Bob Woodward and Carl Bernstein, Assistant U.S. Attorneys Silbert and Seymour Glanzer called Washington *Post* lawyer Joseph Califano and asked him to tell Woodward and Bernstein to stop bothering grand jury witnesses. When their prosecutorial concern was relayed to reporters Woodward and Bernstein, they were shocked at this approach: "We have just come from a one-hour discussion with Silbert and Glanzer. Those guys have some nerve! They never raised the issue with us." The investigation into the nefarious activities of then Vice-President Spiro Agnew was exposed in the press. Whatever the source of the leaks about Agnew—the U.S. Attorney's office, Agnew's own counsel, counsel for other individuals involved in the case, grand jurors, witnesses—it was apparent that the secrecy of the grand jury proceedings had been violated.

This kind of activity by so many of those involved in the criminal justice process—defense attorneys, prosecutors, witnesses, and, more often than most citizens realize, judges—makes reporters particularly skeptical about claims of sanctity for the grand jury process. At least one eminent jurist has privately shared the view that reporters have a right to go after grand jurors, the federal rules about secrecy notwithstanding. The jurist argues that federal rules requiring lawyers, grand jurors, stenographers, and others officially concerned with grand jury proceedings to maintain the secrecy under penalty of contempt cannot be violated by a reporter who simply seeks information from those sworn to secrecy. He believes that those explicitly subject to the secrecy rule must beware of the inquisitive reporter.

There is a profound public interest in grand jury and criminal justice systems. For whatever reasons, criminal justice systems do not work in these United States. Crime continues to rise, jails continue to spew the stench of human cesspools, courts continue to be clogged, some defendants apparently guilty continue to walk the streets free, and other defendants apparently innocent continue to be harassed by government officials. As an integral part of the criminal justice system, the grand jury is certainly a subject of great public interest.

In this context, it is eminently reasonable for reporters and editors to state: It is for the judges to maintain their own secrecy, to exercise their core power over those they control—prosecutors, jurors, lawyers, court clerks, and other "officers of the court." The function of reporters is to find news and to print it. Judges do not hesitate to use their power to hold secret hearings, even during public trials. The sharp increase in secret *voir dires* of potential jurors, bench conferences, and *in camera* hearings during criminal trials provides overwhelming evidence of the judicial ability to bend the inconvenient concept of public trial to the more comfortable surroundings of secrecy.

All journalists complain about these secret proceedings; many deny the right of judges to conduct them. The core remedy of a free press is to expose such judicial practices on its newspaper pages and television broadcasts. An integral element of such exposure is to seek out information from those involved in secret judicial bench or chambers proceedings. Journalists should not be subject to contempt for revealing what, if anything, they discover. The alternative remedy—for the press to litigate to enforce its constitutional rights before the same judge that has decided to cloak his proceedings in secrecy—is not considered a particularly satisfactory one by most journalists. The press regards judges in such circumstances as having a flagrant conflict of interest in ruling on such matters.

The core power principle should also guide the executive branch in the national security area. Journalists confront more difficult decisions here because of the possibility of danger to human life and because society has elected to impose criminal sanctions on those who aid and abet the enemy by revealing state secrets. With respect to national security, most reporters and editors hold that national secrets should be safeguarded by those who determine what the secrets are. The press will continue to listen, as it should, to the pleas of officials not to publish and to make its decisions to publish or withhold publication on a case-by-case basis. No editor or reporter publishes everything he or she learns, particularly in the national security area, because each is sensitive to danger to human life and to the nation's security.

The Glomar Explorer experience is illustrative. At least nine independent news organizations learned that the Central Intelligence Agency had been able to raise from the ocean depths a portion of a Russian nuclear submarine. CIA Director William Colby personally telephoned and visited the heads of several of those news organizations. He pleaded that the CIA had obtained only one-half of the Russian submarine; that the Agency intended to return for the other half which was thought to contain sophisticated Russian military equipment that might give the United States significant insights into Soviet capabilities, and that publication of the story would abort the proposed mission. Most news organizations initially complied with the Colby request. Eventually, the story broke. At that point, all the news organizations wrote what they knew, not out of irresponsible competitiveness, but because the reason for withholding publication no longer existed.

The other celebrated case involves the Pentagon Papers. There Daniel Ellsberg copied a variety of classified documents that he turned over to the New York *Times.* When the *Times* was temporarily enjoined from continuing publication of the Pentagon Papers stories—the first prior restraint sought by the U.S. government in our history—Ellsberg made the papers available to the Washington *Post,* the Boston *Globe,* and other news organizations. Those who published were accused of theft and crimes against the national security.

The Pentagon Papers case provides some significant lessons:

● First, of the thousands of pages of material that Ellsberg copied, only a small number contained information that, if revealed, would endanger the national security. Then Deputy Secretary of Defense David Packard told Washington *Post* editorial page editor Philip Geyelin in the summer of 1971 that "only 27 pages [of the Pentagon Papers] gave us any problem."

● Second, none of the concerned news organizations released sensitive diplomatic portions of the Pentagon Papers. Those portions were either securely locked up in newspaper files or returned to the U.S. government.

● Third—and perhaps most important—the case demonstrates the futility of approaching such problems from traditional legal concepts of conversion and theft insofar as reporters and editors are concerned. Daniel Ellsberg was accused by government officials and numerous others of stealing the Pentagon Papers. In private and public, accusations were leveled at the New York *Times* and Washington *Post* that those newspapers were recipients of stolen property. There were demogogic attempts by government officials to brand them as criminals or at least as tortfeasors who had converted property. But if the Pentagon Papers case teaches any lessons, it is the futility of applying the ordinary technical rules relating to receiving stolen property to a situation where a government official copies a government document and turns it over to a newsman.

Whatever the proper characterization of Daniel Ellsberg's conduct, it misses the point to discuss the actions of the newspapers in the Pentagon Papers case as though they were simply recipients of stolen property, like a hot car, television set, or transistor radio. The salient property involved was information, and it was information produced by and entrusted to government officials in the course of their work as public servants. If Ellsberg had orally passed information in his head to the New York *Times* and Washington *Post*, there would be no such allegations. The essence of what was involved was Ellsberg's failure to keep a secret. Perhaps he violated a contract or oath he had signed as a condition of becoming privy to information other government officials determined should be classified; but in such circumstances it seems spurious to charge journalists as recipients of 27 pages of stolen information.

We suggest a rule comparable to the gag order approach proposed earlier. Those who determine what information is classified bear the responsibility to keep that information secret. If one of their own—in the Ellsberg case, a former Department of Defense employee—fails to keep such information secret, they should exercise their core power and take their legal recourse, if any, against that person. But the press, acting in the exercise of its First Amendment rights and fulfillment of its First Amendment responsibilities, should be free to seek out any information in possession of the government. Once the press obtains such information, it should have the right, subject to its own editorial judgment, to decide whether to publish, without the chilling fear of criminal liability for publication.

The Freedom of Information Act provides all citizens certain rights to government information. But the press, as a uniquely enshrined constitutional institution, seeks access to government information under the First Amendment as well. The right to gather news would appear to be as basic to a free press as the right to publish. Without the right to acquire information, no verbally inflated characterization of a press as free can disguise its decisively diminished value.

In *dictum* in *Branzburg v. Hayes*, the Supreme Court majority opinion declared that news gathering was anointed with the constitutionally sacred oil of First Amendment protection. In the course of his dissenting opinion that a reporter's confidential relationship with news sources should be constitutionally protected, Justice Stewart wrote:

> A corollary of the right to publish must be the right to gather news. . . .
>
> No less important to the news dissemination process is the gathering of information. News must not be unnecessarily cut off

at its source, for without freedom to acquire information the right
to publish would be impermissibly compromised.

In spite of the *Branzburg* court's refusal to protect confidential reporter-source
relationships, it appeared that the constitutional right to gather news was recognized by all nine members of the Court.

Subsequent events, however, have provided sinister contrary evidence. In
Saxbe v. The Washington Post Co., 417 U.S. 843 (1974), the Supreme Court
declared that the press has no constitutional right to interview federal peniten-
tiary inmates even when they desire to be interviewed and there is no demonstration that such interviews pose a problem for prison administration. In an
opinion for the Court's majority, Justice Stewart declared that the press has only
the same constitutional right of access to information as that available to the
general public.

In a 1974 speech at the Yale Law School, Justice Stewart elaborated on
his views of the First Amendment. He termed the free press clause a *structural*
provision of the Constitution because it does not protect specific liberties and
specific rights of individuals, but rather extends protection to an institution, the
publishing business. This is an important distinction, for it differentiates the
freedom of the press from the freedom of speech clause, and permits the granting
of special protection to the institution of press.

Of course, this distinction also poses difficult questions. What, for example,
is the scope of the institution to be protected by the free press clause? If the
letter writer is not protected by the free press clause, is the lonely pamphleteer?
However "the press" is ultimately defined, Justice Stewart seems to view it as an
institution accorded unique constitutional protection. It is difficult, therefore,
to understand his opinion for the Court in the Washington *Post* prison case,
which hinged on a determination that the press had the same right of access
available to the public generally.

Justice Stewart offered another reason for that decision in his Yale Law
School speech:

> The press is free to do battle against secrecy and deception in
> government. But the press cannot expect from the Constitution any
> guarantee that it will succeed. There is no constitutional right to
> have access to particular government information or to require open-
> ness from the bureaucracy. The public's interest in knowing about
> its government is protected by the guarantee of a Free Press, but the
> protection is indirect. The Constitution itself is neither a Freedom of
> Information Act nor an Official Secrets Act.

In view of this statement, it appears that Justice Stewart believes the government has inherent power to determine what shall be made available to the

public, and the press has no constitutional right of access to any information the government desires to withhold. This conclusion fails to take account of the fact that the public interest in knowing about its government, which is the essential objective of the First Amendment freedom grant to the press, cannot be guaranteed without recognition of a constitutional right to gather news. Such an interpretation affords the people no practical remedy if the government adopts a policy of secrecy in its operations.

PRIVACY

In his book *Privacy and Freedom* (New York: Atheneum, 1967), Alan Westin defines privacy as "the claim of individuals, groups, or institutions, to determine for themselves when, how, and to what extent information about them is communicated to others." Others have more simply defined it as "control over knowledge about oneself," for example, Fried, *Privacy*, 77 Yale Law Journal 475, 483 (1968).

Most discussions of privacy in the textbooks and articles by the civil libertarians reflect the 1984 fear factor. Their concerns relate to electronic surveillance, government searches and seizures of homes and persons, psychological and polygraph testing, and the unprecedented accumulation of data by the major public and private institutions of America. With a qualitative assist from computer technology, credit bureaus, governments, large corporations, employers, and newspaper morgues possess burgeoning data banks of information about individual Americans. Privacy issues, like those resulting from the electronic tattooing of the American citizen, are of little concern to the newspaperman, except insofar as they are newsworthy in themselves.

When the reporter and editor talk about privacy, they speak of their right to print facts that they consider are not or should no longer be private. The most glamorous issues arise in connection with public officials. But the problems in newsrooms more often arise in connection with private individuals who find themselves the potential subject of public attention.

The basic law of privacy invasion has been simply stated for years:

• Appropriation of an individual's name or likeness to advertise another's product or promote his business without the consent of the individual constitutes an invasion of privacy.

• An uninvited entry into an individual's home, or eavesdropping or prying, or trespassing to take pictures, can also constitute an invasion of privacy.

• Publicity which places private aspects of an individual in a false light in the public eye creates a cause of action for invasion of privacy somewhat analogous to libel.

• Where statements or depictions are humiliating but true (thereby precluding a libel suit), an actionable invasion of privacy may nevertheless be involved where the facts are indeed private (that is, not part of the public record or visible to public scrutiny) and, if made public, would outrage the community's notions of decency.

The briefest reading of these basic principles of the law of privacy provides no answers to the difficult questions reporters and editors face daily. True, some judgments are almost self-evident. Under these rules, and under basic standards of decency, most newspapers will not publish the names of rape victims. Nor will they publish the names of juvenile offenders, unless they are charged as adults with crimes so heinous or so public that they become a matter of general interest. But the ethical and legal landscape of privacy can become a mine-field for the aggressive reporter.

Item. Once then-powerful House Ways and Means Committee Chairman Wilbur Mills' girlfriend, the Argentine Firecracker, dove into the Tidal Basin in the early morning hours, the lid was off a widely known fact in Washington: Wilbur Mills was on the bottle. Prior to that time, although many reporters in the nation's capital knew that Wilbur Mills was drinking too much and was often drunk at nightclubs, not one had written that fact. Nor had any editor pressed to have the story written.

Should the editors have waited until the incident occurred?

Item. When Joan Kennedy was picked up for drunk driving in Virginia, the Washington *Post* placed the story on the first page of the Metro Section of the newspaper. Wilbur Mills' drunken escapades were carried on its front pages on the same day. Was the distinction because the Washington *Post* tilted more toward the Kennedys than toward Wilbur Mills? Or was the distinction because Joan Kennedy was only the wife of a public figure, whereas Wilbur Mills was a powerful public figure himself? Would the Joan Kennedy story have been on page 1 of the Washington *Post* if her husband had not withdrawn from the presidential race? Would those reporters and editors who knew about her drinking problem long before the Virginia arrest have written about it, if her husband were an active presidential candidate?

In terms of the press performing one of its highest duties—the coverage of public officials elected or appointed to conduct the people's business—the question is the extent to which newspapers publish information about their private habits. In newsworthy terms, these habits largely relate to drinking, mental stability, and sex.

In general, the media have been loath to undress even the most public personalities on the pages of their daily newspapers or in the film clips of their television news shows. Journalists know how hard it is to isolate precise facts and are unwilling to publish information that is not firmly in hand. At Georgetown and Manhattan cocktail and dinner parties, they revel in gossip about the private lives of public figures, particularly with respect to drinking and sex. But publication is another matter.

The general rule most journalists claim to follow is that a public person's private habits merit revelation only when they affect that person's public performance or result in public acts, such as an accident or an arrest. Increasingly, young journalists argue that this is a cop-out. They note that more is printed about the private lives of celebrities than of public officials who have far more power over our lives than movie and television stars.

Drinking habits tend to present the most difficult problem. When we were preparing for the Washington Conference on the Media and the Law, we met with Professors Nesson, Miller, and Sachs at the Harvard Law School to review drafts of the hypothetical cases published in this book. During that luncheon, all three professors pressed editor Simons as to why newspapers do not publish that Congressman X, House Leader Y, or Senate Committee Chairman Z is a chronic alcoholic, or was drunk at a committee meeting, or on the floor of the House or Senate. Simons rejoined: "How do we know that he is drunk? The accurate determination of that condition is by no means simple in a drug-plagued society. Sometimes illness or drug therapy mimics the disease."

"Isn't that just as important to report?" the three professors asked. "Don't the people have a right to know whether their elected and appointed officials are capable of conducting the public business? In making that determination, isn't it relevant whether they can devote their full mental and physical faculties to that business?"

The questions are well taken, and the nation would probably be better off if, to the extent that such information can be accurately obtained, more were printed and televised on the problem of alcoholism in the nation's capital, among the nation's elected and appointed public officials. But alcohol is not the only private problem. What of the private sex lives of public officials? Are they relevant?

Until the recent rise of the gay movement, it was generally considered important public information if a government official with access to classified information were discovered to be homosexual. The argument essentially was that a person could be subject to blackmail by a foreign power. In today's world, if a newspaper discovers a homosexual State or Defense Department official with all kinds of special clearances, is that an item worthy of publication?

Walter Jenkins provides a classic kind of privacy invasion allegation by an administration in power. Jenkins was arrested one night in the YMCA of the District of Columbia in the course of an attempted homosexual engagement in the men's room. The White House tried to eliminate his name from the police blotter. Superlawyers Abe Fortas and Clark Clifford visited Washington newspapers in an attempt to kill the story. Why destroy Walter Jenkins, they argued, the president, Lyndon B. Johnson, will never permit Jenkins back in the government and that takes care of the national security problem. Nevertheless, the newspapers published the story. Was this a legitimate story to print? Blackmail possibilities were present. Jenkins had access to highly sensitive national security information as well as detailed knowledge of the operation of the Johnson White House. The clincher in this particular case was a public incident: Jenkins was arrested. But suppose there had been no arrest, simply an unimpeachable witness to the performance of a private homosexual act. Should the newspapers publish?

Are there other relevant considerations in determining what is private? For example, if a senator is pressing for special legislation to protect the American family, is the fact that he has been divorced half a dozen times or broken up three or four families relevant? When a woman is campaigning on a pro-right-to-life ticket, should the press print the fact that as a 15-year-old minor she had an abortion? If a 60-year-old public official committed a murder in his teens that a reporter has just discovered, should his newspaper reveal it? Suppose it was only manslaughter?

Few of these questions are easily answered. It seems likely that they will be decided on a case-by-case basis. What appears increasingly clear, from legal and journalistic vantage points, is that individual rights of privacy are abandoned by public figures once they voluntarily enter political or other public arenas. There is almost no legally protected privacy interest for a U.S. senator or congressman, should the press decide to publish. In these situations, the only privacy protection is the judgment and good taste of most of our television broadcasters and daily newspapers.

Certainly the wife of a president is a public figure. Even the private aspects of her life have been recognized by the participants themselves to be matters of public interest. The mastectomies of Betty Ford and Happy Rockefeller were major public events, with detailed and intimate briefings about the patient by the doctor. In these situations, the central question in the skeptical minds of the press is whether or not the information is accurate.

Less clear and more difficult is the problem with children of public figures. There is a tendency to hang the children for the fame of their parents. When a young Kennedy or the son of a prominent judge is caught with pot, it is always printable, sometimes front-page news. In a sense, this is unfair to the children of public figures. Yet many politicians enthusiastically exploit their families for their own political purposes. If a politician uses his family to further his career and volunteers it to the public, is he not in effect putting his family into the public arena?

The health of public officials is another matter. Most reporters are familiar with the evasions and dissembling that surrounded the final months and years of the Woodrow Wilson and Franklin Roosevelt administrations. Lyndon Johnson, particularly sensitive to this issue because of his heart attack when in the Senate, overwhelmed the press with information about his gall bladder operation, even displaying the scar. Dwight Eisenhower's press secretary, James Haggerty, presented detailed stitch-by-stitch reports on his ileitis operation and a day-by-day account of his heart attack recovery. It is generally accepted that the health of presidents and vice-presidents is of special importance; but that does not prevent them from attempting to hide the facts from the people. During the 1972 presidential campaign, Senator Thomas Eagleton kept his medical history to himself, attempting to avoid the issue of the past mental health of a vice-president. Once exposed by the press, his medical history raised questions of such importance about potential mental stability under the extraordinary pressure of a possible presidency (and about precisely what he had or had not disclosed to Democratic presidential candidate George McGovern) that Eagleton was forced to resign from the Democratic ticket.

Is not the health of other public figures equally important? The courts, particularly the Supreme Court, however, seek special protection. While it has, on one occasion or another, ordered all manner of citizens and institutions to divest themselves of all kinds of information, including most sensationally in 1974 the president of the United States, the Court itself is one of the most reclusive institutions in the free world.

Washington *Post* reporter John P. MacKenzie chronicled the attitude of the Court in connection with the health problems of Justice William O. Douglas. On New Year's Eve 1974, Justice Douglas suffered a stroke that disabled him from functioning as a full member of the Court. No information was released on the significance of Douglas's stroke. As MacKenzie put it: "Inquiries about Douglas's health were stonewalled at the Court's press information office."

The Court press officer, Barrett McGurn, even dissembled with the media. When Douglas returned to work from Walter Reed Army Hospital, McGurn said nothing about the paralysis of Douglas's left arm and leg, merely passing the word from Douglas that "the Justice is using a sling on his left arm which he said he injured in a fall against a wall at the time he became ill."

Pressured by rumors that circulated Washington, Douglas appeared on the bench on March 24 and the following day permitted some television cameras to film him talking with some reporters. That meeting itself raised special concern over his ability to return to judicial duty and caused many to wonder whether his tenure would be ending shortly. However, until his retirement on November 12, the press and the public were provided with surprisingly little information concerning the gravity of his illness.

Was the press trying to intrude on Mr. Justice Douglas's privacy? Hardly. It is difficult to see why any Supreme Court Justice, or indeed any federal or state judge, deserves any more privacy than officials in the executive and legislative branches of the government.

ACCESS TO THE MEDIA

A Florida right-of-reply statute provided that a candidate for nomination or election assailed in the media with regard to his personal character or official record had the right to demand that the newspaper print, free of cost, any reply the candidate desired to make to the newspaper charges. Failure to comply with the statute constituted a criminal offense, a first-degree misdemeanor. In *Miami Herald Publishing Co. v. Tornillo*, 418 U.S. 241 (1974), the Supreme Court held the Florida statute unconstitutional.

Proponents of the Florida law argued that the statute was consistent with First Amendment values when interpreted in light of the communications revolution which has overtaken this nation. Their argument ran along these lines:

In 1791, when the Bill of Rights was enacted, the press collectively represented a broad range of opinion. Entry into the field was cheap, pamphlets were meaningful alternatives to newspapers, and varied marketplaces of ideas flourished. As a result of technological advances and economic factors, newspaper chains, national papers, national wires and news services, and one-paper towns are dominant today. The power to inform rests today in the hands of a few, who are singularly influential in manipulating popular opinion. Economic factors make entry into the market almost impossible. Only the government can remedy this situation and the government must take affirmative action to ensure fairness and accuracy and provide for accountability and access.

In an opinion for a unanimous Court, Chief Justice Burger rejected the arguments for access, reasoning:

- In prior First Amendment decisions, the Court has consistently expressed a sensitivity to the constitutional problems involved in imposing any form of forced access on the press.
- Although a responsible press is a desirable goal, press responsibility is not mandated by the Constitution and cannot be legislated.
- The effect of the Florida statute would be to reduce political and editorial coverage because editors would be faced with the need to make free reply space available if they printed certain material.
- The statute fails to clear First Amendment barriers because it intrudes into the function of newspapers to select what will be printed.

It is important to note that the Court did not reject the proaccess description of the press as noncompetitive and uniquely powerful. Rather, the Court accepted these facts as true and nonetheless ruled that the First Amendment prohibited governmental intrusion into the editorial function of the press.

Despite the Supreme Court *Tornillo* decision, there are situations in which a newspaper might be required to provide space for free editorial comment. In a concurring opinion, Justice Brennan, joined by Justice Rehnquist, stressed that the Court's opinion implied no view on the constitutionality of statutes that afford plaintiffs, able to prove defamatory falsehoods, the remedy of requiring publication of a retraction. The Court may someday rule that such a statute is constitutional. Another troublesome question may be presented if a public official or public figure seeks access for a retraction, and that party is able to prove falsity but cannot meet the *Times-Sullivan* burden of proving actual malice. Suppose he wishes to purchase advertising space and print his own version of the facts?

THE BROADCAST MEDIA

The fairness doctrine requires that each side of public issues discussed on broadcast stations be given fair or balanced coverage. Two aspects of the fairness doctrine provide access time to specific parties:
- When a personal attack has been made on a figure involved in a public issue, the individual attacked must be offered an opportunity to respond.
- Where one candidate for office is endorsed in a broadcast editorial, the other candidate must be offered reply time to use personally or through a spokesman.

In *Red Lion Broadcasting Co. v. FCC*, 395 U.S. 367 (1969), the Supreme Court rejected the broadcaster's challenge, on conventional First Amendment grounds, to the fairness doctrine in general and the specific rules in particular.* The Court reasoned that although broadcasting is a medium affected by First Amendment interests, differences in the characteristics of news media justify differences in the First Amendment standards applied. The Court applied a different standard to broadcasting, arguing that the limited number of airwaves and the FCC licensing system justified this result.

Red Lion opened more doors than it closed, as Fred Friendly indicates in his book, *The Good Guys, the Bad Guys and the First Amendment* (New York: Random House, 1976). More recent judicial decisions signal that the fairness doctrine is sailing in turbulent judicial seas. David Bazelon, Chief Judge of the United States Court of Appeals for the D.C. Circuit, forcefully argued for a complete reexamination of the fairness doctrine in his dissenting opinion in the *Brandywine-Main Line Radio, Inc. v. FCC*, 473 F.2d 16 (D.C. Cir. 1972). Judge Bazelon asserted that our fears of a broadcast monopoly seem dated. The number of commercial broadcasting stations on the air as of September 1972 was 7,458; as of January 1, 1971, daily newspapers totaled only 1,749. He pointed out that the overall effect of the fairness doctrine may well be censorship of the robust debate and controversy it was promulgated to encourage.

---

*Justice White delivered the opinion of the Court; Justice Douglas took no part in the Court's decision.

The Supreme Court followed *Red Lion* with its decision in *Columbia Broadcasting System v. Democratic National Committee,* 412 U.S. 94 (1973).*
There the Court held that neither the First Amendment nor the Communications Act requires broadcasters to accept paid editorial advertisements. En route to the Supreme Court, a majority of the D.C. Court of Appeals had held that "a flat ban on paid public issue announcements is in violation of the First Amendment, at least when other sorts of paid announcements are accepted." That court concluded that a broadcaster's policy of airing commercial but not editorial advertisements amounted to constitutional discrimination.

In reversing the court of appeals, Chief Justice Burger, writing for a mixed plurality of the Court, first traced the history of the Communications Act and determined that "Congress intended to permit private broadcasting to develop with the widest journalistic freedom consistent with its public obligations." By way of illustration, Burger pointed out that the fairness doctrine rejects the concept of across-the-board access and places responsibility on the broadcasters to ensure fair coverage. As he sees it, the basic principle underlying that responsibility is "the right of the people to be informed, rather than any right on the part of the government, any broadcast licensees, or any individual member of the public to broadcast his own particular views on any matter."

Even assuming that the actions of broadcasters constituted governmental action, the Chief Justice determined that broadcasters were not required by the First Amendment to accept political advertising. He reasoned that the First Amendment should be evaluated in view of the public interest, and concluded that the Commission was justified in determining that the public interest would not be served by a system so heavily weighted in favor of the financially affluent.

In *National Broadcasting Co. v. FCC,* 43 U.S. L.W. 2133 (D.C. Cir. Oct. 8, 1974), the Federal Communications Commission determined that NBC violated the fairness doctrine by presenting a one-sided presentation of an issue of public importance, the abuse of private pension plans. NBC took the position that although the program was newsworthy, there was no controversial issue about abuses in *some* pension plans. The D.C. Circuit reversed the Commission, holding that where a broadcaster has made a reasonable judgment that a news program was not controversial, the fairness doctrine does not permit the FCC to make its own determination of the subject matter and require an opposing view to be presented.

The *Democratic National Committee (DNC)* and *National Broadcasting Company* cases raise difficult questions which remain unanswered. Does the

---

*Chief Justice Burger wrote the opinion of the Court in which Justices White, Blackmun, Powell, and Rehnquist joined. Justices Stewart, White, Douglas, Blackmun, and Powell filed separate opinions concurring with the Court's judgement. Justice Brennan filed a dissenting opinion in which Justice Marshall joined.

jumble of opinions in the *DNC* case mean that broadcasters have complete control over when to accept paid political advertising and from whom? Are all shows dealing with abuses in various programs noncontroversial because such abuses almost always exist? Is a program focusing on campaign financing abuses only in the Republican party noncontroversial because some such abuses do exist?

Any general summary of the law of access to broadcast media today is treacherous to attempt but it might be along these lines:

1. The broadcast media have an obligation under the Communications Act to present a balanced presentation of controversial issues of public importance. While this agency-enforced obligation has been held not to violate the First Amendment, the courts are likely to review any actions regulating access in this area with scrupulous skepticism.

2. It is constitutional for the FCC to require the broadcast media to grant access to specific individuals under the personal attack doctrine and political editorial rule.

3. The broadcast media are not constitutionally required to accept paid political advertising, so long as they reject all such advertising.

4. With the exception of the personal attack doctrine and political editorial rule, the broadcaster is given the right to select who shall appear on his station so long as he provides for a balanced presentation of controversial issues of public importance.

To all of this an important caveat should be addressed: the fairness doctrine is still being tested and reevaluated, and it is impossible to predict the contours it will eventually follow.

Courts have generally verbalized two theories to explain the distinction between the treatment accorded print and broadcast media. First, different First Amendment standards apply because governmental involvement in the granting of broadcast licenses entitles the government to play some role in broadcast regulation. We see this as a theoretical basis for government regulation of licensees, but not as public interest justification for the fairness doctrine.

Second, different First Amendment standards apply because of the technological differences between print and broadcast media. Some regulation is necessary to prevent chaos on the airwaves. Airwaves are a limited commodity, not everyone can speak over them who desires, and certainly not everyone can speak simultaneously. Therefore, it is consistent with First Amendment interests for the government to insure a balanced presentation of views. To the extent recent technological advances undermine the scarce resource argument and make entry into the broadcast media as easy as entry into the print media, we believe this theory loses some of its validity.

There remains a third, often unstated but deeply held, reason for distinguishing between broadcast and print media—the unprecedented power of television communication. Today, 97 percent of all American homes have at least one television set, and the average set is turned on seven hours each day. Whereas in 1959 some 51 percent of all Americans received most of their news from television, today that figure is over 64 percent. Three networks dominate television public affairs and news coverage. Televising the Vietnam war had a far greater effect on American attitudes than did published reports. This nation's attitudes toward another depression would be substantially different from its attitudes in the 1929 depression if citizens witnessed food lines and starving Americans on living-color television. So many jurists informally have cited facts such as these that we are convinced it affects their decisions in fairness doctrine cases.

ECONOMIC, ETHICAL, AND MORAL CONSIDERATIONS

Running through the legal and journalistic questions discussed in this essay are difficult economic, ethical, and moral considerations.

The economics of the newspaper business are treacherous. Most newspapers operate on a very narrow profit margin. Our judicial system is an expensive forum in which to assert and defend rights. Lawyers are expensive; even court stenographers and brief printers are expensive. In a major city today, a court stenographer providing hot (daily) copy for a litigator trying a case may charge as much as $500 each day; an average-length appellate brief can cost $2,000 to be printed. Good big-city lawyers no longer come for anything less than $100 an hour; most charge substantially more. Only the largest and most successful newspapers can effectively move along this legal gold coast. Hundreds of thousands of dollars are spent by such papers to defend their rights—money most journalists think should be spent in other activities.

For the smaller paper, the financial terrain for assertion of First Amendment rights can be insurmountable. Rarely can such papers afford the kind of legal talent necessary to wage significant First Amendment battles. Moreover, most of these issues are not decided in lower courts. The rhetoric of the Supreme Court filters down into federal district courts and state and local courts through the biases, prejudices, incompetence, and sheer laziness of too many judges. Case after case is tried that should be dismissed on motion for summary judgment or motion to dismiss. Trial after trial is reversed. Affluent plaintiffs suing for libel, invasion of privacy, or attempting to subpoena reporters keep going back to the mat. There undoubtedly have been libel suits pursued in order to break a newspaper financially, or frighten it from printing about the plaintiff again.

Judges tend to say that if newspapers are careful, they will be protected in the courtroom. It is time they put some legal muscle behind their assurances. When frivolous libel suits are brought—indeed in most situations when public figures bring libel suits and lose them—we believe that legal fees and court costs should be assessed against the losing plaintiff. For the very expense of protecting the First Amendment rights of the newspaper can have an enormously chilling effect.

As we have seen in the course of this essay, there are few hard rules of law that apply in the tough day-to-day problems that national, state, and local newspapers face with legislatures, chief executives, courts, and city councils. But legal problems are often dwarfed by the perplexing ethical and moral issues that alter journalism in the 1970s. The day-to-day professional lives of most good reporters and editors are shadowed by a series of moral and ethical challenges. Sometimes they do not think about them as carefully as they should. Often there is inconsistency from paper to paper, and from section to section within the same paper. What a gossip columnist might publish in a society or style section would not be acceptable to a hard-news reporter for the front page.

If a group of reporters and editors in any room were asked whether they would physically steal a document in order to obtain a story, the answer would be a chorus of honorable "No's!" All, however, could be charged with "stealing" with their eyes (even upside down). Moreover, asked if they would publish newsworthy documents stolen by a third party and passed on to the paper, most would probably print them or the information they contained. There might (or might not) be questions about whether they actually knew the documents had been stolen. What is the difference? We have tried to suggest in this essay that the difference is not simply a cop-out on morality, a refusal to recognize a moral dilemma. Rather, the appropriate scope of editorial responsibility must be defined. That responsibility is to publish the news. Provided that they do not steal themselves, journalists should not be held criminally liable for theft simply for publishing information.

Other questions arise where news sources want to be paid for information. Most daily newspaper reporters consider such information tainted. Editors and publishers consider it too costly and also believe that such payments would discourage persons from revealing information until they could auction it off. Nevertheless, television networks have rarely hesitated to pay for information. CBS reportedly paid H. R. Haldeman at least $25,000 for the Mike Wallace interviews. And book publishers increasingly bid for newsworthy information.

One of the most troublesome aspects of paying for news is the danger that the payment itself undermines credibility. The best journalists feel singularly dedicated to maintaining credibility. They regard credibility as the most precious commodity of journalism. They will go to tremendous lengths to check out a tip or a story. Most will not publish until completely satisfied that they have all the information available—at least within the deadline restrictions and institutional limitations of newspapering.

Among good reporters the rule is to call "the other guy." Put another way, if someone attacks an individual, the attack should not be printed without providing an opportunity to answer. Blind criticism from confidential sources who refuse to identify themselves should not be allowed, although such a rule can be difficult for editors to police.

All this does not mean fairness in any sense of reporting, inch for inch, all sides to the same story. It does mean fairness in hearing out the other side and making an independent judgment.

This understanding of a journalist's sense of fairness is critical. Recent years have witnessed increasing attempts to use the courts and/or the state or federal legislatures to impose on newspapers something analogous to the fairness doctrine that applies to broadcasters. Proponents of such moves intone the lofty rhetoric of fairness, accuracy, and objectivity. Fairness and accuracy are essential to credibility; but these are the responsibility of reporters and editors. Objectivity is a difficult goal in the newspaper business. There is no way an editor can wrench out of reporters the inculcations of 25 or 40 years of personal experiences that seed biases. What those reporters must do and be trained to do is give each side a chance to present its case, particularly on controversial stories, and then write as accurately as they can. This is a painstaking, sometimes tedious business. But when it works well, it is the essence of good journalism.

A truly fine newspaper is not a public-relations operation, or business blotter, or a booster for the community in which it is published. It is not a mouthpiece for the government or a quasi-governmental publication for official statements and pronouncements. Nor at the same time is it an activist cause-oriented instrument in the hands of an elite group of the leaders or individuals who think they have the sole perception of what society is or should be. A newspaper certainly is not the last word on the news. Nor is it even a comprehensive, utterly fair, totally accurate, always excellent, completely objective chronicle of its times. And it does not have to be correct all of the time. Nor could it be, putting out a totally new product every day of the year.

A truly excellent newspaper is a collection of bright, eager, and hard-working human beings, reporting what they see as best they can, trying to determine what is new and profound, significant or funny, sad or telling, different or important. More often than not, what is printed has more to do with what is wrong than what is right; more to do with keeping people honest than with honest people; more to do with eliminating dark places than reflecting sunlight; but, always, mostly to do with seeking truth.

The journalist perceives his right to seek the truth as stemming solely from the First Amendment. But judges see themselves as informing the First Amendment with robust constitutional energy. As one judge said at the last conference session:

> Where, ladies and gentlemen, do you think these great constitutional rights that you were so vehemently asserting, and in which you were so conspicuously wallowing yesterday, where do you think they came from? The stork didn't bring them. These came from the

judges of this country, from these villains here sitting at the table. That's where they came from. They came because the courts of this country at some time or place when some other agency of government was trying to push the press around or, indeed, may be trying to do you in, it's the courts that protected you. And that's where all these constitutional rights came from. . . . It's not that it was done for you, or that it was done for ourselves. It happened because it is our understanding that that's what the Constitution provides and protects. But let me point out that the Constitution of the United States is not a self-executing document. . . .

If you look at the literal language in the First Amendment of the Constitution of the United States, it says, "Congress shall pass no law abridging the freedom of the press." That's all it says on this subject, absolutely all. It doesn't say a word about what a state can or can't do. It doesn't say a word about a reporter's privilege before a grand jury. . . . The very fact that these protections are available is attributable to the creative work of the judiciary over the last 190 years.

If you say it's self-evident, that this was always clear, let me tell you that it wasn't always so clear. If you went back to the original understanding of our ancestors, back in the early years of the nineteenth century, you would find that their understanding of this clause and the Constitution in their judgment allowed them to enact the Alien and Sedition law. And if those laws were still on the books, Richard Nixon would still be president of the United States, Spiro Agnew would still be vice-president of the United States and all of you people would probably be in prison.

The journalists of this nation might not agree with the assessment of that eloquently angry jurist. But the creative work of the judiciary, particularly over the last 25 years, has given much of the vitality to the robust debate that newspapers and television foster under the banner of the First Amendment. What concerns journalists most about such statements is having their First Amendment fate in someone else's hands. And the recent turn of the Supreme Court—particularly in the *Branzburg* confidential news source decision, the denial of access to prisoners, and the potential mischief in the lower courts that may result from *Gertz*—is of profound and chilling concern to reporters and editors.

Yet, if an essence of freedom is the absence of law, certainly another essence of freedom is the need for order. Somewhere between the robust hurly-burly of the newsroom and the somber quiet of judicial chambers we must find the balance. Both are critical to the preservation of individual liberty and the maintenance of an informed citizenry in our nation. What weakens one can in a sense weaken the other. The demand of judges that the press, like every other institution of American society, be accountable to the courts should be tempered by their recognition that with extremely rare exceptions such accountability must be self-imposed by reporters and editors.

The central issue presented is who shall decide—the press or the courts or the government? This is the one issue that pervades all discussions of the media and the law. Is it the role of the jurist or journalist to decide what shall be made available to the public and when, what shall be withheld and for how long?

To the extent the press wins the right to decide, First Amendment values seem well served. Unfortunately, the Supreme Court has been inconsistent in this regard. On specific questions, most Supreme Court Justices have vacillated with Hamlet-like self-doubt, expressed in soliloquy opinions. They have made it difficult, if not impossible, for lawyers to determine underlying rationales that would render First Amendment advice and litigation persistently predictable and too expensive for most newspapers and broadcasters to assert their rights with the unyielding vigor the First Amendment encourages and demands.

THE CASE

Harlow Mason is an investigative reporter for the Federal City *News*. He has come into possession of two documents which he considers highly newsworthy. One is a chapter of an unfinished personal memoir written by Winston Bridges, former director of the CIA (1963-73), now the U.S. ambassador to Hinterland. The memoir is in manuscript form and carries a typewritten legend at the top of each page, "Not to be published until ten years after my death or 2000 A.D., whichever is later—WKB." The second is a memorandum to Bridges from Brian McKinley, Director of Counter Intelligence, dated June 17, 1967, classified TOP SECRET/LORDS/Group I. It appears to be a source document which is described in the text of the memoir.

In the chapter of the memoir which Mason has obtained, Bridges describes the circumstances under which he initiated the Agency's domestic surveillance program. He describes how, in the summer of 1967, a key U.S. agent, deeply infiltrated into the Hungarian government, passed information to the Agency that the antiwar movement in the United States was receiving extensive aid and counsel from the Soviet Union. The agent (code-named Duke) reported a series of contacts between leaders of the antiwar movement and agents of the Soviet government, and described the movement of funds from Soviet-connected sources to front groups and persons in Sweden, thence to individual American citizens who made contributions to antiwar groups.

Bridges states in his memoir that initially he was too skeptical of the information to act on it, but that Brian McKinley, his Director of Counter Intelligence, overcame his skepticism by submitting a highly classified memorandum to him outlining the development of Duke as a spy, detailing every past contact Duke had had with Agency personnel, reciting and evaluating all information which Duke had passed before, and stating McKinley's conclusion that Duke was the most important and reliable source in the entire Lords spy network. (It is this document, in addition to the memoir, which Mason has obtained.)

This memorandum, according to the memoir, convinced Bridges to initiate a limited program of domestic surveillance to attempt further verification of Soviet support for the antiwar movement. Such surveillance, according to the memoir, confirmed that the Soviet Union was indeed actively supporting the antiwar movement, and that Duke's information had been accurate. Duke, according to the memoir, continued to rise in the Hungarian government and to supply increasingly vital intelligence information on Communist military, political, and economic activities.

Mason has prepared a story describing the memoir and the Lords report. He wants the paper to run his story and to print the memoir and the Lords report in full.

Questions

1. How should the managing editor of the Federal City *News* deal with Mason's story?

2. Should it make a difference to the editor how Mason obtained the documents?

a.   Suppose that Bridges had reported a month previously that the study in his home in Hinterland had been burglarized and that some drafts of his memoirs had been stolen.

b.   Suppose that the documents had been copied by a secretary in the State Department when Bridges was there on a visit, then passed to Mason in exchange for $2,000.

c.   Suppose that Mason, while at a cocktail party in Washington for Bridges, wandered into the study, saw Bridges' briefcase, opened it, glanced through the papers, then, realizing that he did not have time to absorb their contents, stole them.

3. Suppose that the Agency and Bridges learn that the Federal City *News* has the documents. How should the paper respond to a demand from the Agency and/or Bridges for return of the documents on the ground that they are stolen property?

4. Should the paper hold back all or part of the story based on the CIA's off-the-record representation that publication of the documents would blow an extremely high-level existing network of spies, and would result in at least some agents being killed? How should such a decision be made? (That is, by whom, and by what criteria?)

5. Suppose the Agency and Bridges file papers before Federal Judge Keptman to enjoin publication, claiming:

a.   irreparable damage to national security;

b.   violation of contracts signed by Bridges when he was director that he would never publish anything relating to Agency work without first submitting the manuscript to a security clearance by the Agency;

c.   the right to return of stolen property;

d.   copyright violation.

How should Judge Keptman respond?

6. Suppose that the Agency submits to Judge Keptman an affidavit written by the current director of the CIA stating that (a) disclosure of the memoir and the Lords documents would reveal the identity of a top CIA spy who is currently the Minister of Finance in Hungary, and would reveal also as many as 22 other agents currently operating in communist countries; (b) that it is impossible to extricate these agents (and in some cases, their families) from positions of personal danger in less than three weeks; (c) destruction of this spy network would irreparably damage U.S. intelligence capacity, hence U.S. national defense; and (d) the information in the affidavit is so sensitive that it cannot be disclosed to anyone, and no more information on the subject can be disclosed even to the judge.

7. Should Judge Keptman take any steps to insure that the process of the court is not being manipulated by the CIA in order to give credibility to a planted, self-serving news story?

PROCEEDINGS

PROFESSOR CHARLES NESSON (Harvard Law School): Editor, how would you decide this case? A reporter comes in to you one morning and puts this story [Case I] in front of you. What do you have to say to him?

1ST EDITOR: The first thing I'd do is ask him very forcefully and very carefully how the hell he got this document.

MR. NESSON: Why would you do that?

1ST EDITOR: Because there's a smell that he didn't get it properly.

MR. NESSON: And you don't like smells?

1ST EDITOR: I don't like impropriety. I don't mind smells. (Laughter)

MR. NESSON: Okay, I'm the reporter. Ask me the question.

1ST EDITOR: All right, where did you get it?

MR. NESSON: (Turns to a reporter-participant): Do you tell him?

1ST REPORTER: Yes.

MR. NESSON: Where did you get it?

1ST REPORTER: Do I have to use the facts for this exam?

MR. NESSON: Yes.

1ST REPORTER: I would not have stolen it. I would only have acquired it as it comes to me, probably through a third party.

MR. NESSON: Well, let's take it the easy way. You have some worries about being a thief, I take it. And your editor has some worries about your being a thief. You tell me how you would have gotten this for real.

1ST REPORTER: I probably would have written a story that put me in contact with the source. Again, the source probably would have gotten the document to me through a third party.

MR. NESSON: Now somebody talks to you and says, "I'm a friend of Bridges, the former CIA director, and I've come across some very interesting papers which you might be interested in," something like that?

1ST REPORTER: In my case, I think it would have come from a story, something like that.

MR. NESSON: Do you ask him where he got the documents?

1ST REPORTER: No, I don't.

MR. NESSON: So he might have stolen them?

1ST REPORTER: I'm assuming this; I don't know for a fact there has been a burglary report. If I had known that in advance, I'd probably ask him how he got the documents, but I don't see how I would know now.

MR. NESSON: And suppose he tells you that he's not interested in telling you how he got the documents?

1ST REPORTER: There's not enough of a reason for me not to accept the documents.

MR. NESSON: Now it looks good. You've got it. You asked him the question. You did your duty. (Turns to the 1st Editor) How about that, is that what he tells you? Is that good enough for you?

1ST EDITOR: And he satisfies me that he did not steal it?

MR. NESSON: He tells you that he did not steal it. Does that satisfy you?

1ST EDITOR: Yes.

MR. NESSON: You just take your reporter's word for it?

1ST EDITOR: Yes. I examine it. They've got to convince me, which isn't as hard as it sounds.

MR. NESSON: And is that as far as you go then?

1ST EDITOR: No, then we go through the story point by point. I'm presuming that we don't know any A, B, or C yet. Also, that we're really dealing with a story that starts with the fact there is possession and the CIA has information which says foreign powers heavily infiltrated the antiwar movement. This is news by any definition and we explore the story, explore each part of the background. I doubt if the reporter's only source is this. He will have talked to people in the antiwar movement and will have talked to other agencies of government. In this kind of story there is a spectrum of public knowledge; people who will gladly give you information, provided it's true, that will tend to confirm this story.

MR. NESSON: Let's just suppose for a minute, Mr. Editor, that there's at least something here. Suppose the reporter said to you, "I stole the document"?

1ST EDITOR: That's the end of it.

MR. NESSON: You wouldn't print it?

1ST EDITOR: No.

MR. NESSON: Really hot news?

1ST EDITOR: No.

MR. NESSON: Just because it's stolen you wouldn't print it?

1ST EDITOR: Yes.

MR. NESSON: Does it make a difference to you that somebody stole it and gave it to your reporter instead of the reporter stealing it himself?

1ST EDITOR: Yes, I'm afraid it does.

MR. NESSON: What sort of difference does it make?

1ST EDITOR: Well, along about this time I'd call my lawyer. (Laughter)

MR. NESSON: I'll allow you to do that. We have a good selection up here.

1ST EDITOR: But yeah, a reporter can't steal papers. We have to get out information legally, barring some major —

1ST TV REPORTER: News developments. (Laughter)

MR. NESSON: He says barring some major news developments.

1ST EDITOR: I'm thinking in terms of the question which comes up in one of the other cases of, is the grand jury process being perverted in some way and maybe that there are circumstances in which I would be interested in grand jury minutes, if I'd had that knowledge.

MR. NESSON: What would you say was the biggest national security news story in the last four years?

1ST EDITOR: The Pentagon Papers.

MR. NESSON: Suppose the Pentagon Papers had been stolen by somebody, would that make a difference to you?

1ST EDITOR: No.

MR. NESSON: You'd print them? Suppose your reporter had stolen the Pentagon Papers?

1ST EDITOR: I would not have printed them.

MR. NESSON: You would not have printed them? (Turns to another Editor-participant) Do you feel the same way?

2ND EDITOR: There might be another way to find out—to get that same information.

MR. NESSON: I'm talking about the documents, the text. Somebody comes to you and they've got a document and it's stamped top secret, Lords/Group I. You're going to get that document some other way?

2ND EDITOR: One could see whether it existed in some other way. One could begin to ask questions about it to see whether there were other ways to ascertain the information contained therein.

MR. NESSON (Now addresses all media participants): Let me put it to you. Do we have an editor in the room who would print a story that was stolen by his reporter?

2ND REPORTER: I'm not an editor but under some circumstances I would print a story about a stolen document, stolen by my reporter.

MR. NESSON: How do you respond to our first editor?

2ND REPORTER: Well, particularly with respect to government documents, it's a question in my mind whether unauthorized possession can ever constitute theft. It's different, I should think, than the manuscript we're talking about, this man's intellectual property.

MR. NESSON (Turns to 1st Editor): What do you say to that? He's asking you the question, "What's really been stolen here?"

1ST EDITOR: Well, I don't know. I don't think anything has been stolen, but if the reporter has actually said, "I swiped it from the desk of——"

MR. NESSON: Yes, our second reporter says, "Swiped what?" What did you swipe?

2ND EDITOR: The ideas.

MR. NESSON: No, you swiped the document. You swiped the top-secret Lords report. I went to a Xerox machine and I made a copy of the document.

1ST EDITOR: What?

MR. NESSON: I went to a Xerox machine and I made a copy of the document. That's different?

1ST EDITOR: No.

MR. NESSON: I see, so as long as we take copies of documents . . .

1ST EDITOR: No, no, excuse me. You haven't understood me. I think if a reporter steals it and then takes a Xerox of it and says, "Well, I . . " you know, and then returns the first one, he has still stolen it by my definition.

MR. NESSON (Recognizes another Reporter-participant)

1ST TV REPORTER: I think there's a point—a shading of a point—that's being missed here and since I'm not an editor, I don't have to be hypocritical. A certain amount of larceny goes on in the news business all the time. The question is what degree of larceny goes on. Is it stealing to read something upside down on a person's desk? If there is such a thing as stealing ideas or words, hasn't that already begun to happen, and what reporter or former reporter here hasn't done that or tried? You get a document and you know the document's stolen and you say, "We can't use a stolen document because we can't be in the position of using a stolen document. It would be very bad for us if it were found out. Get it back there after we've made a copy." Now that we know it exists and someone has it, can we get another copy of it somewhere more legitimately? If not, can we develop a story knowing the contents of it by asking a lot of questions of the right people and develop an original story which we can say comes from other sources? The question of whether you use a document or don't use a document is in most cases too simple a question. You try to find a way in which you do and do not at the same time use a document.

MR. NESSON: If I understand you right, what you're suggesting is that you try to figure out a way to use the document so you're really not exposed to charges?

1ST TV REPORTER: Yes.

MR. NESSON: Purely pragmatic. I mean, you're just operating with the information?

1ST TV REPORTER: That's a blunt way of putting it.

3RD REPORTER: I think that's wrong. (Addresses 1st TV Reporter) You're saying we've got this thing in our newspaper or radio station because our intrepid reporter has stolen it and then we can give it back and figure out some other way of getting the story. I would hope that we don't have this kind of reporter working for us with that way of doing business and that we would have trained him so that he didn't steal it in the first place.

(2ND Reporter speaks out): People are sliding off this business and onto the business of theft much too easily because . . .

MR. NESSON: Put us back on it.

2ND REPORTER: All right. I assume that most of us think that theft means the unauthorized possession of something of which someone else has a possessory interest. I don't know that any government official has a demonstrable or even an arguable possessory interest in the contents of public documents that belong, I think, to some kind of mass known as the public. And the public, therefore, has some reasonable access to it and . . .

MR. NESSON: He wasn't stealing the document, he was just liberating it?

2ND REPORTER: He was not stealing it because the source from which he filched it didn't own it.

MR. NESSON: You would then distinguish the two documents that we have here: one, the highly classified Lords document . . .

2ND REPORTER: Yes.

MR. NESSON: You would say fine, no problem with that?

2ND REPORTER: That's right.

MR. NESSON: But there is a big problem with the other document?

2ND REPORTER: Not a large problem because I think it's derivatively public. The memoir derives solely from the man's public service and experience. I have some problem with the intellectual commercial property right that he will or has asserted in his memoir.

(1st Editor speaks out): Regarding the classified document, it seems to me, as you describe it, there's almost no chance for an argument that it's been inappropriately classified. That's what worries me about this particular document, whereas in the Pentagon Papers case, that argument was there to be made and begged to be made.

MR. NESSON: Let's hold off on that just a minute if we can. I want to find out from reporters here whether it is a fact that they would not steal a document. Now of course you all say, "No, of course we'd never do that." Our first TV reporter says, "Well, we peek a little." There's at least some suggestion that maybe Xerox copies make a difference. We're talking about the CIA here. We're talking about a vital organization which has operated in secrecy. We're talking about an organization where there are public issues of tremendous importance that people need to decide about. We're talking about an organization which has been engaged in secret wars and assassinations and you are going to stop at just picking up a little document to expose all that, is that right?

1ST EDITOR: Well, now you say "just picking up." Are we walking down the street and suddenly there it is on the sidewalk to be picked up? I would pick it up.

MR. NESSON: Suppose you walk into a study and there it is sitting on a desk?

1ST EDITOR: When you walk into whose study?

MR. NESSON: I don't know. In this case we have the situation of walking into somebody's study who's having a little party for Mr. Bridges.

2ND EDITOR: Why did Mr. Bridges write this memoir if this information is so invested with national security issues? Where was his failure of responsibility?

MR. NESSON: Well, remember that he wasn't going to publish this until 2000.

2ND EDITOR: He wrote it and he left it exposed on a desk. That's not very responsible for a man who had taken an oath of office.

MR. NESSON: So tough luck on Mr. Bridges?

2ND EDITOR: Well, I think it's a factor. You're asking these questions in an either/or way that just doesn't happen in our life. I mean, it isn't that classical, it isn't that austere—would you do this or would you do that. When we make these decisions, if these decisions come to us to be made, there is a whole world that comes in with it and a whole lot of nuances that are being left out entirely as you strive here to get this case established. You ask, "Would you do this," and if we say "Yes," then you go on to the second step, and then pretty soon you've got us in a corner, right?

(1ST TV REPORTER chimes in): Granted use immunity, I would say that I would take it in order to make the point.

MR. NESSON: All right, we have one here.

1ST PROSECUTOR: Well, Professor Nesson, what do you mean by this problem in terms of levels? I'm not too sure I understand what you're saying. Are you talking about ethically or legally? Are you concerned about the legal exposure?

MR. NESSON: I'm not talking about either. What I'm talking about at the moment is what the editor does, sitting at his desk, when a reporter comes to him; what kind of questions the editor asks the reporter; and why and what difference do the answers make. So far what I've heard is, "Yes, I will ask him whether he stole it." I've heard our first reporter say, "Yes, I will tell him if I did," and I've heard our first editor say, "Therefore, no matter what the story, I won't print it. I'll try and get it some other way. I'll try and limit my exposure but I won't print that story."

1ST PROSECUTOR: I think it's more than exposure that they're concerned about; I think a reporter might be concerned about the fact that maybe the editor would fire him for stealing the document.

MR. NESSON (Turns to first reporter): Would you be worried?

1ST REPORTER: No because I've worked for the editor for 15 years and he knows I wouldn't steal it. I don't even think the question would be necessary.

MR. NESSON (Turns to 1st TV Reporter): Would you tell the editor?

1ST TV REPORTER: Would I tell him if he asked me?

MR. NESSON: Yes, you bend a little bit, it's a big issue . . .

1ST TV REPORTER: No, I make it a policy not to withhold essential facts of my professional dealings with my boss. I would tell him, yes.

2ND EDITOR: The first thing an editor would do, as a matter of fact, is not ask whether it was stolen or not.

MR. NESSON: Or would he say, "Where did you get it?"

2ND EDITOR: No, he wouldn't even say that. The first thing he asks is, "What does the document say, does it matter?" If it doesn't matter . . .

MR. NESSON: There's another point we should have gone into.

(1ST EDITOR speaks out): One second, just to put something in perspective. When you've got a story like this, the fact of the matter is that there is an instant realization on the part of the editor and all his editors that they are headed for rough seas and they really are. It's going to be a thorny issue. It's going to involve the public's right to know. It's going to involve the image and the reputation of the newspaper. It's going to involve everything, so you start instinctively striving from the word go not to get yourself into a posture where your case is weak. Almost immediately, if you are in possession of a stolen document, you prepare to go all the way to the Supreme Court where many of the justices will throw statutes at you and say to the government, "Go after them on that." [See, for example, 18 USC secs. 793, 797, and 798 which prohibit disclosure or publication of certain classified information.] There is a little caution light that starts blinking when somebody says, "I've got a document," and it does condition your entire behavior from then on, I promise you.

3RD EDITOR: Well, another question that an editor should ask at that point, being presented with highly explosive material like this, is to question the authenticity of the document and of the sourcing. You know, in basic training in intelligence, you go through authenticity and you go through the sourcing and there are two different characterizations, scales on these things and why. Is it possible that this is part of a large plot, black information being given out to embarrass somebody, which is a kind of question one should ask along with the sourcing on the thing. I would have doubts about some of these things presented that way. Why would somebody want to tell me this?

MR. NESSON: Well, let's come to authenticity in just a minute. I grant you that it's a real question. I want to come back to our first editor and stay with him for just a minute. (Turns to 1st Editor): What you're saying is that somebody comes in with questionable documents and it lights red lights for you. It's going to be trouble. What you've told me is that if a certain red light goes on, you don't print it. That solves all problems, right?

1ST EDITOR: Yes, it does for me in this instance.

MR. NESSON: Except how about me? I'm the reader out there and the public. I want to see the thing.

1ST EDITOR: Well, I've got an enormous interest in you and I would not claim to say that I would not read this document.

MR. NESSON: You have said that you would not print the document.

1ST EDITOR: That's right, but if the document tells me that there is information of a reliable and extraordinary quality coming into the United States about the infiltration of the antiwar movement by a foreign power, if I am in possession of that information, however the hell I got it, and I am free to look for supporting information then I would set about doing that right away. I would go to these people, try to prove the story out, try to work it out. I'd see if I could corroborate it, see if I could find some corroborating evidence.

MR. NESSON: Why does it make a difference to you that it was your reporter who stole the document rather than someone else who simply gave it to your reporter?

1ST EDITOR: Well, I think it's called 793 A thru F.

MR. NESSON: Just pure legal liability that's involved?

1ST EDITOR: Well all a major newspaper has got to do is get indicted and convicted of theft and you've lost an awful, awful lot.

MR. NESSON (Turns to 2nd Editor): Do you feel the same way?

2ND EDITOR: It's not nice to steal. (Laughter)

MR. NESSON: Well, we can all agree on that.

2ND TV REPORTER: Let's put a nuance to that. Let's say that the reporter talked to Bridges beforehand and said, what about the infiltration of Communist governments in the antiwar movement? Bridges said, I can't tell you about it but why don't you go into my study and have a cigar.

1ST EDITOR: That's an invitation to share. That's not stealing.

2ND TV REPORTER: Yes, but I mean in a legal sense he still takes the document. We do that all the time.

1ST EDITOR: I don't know enough about defense attorneys, but I suspect that it would be pretty tough to prove theft of the document.

2ND TV REPORTER: No. You're still taking an official document.

1ST EDITOR: Oh, the officialness of it doesn't worry me at all or the classification.

2ND TV REPORTER: I think I'm saying reporters do that all the time.

1ST EDITOR: Yes, and so do prosecutors.

MR. NESSON: Are we clear on what's been stolen? It went by kind of quick. Is it the piece of paper that we're worried about? Is it the information?

1ST EDITOR: No, it's the document itself. The question is, would we run it—a stolen document.

MR. NESSON: The arrangement of the words?

1ST EDITOR: This piece of paper.

MR. NESSON: Piece of paper.

1ST EDITOR: Here's the message, the Lords.

MR. NESSON: No problem if he takes a copy.

1ST EDITOR: I don't think you're out of it if you've got a Xerox copy of it instead of the original.

MR. NESSON: Why not, you've still got your piece of paper?

1ST PROSECUTOR: He meant—he means—that he doesn't think that he's dismissed his legal liability by having a copy.

1ST EDITOR: So long as it was my reporter who stole it in the first place.

MR. NESSON: What if the CIA happens to open mail sent to a newspaper. It opens anything that comes from a foreign source and makes a Xerox copy but then sends the letter on to you. Are they guilty of theft?

1ST EDITOR: Well, they're guilty of something.

MR. NESSON: Maybe, but is it theft? Have they stolen the letter?

1ST EDITOR: Ask a lawyer, I don't know.

MR. NESSON (Turns to 1st Gov't. Official): Has the letter been stolen?

1ST GOV'T. OFFICIAL: I think someone is guilty of something but not guilty of theft. But you know, there's another question about Mr. Bridges, did he have the right to give that information away. If it was under his agreements and so forth, he didn't have a right to give it away.

1ST EDITOR: Well, I think that obligation is on him. If he gives it to a reporter, you know, we're right now on facts of the Pentagon Papers.

1ST GOV'T OFFICIAL: The reporter is profiting from a misdeed that he did.

MR. NESSON: Let's stay with theft for just a minute—we'll come to Mr. Bridges . . .

2ND EDITOR: So let the CIA sue him.

MR. NESSON (Ignores 2nd Editor's comment; addresses 1st Editor): You want to find out from a lawyer whether it's theft, right?

1ST EDITOR: Yes.

MR. NESSON: Well, let's find out. (Picks on 1st Judge): Judge, would you advise our editor friend?

1ST JUDGE: I think that technically there is a difference between having the document itself, the original document, which would be theft, and having a copy of it and there's a difference between the reporter from the paper taking it, stealing it himself, and receiving it. Now if the document is the original document and is put in his hands and it was stolen, he may be guilty of receiving stolen property. If he gets a copy, he may not be because when you're getting a copy, you're dealing not with the physical property, you're dealing with copyright laws and I don't think that either of the documents here—the CIA Lord's report or the private memoir—are copyrighted so you're free on those grounds. Now these are legal technicalities and I agree with the editor that it really doesn't make too much difference in the exact physical form that he gets it in regard to his problem of what he should do with it and in regard to the problem of morality involved with his employee.

MR. NESSON (Turns to 1st Editor): Is it clear now?

1ST PROSECUTOR: Professor Nesson, I don't think that you would have a copyright problem here because in a copyright problem the question is whether you're stealing the words themselves and the arrangement of the words and there's no effort to really misappropriate that.

1ST JUDGE: That's the distinction I was trying to make. There's a gap in the law that may not afford complete protection from one point of view. And from another point of view it may not cause any problem to the newspaper if it wishes to print this. The copyright covers the intellectual ideas in it if it were copyrighted, which it isn't. Theft of property covers the physical property, the document itself. When you get a Xerox copy of the document itself without the original complicity of the newspaper, then you may be home free as far as the legal liability of the editor. It's his judgment as to the content and as to what he will do with it.

1ST EDITOR: Well, I don't believe Xerography has so changed the law here that if my reporter stole it, takes it to a Xerox machine, and comes back and gives me the Xerox copy I'm off free. I don't believe that.

1ST JUDGE (Advises 1st Editor): No. No. But suppose the document has been copied by a secretary in the State Department, not by your reporter. Then the actual physical document given to your reporter is not a State Department document per se, at least physically.

1ST EDITOR: Now, he's been given it. Now Case I talks about money and that's another thing that is a no-no as far as I'm concerned.

1ST JUDGE: I didn't see the money part but that raises another problem.

1ST EDITOR: He was given it by this secretary. I have no problems. I mean, I've got another problem, but I don't have the theft.

MR. NESSON: In other words, she steals it, she gives it to the reporter, and you don't have a problem?

1ST EDITOR: I don't think so. Now, I admit that in a Biblical sense. I'm not sure I see all that much difference, but I haven't been informed by lawyers that there is so . . .

1ST JUDGE: The observations of our first TV reporter on the thing being a shading I think are applicable here. It's the whole shading of minor thefts of ideas and on down the line. As far as the law is concerned, you're in better shape if you don't have the original document.

MR. NESSON (Addresses 1st Judge): Do you have any problem dealing with this whole subject in terms of theft; that is, does it make sense at all to be talking about property whereas what we're really dealing with here is some notion of information?

1ST JUDGE: Well, there are two basic problems in this first case. One is theft and the other is the national security interest. The newspaper being in receipt of the original stolen document may be in a position of receiving stolen property just like a used car dealer who takes a stolen car. That's one position but only part of it.

MR. NESSON: Yes. But what I want to put to you is, isn't it clear on this problem that the main things that should govern the issue of should they print or shouldn't they print has got nothing whatsoever to do with ordinary notions of property.

1ST JUDGE: That is probably the ultimate and decisive thing when you get down to the question of the content of these documents and of the justification for printing them. Of course, here there's far less justification, in my opinion, than there was in the Pentagon Papers. Here it is hard to point out any great benefit to the U.S. public or benefit to any kind of our processes by printing something that will expose a spy ring operating, supposedly, in the best interests of all American citizens overseas. And then when you come to the domestic part of this problem, I'd say . . .

(Simultaneous remarks)

MR. NESSON: I'd like to slow you up on it a minute.

1ST PROSECUTOR: I don't see where it's receiving stolen property anyway. Under the law you have to have a specific intent to defraud. There's no specific intent to defraud here by the editor if he receives that document—even if it is taken.

MR. NESSON: What about the reporter who pays money to the secretary?

1ST PROSECUTOR: Well, if there was a preexisting agreement, you might have a case. But there was no preexisting agreement here. Payment came afterward. (Laughter)

MR. NESSON: In other words, your notion is that if somebody knows that something is stolen and receives it in exchange for money, he's not guilty of receiving stolen property.

1ST PROSECUTOR: Well, that's not in the problem here.

(2ND REPORTER speaks up): But suppose during a week in which a reporter steals a document he receives his salary. All right? And one assumes that part of his compensation is for professional output. And one item of professional output that week was the "theft," quote, unquote, of a public document. Now has the publisher or the managing editor, whoever signs the paycheck, engaged in any less of a purchase or acquisition through illicit means?

MR. NESSON: A little bonus.

2ND REPORTER: Bonus? No, that's different.

(Laughter and simultaneous remarks)

MR. NESSON (Asks the 1st TV Reporter to comment)

1ST TV REPORTER: I don't like checkbook journalism.

(4TH EDITOR chimes in): The point that the first editor made earlier as an editor, and I'm an editor, which seemed to have passed everyone, is that he has to protect the integrity and the credibility of the property he works for. He can't be indicted and go to court without a case. And this is why he is not going to risk, nor would I, taking stolen property in return for a story.

1ST EDITOR: No matter how bad you want it or need it.

MR. NESSON: Suppose he doesn't know it's stolen? Would he pay for it? Would you pay for it?

4TH EDITOR: If I didn't know?

MR. NESSON: Yes, one of your secretaries hands you a document, and as our first prosecutor points out, we don't really know whether it was stolen or not.

4TH EDITOR: The only materials we ever buy are from impecunious professors. (Laughter) As a matter of fact, we don't buy material. I don't think we would pay for the best story in the world.

1ST EDITOR: Well, I could give you an actual example of where someone was offered the contents of Howard Hunt's desk by a lawyer representing a client who, it was suggested, had been sent by an official of the Committee to Re-elect the President to clean out Howard Hunt's desk on June 19, 1972.

MR. NESSON: And what would you have done?

1ST EDITOR: We would not pay for it. We would have tried like hell to suggest that it was in the public duty to make these available for no money.

MR. NESSON (Now turns to 3rd Editor): Would you pay for that?

3RD EDITOR: Would I pay? Absolutely not.

1ST EDITOR: The dangers of a set-up there are obvious enough to not . . . (Laughter and simultaneous remarks)

MR. NESSON (Calls on 3rd TV Reporter): Can you speak for the broadcasters a little bit? Would you pay for material, news?

3RD TV REPORTER: That same material was wafted past us.

MR. NESSON: Smelled too bad for you too?

3RD TV REPORTER: I'm not on a level to make those decisions, but it wasn't on my network.

MR. NESSON (Turns to 4th TV Reporter): Would you have taken it?

4TH TV REPORTER: Would I have taken it?

MR. NESSON: Excuse me. Would you have paid for it?

4TH TV REPORTER: Oh, paid for it. No, I don't think so. I would not.

MR. NESSON (Turns to 2nd TV Reporter): You?

2ND TV REPORTER: No.

MR. NESSON: How about, let's say, an interview with Mr. Liddy? (Laughter)

MR. NESSON (Asks 4th TV Reporter): How about you? Can you tell me what the difference is?

4TH TV REPORTER: As a matter of fact, we have turned down various star figures in recent times because of their requests for money.

MR. NESSON: Mr. Liddy, Mr. Colson?

4TH TV REPORTER: Well, not Mr. Liddy, no, but Mr. Dean.

MR. NESSON: Mr. Dean?

4TH TV REPORTER: Yes.

(1ST EDITOR speaks): You've got the two major no-no's, so far as the postulates here, that you stole a document and you bought a document, neither of which is ethical, as far as I'm concerned.

MR. NESSON: So you would say that whoever paid Mr. Liddy to go on TV with his interview was acting unethically.

1ST EDITOR: Well, I mean . . . No, I think they've got a right to do that. That's different.

MR. NESSON: Why is it different?

1ST EDITOR: Because one is kind of a show business thing, and the other is . . .

MR. NESSON: I see. I see. That's just show biz, that broadcast guy.

(Laughter)

1ST EDITOR: It certainly is, to interview and trot out . . .

MR. NESSON (Recognizes 5th Editor)

5TH EDITOR: I think you always have to weigh all of the values that enter into this kind of equation, and your answers are going to be different, according to your judgment of what is the best way to handle your own responsibilities. You have a responsibility to your paper. You have a responsibility to your broadcasting enterprise. You have a responsibility to the public. Now, buying news is repugnant, I think, to any professional journalist. And yet I think there might be instances where you felt that the only way that you could get important information before the public might be to pay something for it. I think that in that case you might do it.

MR. NESSON: Would you articulate for me why it's repugnant?

5TH EDITOR: Well, because we believe, I think, that we operate through enterprise and through ethical activity, and there's something a little bit unethical about buying information for which we have a professional staff that is supposed to obtain it in the normal course of their work.

MR. NESSON: That doesn't wash. I mean, isn't buying stuff the American way?

5TH EDITOR: No, I think it has an element of bribery in it, actually. You're paying somebody to do something which is improper, and he knows it.

MR. NESSON: Excuse me, what's improper about it?

5TH EDITOR: Well, he's violating his obligation to whoever his employer is.

MR. NESSON: So you recognize that it's improper for him to give you information. And yet you go around, will hound that man in every way you can in order to get him to give it to you for nothing.

5TH EDITOR: Yes, we would.

MR. NESSON: Well, that's a cheap thing, isn't it?

5TH EDITOR: I don't think so.

(Laughter)

MR. NESSON: Well, why isn't it equally improper for you to go around and hound that man, to try to convince him it's his public duty to violate his obligations to his employer?

5TH EDITOR: Well, I think that sometimes he might feel that he had a higher obligation, and that it had something to do with something more than money.

MR. NESSON: We still haven't got an articulation. Does somebody else want to try?

1ST TV REPORTER: Weakly, in a very weak way?

MR. NESSON: Sure.

1ST TV REPORTER: There is a point to be made that those who have to maintain security of documents may be living in a fool's paradise if we help them by not trying as hard as we can to get the information. In fact, in so doing we sometimes help to expose for those in charge of security the weaknesses of their security apparatus. And if we come across a document like this, or if it's available to us, and we don't use it, we may be lulling the official into thinking his security is better than he thinks it is.

MR. NESSON: I take it that it would be totally improper to suggest that there's a phenomenon that operates here that's similar to the antitrust problems. That is, it would be very bad for business to start buying information. And God knows, look at what salaries are now paid in the ABA and the NBA. Who knows what the cost of information would be in two or three years?

1ST GOV'T. OFFICIAL: Well, some government agencies pay for information abroad without any hesitation. (Laughter) It's a purely practical problem that you can get yourself the subject of fabrications very easily if you're too generous with money and if you're too quick with it. There appear to be a whole variety of procedures where, if somebody comes and offers something particularly attractive for X number of dollars, an attempt is made to get it before any money is offered.

MR. NESSON: Very interesting.

1ST GOV'T. OFFICIAL: I would comment on another thing, though. I wonder if there's a difference between paying Mr. Liddy for an article in the Sunday magazine section and paying him for an article in the daily paper.

MR. NESSON: Well, let me just stick with your initial, very interesting observations. Now you obviously have some advice for our first editor as to how he should be conducting his business. Right?

1ST GOV'T. OFFICIAL: No, because he doesn't want to buy the information at all.

MR. NESSON: Well, he says he has to get it. I mean, after all, he's involved in letting people like me know what goes on. That's his sole obligation.

(4TH EDITOR breaks in): Intelligence agencies aren't hauled into court. Newspapers could be.

MR. NESSON: We don't know about the CIA. (Laughter)

1ST GOV'T. OFFICIAL: I'm thinking of a situation abroad, where the intelligence agencies can get into a great deal of trouble by buying advice and information. It's called espionage.

MR. NESSON (Recognizes 2nd Editor)

2ND EDITOR: I think your earlier questions and the things that we're talking about now, such as would we use a stolen document and why we are so chary of it and why we won't pay, tie together, for us in the media, at least newspapers. It comes back to what is our stock-in-trade as we perceive it, which is our credibility with our readers. For logical reasons or otherwise we feel that to pay for information and to make a habit of purveying documents that we stole would cost us that credibility, and we would lose the base of our professional existence.

1ST EDITOR: And the richest newspaper would become the purveyer of the most information. It's totally evil, wrong.

MR. NESSON: Our second editor says the newspaper will go out of business; they will lose their credibility; they will cease to be believed; and that's going to be the end of reputable journalism.

1ST EDITOR: Buy one dog and you're out of business.

MR. NESSON: And you say it's because the richest newspaper is going to get all the news.

1ST EDITOR: No, I don't say that, but I say that . . .

MR. NESSON: Didn't you just say that?

1ST EDITOR: Well, I didn't specify it like . . . (Laughter) It's wrong; it's repugnant. It is.

2ND EDITOR: But it breaks down; it's not an absolute. And I think you're looking for absolutes. At least you're appearing as if you're looking for absolutes.

MR. NESSON: Our government official isn't looking for absolutes. He suggests that some government agencies buy information when they can get good information. And he suggests further that governments have lots of guidelines for getting it, and don't buy information when they can't get good information. What's the matter with that?

(Simultaneous remarks)

1ST GOV'T. OFFICIAL: I'm concerned about credibility, too. The government has got to make sure that the information it gets is accurate information and not fabrications, so it, too, is concerned about the credibility to its readers, a rather limited circle.

2ND EDITOR to 1ST GOV'T. OFFICIAL: Some government agencies are expected to buy information, aren't they?

1ST GOV'T. OFFICIAL: Yes.

2ND EDITOR: Okay. We're not expected to buy information.

1ST JUDGE: Exactly. There's quite a bit of difference, both legally and morally, between the two businesses. Buying information has been the stock-in-trade of espionage for centuries, and it's legally correct. And if espionage is moral, it's morally correct. On the other hand, the editor's problem may be legally wrong as well as morally wrong. They're two different businesses.

MR. NESSON: Wait a second here. Here we have a problem that's posed in front of all of you, where we have on the one side the intelligence business of gathering information, credible information for its limited clientele; on the other side, the newspapers, in the business gathering information for their clientele. And you're prepared to tell me that the newspaper shouldn't buy information to serve their readers, when they're in the business of buying information all over the place.

1ST JUDGE: Not that kind of information.

(5TH EDITOR speaks up): Well, it isn't that black and white at all. Newspapers and any other kind of publication frequently buy information from experts. We'll ask a scientist to write a piece or somebody with some special, particular knowledge to write a piece, and they're paid for it. There's nothing illegitimate about that.

MR. NESSON (Recognizes 3rd Editor)

3RD EDITOR: This raises a point. A lot of newspapers and magazines are part of conglomerate organizations in the news business, and during the course of Watergate people came to you trying to sell news, and you said, "Well, we don't buy news," and they said, "But you have a book company, you have this, and I'm interested in writing a book. Can we work a deal. I'll give you this for the weekly issue of the magazine, but then can you get me a book contract? And we can work it that way." And this raises another moral question, which you specified before, is it possible to get the same information in a weekly—the Sunday *Times* Magazine or the Outlook section of the *Post*—by paying for it.

MR. NESSON (Asks 1st Gov't. Official): Is that what you had in mind? You raised the Sunday, daily issue. Just go around the post, for example, a little different way.

1ST GOV'T. OFFICIAL: Well, I questioned whether there aren't certain situations where editors do buy information and publish it.

MR. NESSON (Acknowledges 4th Reporter)

4TH REPORTER: I really fail to see why keeping a stable of your own reporters and paying them and putting professional pressure on them to ferret out information isn't paying for information.

1ST EDITOR: Well, buying the AP is paying for information.

4TH REPORTER: I think that's buying information.

MR. NESSON (Recognizes 2nd Gov't. Official)

2ND GOV'T. OFFICIAL: I just wonder if you'd ask your reporters whether they don't feel there's some contradiction or tension between these moral compunctions they feel and the concern about the variety of laws and their First Amendment obligation.

MR. NESSON: Who'd you like to ask that to?

2ND GOV'T. OFFICIAL: Well, I'd like you to ask the entire assembly.

MR. NESSON: Why don't you just ask somebody?

2ND GOV'T. OFFICIAL: Our first editor!

(Laughter)

1ST EDITOR: Rephrase it.

2ND GOV'T. OFFICIAL: Well, you have a variety of compunctions about the criminal law, and I was a little surprised you didn't say that the criminal law, insofar as it interfered with this kind of flow of information, was unconstitutional. I was surprised you didn't say that. And, secondly, I'm wondering about this variety of compunctions you have and whether they don't contradict your First Amendment obligations.

1ST EDITOR: There are restrictions on the First Amendment.

2ND GOV'T. OFFICIAL: Yeah, but I don't know that . . .

(Laughter and simultaneous remarks)

MR. NESSON: What a marvelous argument coming from a government official—has got to be food for thought, Mr. Editor.

2ND EDITOR: The trouble is the instant case. I think you can get your exemption to all our morality if you pose these questions differently. In this case you have three elements. You have the element of an American antiwar movement being directed by the Soviet Union. That's a hell of a news story. But if the public did not find out about it, it wouldn't harm them because the authorities know about it. The authorities are dealing with it.

2ND GOV'T. OFFICIAL: But it might change attitudes toward the movement.

1ST EDITOR: Precisely.

2ND REPORTER: Who's watching the authorities as they watch the movement?

2ND EDITOR: Now let me finish my obviously shot-full-of-holes theory. (Laughter) The second element is the fact that there is an American spy who is the finance minister of Hungary. I don't think any of us would print that—I wouldn't. No problem, as far as I can see. The third element begins to have a problem, and that is the domestic surveillance by the CIA because that begins to violate American law, and there the public interest is immediately discernible. But in the real world it is that type of issue that might possibly change our minds about our normal way of doing business. What is at stake here? What is the story about? How will the public interest be served?

MR. NESSON: Well, let's move on to that. One of the editors was interested in verification. (Turns to that editor): How do you verify a story?

3RD EDITOR: Well, in this case, it was a question of an American spy in Hungary. You can feel around the edges of former agents you might know. You might check into the Hungarians you knew around town. Half of them are KGB. But it's very difficult to verify. The authenticity of a document like that would give me great pause. I suspect at the end we'd wind up running information that would be unverifiable in this area because of the quality of the sourcing and the quality of the document.

MR. NESSON: Would you check the document out with the director of the CIA?

3RD EDITOR: No. I don't know the present director. But I would check . . .

1ST EDITOR: But there would come a time when you would let the CIA know that you had that document.

3RD EDITOR: That's right. Prior to print.

MR. NESSON: Prior to print?

3RD EDITOR: Yes.

MR. NESSON: In order to verify it.

1ST GOV'T. OFFICIAL: I should hope the government were told about it, because exactly what you say about going around to the Hungarians to check on whether there's an American spy network there . . .

3RD EDITOR: No, no, no. You're not going to ask them if there is an American spy.

1ST GOV'T. OFFICIAL: I know, but they're pretty smart, too.

3RD TV REPORTER: Well, I'd say right now that I think that the officials who brought the Pentagon Papers case had harmed their self-interest here because as you know some editors said, after all that litigation was over and they'd been held under a temporary restraining order for 15 days, "Well, we know how we'll deal with this next time. We'll print it all the first day."

1ST GOV'T. OFFICIAL: Mr. Agee went out of the country in order to print it. [Former CIA employee Philip Agee is publishing his book, *Inside the Company,* in Great Britain.]

3RD TV REPORTER: That's right. That's the sort of thing I fear is going to happen. It seems to me that the way this whole discussion started out is an illustration of one of the problems of journalism today. We started out talking about statutes and criminal law, and it's very unfortunate and of course this is my ax to grind, but I don't like to see the way the law has permeated the business of journalism. It should not be legalistic. And when you start out discussing what is really a problem of ethics and journalistic propriety and the way we should run our business, talking about section 614B or whatever, it's one of the problems we're facing and I think we need to back away from the law if we can, and operate in an era of ethics and . . .

MR. NESSON: So you're really wondering why it is that newspaper editors and reporters have to be so concerned with theft statutes for example.

4TH EDITOR: Was the second government official suggesting that editors should use the First Amendment as a crutch in every instance as an overriding constitutional right?

1ST EDITOR: As a *laisser passer* to do anything.

4TH EDITOR: Were you suggesting that we should feel that way, . . .

2ND GOV'T OFFICIAL: We were discussing the fact that you have two enormously important social and constitutional values in conflict here, and they're not resolved by discussing copyright laws or ethics about paying people for things. One could very easily postulate a case in which I hope you'd pay for stories, for example, if somebody told you they had government plans to set up concentration camps. I trust you would buy that story and publish it. I trust you would steal that story and publish it. I hope you would, and that's why I think you're not discussing basic values that are employed. You're discussing all kinds of . . .

4TH EDITOR: Substituting the press for the legal authorities there, is that what you want? In other words, we make the judgment, not you.

MR. NESSON (Turns to 1st Prosecutor): Would you prosecute . . .

2ND GOV'T. OFFICIAL: I think I'd have to plead the First Amendment.

1ST PROSECUTOR: We're getting back to the question that I raised at the start about whether you're talking about ethics or law and now we've really got the issue joined.

3RD TV REPORTER: Well, I agree with him too, but it seems to me that the indictment of Daniel Ellsberg and Anthony Russo on some of those very strange charges such as theft of government pieces of paper is why—and the attempt to suppress the Pentagon Papers is a reason why—editors now have to say immediately, "Oh, oh, I better call my lawyer," when really we should be talking about informing the public.

1ST TV REPORTER: I'd like to reformulate the second government official's doctrine.

MR. NESSON: Shoot.

1ST TV REPORTER: Bought, borrowed, and stolen information must have redeeming social value.

NUMEROUS: Yes. Right.

2ND GOV'T. OFFICIAL: First Amendment social value.

MR. NESSON (Asks 2nd Gov't. Official): How much?

2ND GOV'T. OFFICIAL: Well, you know, there's no way of avoiding the fact that you're going to wind up in court and you're going to have a conflict between the executive need for confidentialities and the First Amendment.

3RD TV REPORTER: Redeeming social value.

2ND GOV'T. OFFICIAL: But I think we ought to discuss the conflict in those terms and not in terms of the copyright law or property law and so forth. They're really doctrines that will fall by the side.

MR. NESSON: And does it follow from that, that the United States government in dealing with these problems should be dealing with them in terms of doctrine other than copyright and theft?

2ND GOV'T. OFFICIAL: Yes, I think it does, I think it may apply the criminal law, but ultimately the validity of the criminal law is going to depend upon the constitutional determination as applied to these facts.

1ST PROSECUTOR: Well, you see, you say apply the criminal law, but the fact is that one of the principal factors of determining whether you would apply the criminal law by any prosecutor would look at this in terms of whether a jury would convict, which is really the ultimate test. And in the case postulated by the government official, no jury would convict anybody.

MR. NESSON: Wait a second, that's your ultimate test, whether you can get the conviction?

1ST PROSECUTOR: Well, . . .

MR. NESSON: That's not the official's ultimate test.

1ST PROSECUTOR: And whether there is a public interest in the prosecution. Of course there are other factors too.

MR. NESSON (Calls on 2nd Prosecutor): What do you think about it?

2ND PROSECUTOR: The ultimate goal is not whether you can get a conviction, it seems to me, but whether you are persuaded, as a prosecutor, that you can get the case to a jury for determination as to whether there's a violation of the law or not. In other words we're not . . .

MR. NESSON: What happened to our official's redeeming social value, what happened to the prosecutor's discretion that he's telling you to exercise?

2ND PROSECUTOR: It's still there.

MR. NESSON: Where?

2ND PROSECUTOR: I was disagreeing because when you make a prosecutorial decision whether to indict or not you first have to determine whether there are any factual inadequacies in the proof and second whether there are any legal problems that perhaps are going to be incapable of resolution. And that will be where you will take into account the official's suggestion that you have a First Amendment value.

MR. NESSON (Turns to Former Gov't. Official): A reporter has just stolen secret papers, showing that there's a concentration camp plan in the United States. He stole them, he didn't make copies of them, he didn't buy them from anybody, he just went and he lifted them. Cold case, cold turkey case. Are you going to prosecute that case?

FORMER GOV'T. OFFICIAL: No.

MR. NESSON: Why not?

FORMER GOV'T. OFFICIAL: Because the suggested activity on the part of the government is so far outside of their own legal responsibilities that the government in turn prosecuting his offense is acting very inconsistently. I don't believe that under those conditions what he is really doing by committing a technically illegal act is other than in the broader public interest and therefore as a prosecutor I think that in the exercise of my discretion I would refuse to prosecute.

MR. NESSON: A justification defense.

FORMER GOV'T. OFFICIAL: Sure. Prosecutors make those kinds of decisions all the time.

MR. NESSON (Turns to 2nd Prosecutor): What do you say to that?

2ND PROSECUTOR: I think he's right.

1ST PROSECUTOR: That's correct. They're made all the time. There are a number of considerations and factors that go into the determination of whether you'll go forward with the case.

2ND REPORTER: Suppose the White House called and said I want you to prosecute.

2ND PROSECUTOR: Let them send a lawyer to prosecute.

1ST PROSECUTOR: That's correct. You would say send down somebody to prosecute.

4TH EDITOR: Well, the point is that simply because three people at this table say they wouldn't doesn't mean the case would not be prosecuted.

2ND REPORTER: Well, the Pentagon Papers . . .

4TH EDITOR: Then it's the responsibility of the editor of going to court with clean skirts or a $2,000 theft that he's got to defend.

2ND REPORTER (Speaking to 4th Editor): What troubles a lot of us, I suspect, is that the judgments are being left to the prosecutors today. Why, for example, is it not just as justifiable for the editors of the New York *Times* to determine that Lyndon Johnson lied to the American people in the course of a presidential election campaign and kept that fact undisclosed, and then when one newspaper goes out and publishes it it is subject to prosecution. Mr. Johnson's behavior, at least in some people's moral universes, may be just as condemnable as the plan to create a concentration camp. And the question is, is it going to be an editor who makes that judgment that that's a condemnable behavioral pattern for a publicly accountable public servant, or is it going to be left to a prosecutor? And one of the unhappy things is that too many times these days I think we in the press think first of calling a lawyer.

4TH EDITOR: Exactly.

2ND REPORTER: I suppose it's an entirely understandable sensation because some of us don't have long purses. You get out in the boondocks, you get a small newspaper and they don't have any purse. So they cannot hire a lawyer, they cannot stand a temporary restraining order for one day, they cannot stand the possibility of a contempt judgment with a fine, even for one day. So we have to think about these legal things. But the question is, when it comes down to making that judgment to publish or not to publish, do you make it upon some legal premises or do you make it upon some other larger, moral premises that only newspapermen feel free to make for themselves?

1ST LAWYER (Asks 2nd Reporter): Don't you ultimately make that decision, one of the factors in the decision whether or not the conduct violated the criminal statute?

2ND REPORTER: Oh, yes, yes.

1ST LAWYER: So in other words you're not really leaving the decision, as I would understand it, to the lawyer, even if the lawyer said you will violate a statute here involved if you publish the material, or if you pay for it. But in the last analysis you are making that decision as to whether to publish or not. Now granted it's small consolation, I suppose, to have the ultimate determination, but that, as I understand it, is what the First Amendment's all about. Because if you go one step further you get into the question of whether, because of the First Amendment, mass media are above any criminal statute or any civil statute. I mean, if you get down to the last analysis you've got to weigh these two factors. Now, I've always felt that in the last analysis the right to publish is about as absolute a thing as there is under our Constitution. The next question that comes in is how much do the individuals in that paper have to be concerned about possible applicability of the criminal law. But to me it's a factor that goes into it, and I think if you move into an area where you say the First Amendment is absolute and supersedes any part of criminal law, or indeed any potential civil liability like taking property of others and utilizing ideas, then you reach a situation where you are in great difficulty.

1ST EDITOR: We're headed into this question of who the hell is any editor to decide whether something is in the national interest or not? The next shade over is who the hell are these editors to decide whether something is, in fact, national security. What frustrates me about this case is you don't have the chance to argue that the government says it's national security and we disagree. It's awfully hard to disagree, you know, to cost five people their lives and to destroy a network of 20 people is in any way in the public interest. Well, 99 times out of 100 you'd never get the case presented to you that way. You'd have a document which said, yes, the Commies are infiltrating the antiwar movement, and you wouldn't have the specifics or you'd have some very few specifics, and as a cynic you'd say, "Boy, they've been trying to prove that for the last five years," and suddenly a reporter comes with a document and it is not above the director of the CIA or his predecessors to have arranged to have that document come into the reporter's possession. And I would be goddamned suspicious of any such document. But the case here is so specific you can't argue that.

MR. NESSON (Turns to 3rd Reporter)

3RD REPORTER: Well, I think that part of this case, the national security issue, is really phony because I think most of us would write the story without going into how the CIA director was convinced that he ought to go into bugging and infiltrating and whatever he did to the antiwar movement.

MR. NESSON: Well, how about that story? What would you put in and what not?

3RD REPORTER: Some of it depends on the degree to which I believe the findings they make. But the elements that are newsworthy are if it's true that the antiwar movement was dominated by foreign or Communist elements, and that the CIA infiltrated and did all that wiretapping, did all these bad things.

MR. NESSON: And I as your reader am not entitled to some verification of the story?

3RD REPORTER: Of course you are.

MR. NESSON: How do I get it?

3RD REPORTER: Well, . . .

MR. NESSON: Just on your say-so?

3RD REPORTER: No, the various ways described earlier of trying to check and see whether the thing is true as best you can.

MR. NESSON: And here you are sitting with a document which provides the verification for the story.

3RD REPORTER: Well, you can use the document. What I'm saying is you don't need the Hungarian finance minister in it. You don't need to know how the CIA first became apprised of the possibility because that wasn't enough for them. They then went ahead and infiltrated to see if this tip they had was worth anything. Now, they might say in court, "Look, if you print anything you'll expose the Hungarian finance minister because somebody would know he did it." And I would say, "Nonsense, if the Russians let him know about it there were so many people in Moscow who knew that the sourcing isn't all that obvious, and what's important is how they verify it by wiretapping, et cetera, in the antiwar movement."

MR. NESSON: But what's important . . .

FORMER GOV'T. OFFICIAL: I would really hope that, to echo a prior suggestion, in a case like this, before a newspaper would print the information leaving out what might jeopardize somebody's life they would first go to the agency, whether it's the FBI or the CIA or whatever, and try to discuss as openly as possible what the potential problem might be. Because it is entirely possible that unbeknownst to you a revelation at this source could take place because of information you printed that didn't seem to be related.

3RD REPORTER: Sure.

1ST EDITOR: But as a matter of fact in this case I suspect that the Hungarian finance minister would have been removed six weeks before any reporter ever got the story, once Bridges had reported that his study had been burgled, and once all of this had happened. The CIA then knows that the agent—the whole network—was compromised, and it would be out. There were three or four CIA agents in the Pentagon Papers case who were named, and no newspaper printed them, and they were all long gone before their names could have been printed without endangering their lives at all.

MR. NESSON: Suppose that the reporter got the material from a friend of Mr. Bridges' in the CIA who thought that Duke was a double.

1ST EDITOR: Now, you're thickening the soup quite a lot.

MR. NESSON: We're back on trying to verify the story, to find out what it's about. This fellow gives it to the reporter because he thinks he's doing a service if he blows this thing.

1ST EDITOR: Right, it's much more likely how he got it.

5TH EDITOR: There's another journalistic device that you can use with a story of this kind, and that's a flat confrontation with the legitimate sources in the story. And even if they deny it, if you print their denial, I think you're getting the substance of the story out before the public.

MR. NESSON: Wait a minute, let me follow that one closely. Undisclosed sources say that "A" robs, steals, and beats his wife. "A" denies it. That's the story?

5TH EDITOR: No, we're talking about a different story entirely. We're talking about something where national and public interest and social values are involved. I think you're talking about gossip in your example.

MR. NESSON (Turns to 1st Reporter): Supposing you had gotten the information under circumstances which indicated from a source inside the agency that in fact there was great suspicion of "Duke," because he might have been a double. Does that affect the way you deal with your editor at all in the story?

1ST REPORTER: You mean do I confide in him all I know?

MR. NESSON: Yes.

1ST REPORTER: Oh, yes. We have to—he has to be in the same position.

MR. NESSON: Suppose you had, in an attempt on your own part to verify the story first, gotten in touch with some people you were friendly with in the agency. They said to you, "Whatever you do, don't print this story." And you decided in your own mind that they were right, really, given all the considerations you shouldn't print it. Do you let that go to your editor?

1ST REPORTER: That situation has arisen a couple of times. Yes, we talk it over. It was a local editor rather than one far away.

MR. NESSON: So even when you make a judgment that material you have shouldn't go, that's something you turn over to your editor to decide?

1ST REPORTER: Yes, because in this particular case I thought that it was a sufficient question of public interest involved in getting it out. But I sympathize with them for not wanting to print, I know what would happen if it got printed.

1ST PROSECUTOR: What would happen if the editor decided to print it?

1ST REPORTER: Some people will lose jobs. You know what I'm talking about is hypothetical.

1ST EDITOR: And you might quit. But that happens all the time, that's not new.

4TH EDITOR: I'd like to know what the director of CIA's reaction would be if I had this information, and confronted him with it. I would have no trepidation in this case of telling him this is damned hot stuff, and I want him to level with me. We're going to print part of it. We will not use the text of the Lord's document, we'll refer to it, and I want to know straight out who we're going to hurt and how badly. What would his reaction be?

1ST GOV'T. OFFICIAL: He'd have to convince you that that was right. I think he'd have to tell you enough of the story, of the reality of the story, to convince you of the seriousness of it.

4TH EDITOR: Obviously, he would prefer that I didn't touch the story at all.

1ST GOV'T. OFFICIAL: Oh, in a perfect world probably yes, but once you have the basic elements of the story then it's up to him to try to convince you to cut it down to something which is manageable but not disastrous.

4TH EDITOR: Do you think many directors of the CIA would have taken this approach?

1ST GOV'T. OFFICIAL: Well, if the director and the editor—and this is the danger in going to him with the story—come to a difference of opinion and the editor says, "I'm not convinced, I'm going to print it the way it was," then the director has a problem of whether he turns to the law. And the editor has given the director the tip.

4TH EDITOR: You are opening a whole new vista to me.

1ST EDITOR: But would you believe his answer?

4TH EDITOR: Yes, I would. Now whether I would . . .

1ST GOV'T. OFFICIAL: I think the director would have to give an editor enough facts to convince him that he could be sure that it was right, not just take the director's word for it. I think the editor would be wrong if he just took the director's word for it.

MR. NESSON (Acknowledges 6th Editor)

6TH EDITOR: When the reporter has the documents a few editors have seen them, maybe someone has typed them in the office, maybe the reporter or the editors have gone around and called a few people. At what point does it no longer make a difference whether it's printed or not, because the security is already violated?

1ST GOV'T. OFFICIAL: It's like a ripple going out in a pond, obviously, but sometimes the Hungarians might not be in touch with your secretary. And obviously they're going to try to be, I mean that's their job to know what's going on around here. But I can envisage things—well, obviously, some of the CIA's most sensitive activities are today known by several hundred people in the government, on both sides of the executive and the legislative. And yet they're reasonably secure still. So the actual numbers isn't the problem, the question is whether the other side is alerted to it, and then jumps on them.

6TH EDITOR: But would this many people, a handful, be a consideration?

1ST GOV'T. OFFICIAL: Not necessarily.

6TH EDITOR: Wouldn't someone have to take steps in any event to kind of render the situation different, with . . .

1ST GOV'T OFFICIAL: Well, the government would probably have to take some steps, protective steps within its own outfit anyway. But I think any move against either a newspaper or the people that got onto it through legislation or through judicial action would obviously blow the thing into very great prominence.

MR. NESSON (Turns to Former Government Official): You wanted to direct a question to our first editor.

FORMER GOV'T. OFFICIAL: Well, he mentioned I think somewhat in passing that he wasn't so sure he would believe a government official when he told him of the sensitive nature of this information and the validity of this source being revealed if it were printed. In fact the FBI had a very similar case of this in which there was the possibility of the revelation of a source in an embassy. The FBI transmitted that information to newspaper editors and they believed it more than the FBI did.

1ST EDITOR: The reason I don't believe the government official is that I consider him to have a higher national duty than to tell me the truth. Moreover, it has been my experience, and I think this is perhaps new in the last 25 years, that government officials lie to reporters with an equanimity that is mind boggling, mind boggling. And if we went around believing what government officials told us we'd be in an interesting line of work but not the one we're now in.

FORMER GOV'T. OFFICIAL: I would say, in general, that that's the basic principle, but where you've got a specific case like this where an individual or a group of families' lives might be in jeopardy, it seems to me you have a somewhat different . . .

1ST EDITOR: I agree in this case; that's why I'm a little bothered by this case, but I would be very suspicious. I would certainly examine the possibility that this was a part of a black campaign to prove that the hippies were dominated by Commies.

FORMER GOV'T. OFFICIAL: Well, I think that's right, I think . . .

MR. NESSON: Well, let's stop here for a minute. (Asks 1st Editor): What are the standards that you are using? You say you agree, and this is a clear case. What's so clear about it?

1ST EDITOR: Because to print the contents of the Lord's documents is going to cost about five or six people their lives. And that hurts.

MR. NESSON: Lives, so that's it.

1ST EDITOR: Yes.

MR. NESSON: That would be a standard.

1ST EDITOR: That is one standard.

MR. NESSON: If any person is going to lose his life, you don't print.

1ST EDITOR: Well, you're going to say in the case of the Pentagon Papers, printing them earlier might have saved 40,000 lives rather than . . .

MR. NESSON: That is what I was going to say.

1ST EDITOR: Well, I believe that in this case it's a fact. I think a prior publication of the Pentagon Papers would in fact have brought an end to the war earlier, and what is the true national interest, you know, whether it's to cut it off or delay it, that's for other people to decide. I know where I stand on it.

MR. NESSON: Well, when a government official is trying to convince you not to print, one of the standards by which you're going to judge what he tells you . . .

1ST EDITOR: How many dead, yes.

MR. NESSON: . . . is how many dead.

1ST EDITOR: That is one of the standards, surely.

MR. NESSON: And if you find that it's four or five you don't print it.

1ST EDITOR: If you find it's one in certain cases you won't. There was a story of a kidnapping in the suburbs. A child had been kidnapped and our reporter found out about it and we got a call from the FBI that night saying, "Look, if you print that, that kid may die. We are in contact with the kidnappers, we expect to get the kid back, and if you print it you might blow that."

MR. NESSON: Suppose you said to the government official, "You say four or five people are going to die, I'll give you a week to pull them out."

1ST EDITOR: Well, I don't think I could do that.

MR. NESSON: Why not?

1ST EDITOR: Well, who the hell am I to tell him that?

MR. NESSON: You're the guy who's writing the newspaper that I read.

1ST EDITOR: Well, I'm a little reluctant to tell him to do anything. I'd resent like hell if he told me to do anything, and . . .

MR. NESSON: You're not telling him what to do, by the way . . .

1ST EDITOR: You just told me I was telling him to pull them out.

MR. NESSON: . . . you're just saying, "I'm going to print this in a week."

1ST EDITOR: Pull them out or you've got seven days. That is an instruction of some kind.

MR. NESSON (Asks 2nd Editor): Do you say anything like that?

2ND EDITOR: What story are we printing here, one that says what?

MR. NESSON: The one that says the reason why the CIA started domestic intelligence operations in the United States was because they had a very reliable agent who gave them information to the effect that this document discusses.

2ND EDITOR: Lots of trouble printing something like that, lots of trouble. Really. I think on balance we wouldn't print that. I think we'd agonize a long time about it, but I don't think we would print it.

3RD EDITOR: There's another question which this whole case has excluded, and this is a thing we all think about, and that's the question of competition. Supposing we know that if we don't print it the source or the secretary in the State Department would run down the street to a rival organization and offer it to them. And then supposing we knew that they were going to run around and they were going to have a big piece on it the next week, and the same thing would apply for the *Post* and the *Times*. The competitive factor sometimes weighs heavily in what you do or don't do. If we don't print it somebody else will.

MR. NESSON: Even leaving the competitive factor out I'm not quite sure I understand why our first editor wouldn't say if it's lives that I'm worried about I'll set it up so we aren't going to lose any lives. I'll wait a week.

1ST EDITOR: Well, is that in the national interest or is that in the public interest, in the First Amendment situation?

MR. NESSON: What have you got then, you've got another standard that's working.

1ST EDITOR: You've got hundreds of them.

MR. NESSON: All right, let's hear some more.

1ST EDITOR: Our national interest is certainly one.

MR. NESSON: And where is the national interest here?

1ST EDITOR: You want black and white answers. I don't know. I suspect that the national interest—on balance with five lives on one side and the public's right to know—...

MR. NESSON: Well, we've gotten those five lives out of here. We've given them a week.

1ST COLUMNIST: Well, obviously there's future information that this same spy could develop.

MR. NESSON: In other words our national interest is in keeping spies in place overseas.

1ST COLUMNIST: I assume the government would argue that.

2ND REPORTER: Is that an interest we must husband?

1ST TV REPORTER: Can I attempt a realistic answer to that? I think we sometimes have a tendency to flounder between absolutes, and the problem of absolutes is we know in our hearts that we don't deal in absolutes on a daily basis. I suspect—I'm not the one to speak for editors and publishers—but I suspect that what really concerns us from day to day is not whether or not we violate the law. There are some laws we would have willingly violated at certain times and have violated if we thought there was a public interest involved. That is part of what exists today, the tension between information and the law. And there's a question of a source to be protected and under present dictates of the Supreme Court that might involve going to jail, if there would be a violation of law. There might even be other technical, criminal acts that we'd be willing to perform as long as we were perceived by a larger public as performing a public interest. The question of how we are perceived is terribly important to us. Maybe more important to us than whether the thing is legal or illegal, is can we justify this to our readers as something that's needed to be done for their interest, and will we be perceived that way. If so, we'll take our chances with the law; we'll take our chances with the government; we'll take our chances with a whole lot of things. But we ultimately depend on that perception from our audience. And can I submit that as one of the overriding standards?

2ND GOV'T. OFFICIAL: Yes, that's the redeeming social value aspect.

1ST TV REPORTER: Well, it's redeeming social value plus whether it will be perceived as having redeeming social value.

MR. NESSON (Recognizes 1st Judge)

1ST JUDGE: I think I go along with that very well, and I think that that is what all the first editor has been quizzed about, and the others, adds up to—the really multiple considerations that enter into any case. Now, if the story is printed in a way that blows a spy network overseas, it's hard to say that that in itself is in the U.S. public interest. The part of the story that could and probably would be printed is about the domestic aspect of it, and if it could be done without blowing the spy network overseas then I would say that it should be done after it's thoroughly checked out. But the evaluation of the public interest in the long run is made by the readers, and our first TV reporter is absolutely right. If the reader perceives that it's not in the long-run interest of the United States, of the people themselves, to have this exposed, then they will react adversely. And so the publication of the story, instead of being a victory by the exercise of the First Amendment rights, actually has put a great strain on the First Amendment. And it has caused a lot of people to think less of the freedoms under the First Amendment than they otherwise would. But if the public perceives that printing the thing really was in the long-range public interest, they're inclined to forget about legal technicalities and say the First Amendment certainly overrides those, and they should publish. But it all adds up in the final analysis and I think the second editor was hinting at that a moment ago, that you've got to serve the long-range public interest, and your readers have got to perceive it to justify it.

1ST COLUMNIST: I'm bothered by that.

4TH TV REPORTER: I am too.

1ST COLUMNIST: I think if we rely on what our readers or our viewers perceive as their own good, we're relying on a very, very thin reed. In all the polls I've ever seen there's no great empathy for the First Amendment out there in the country. I think we have to make these judgments in a very egocentric way on what we think is really the good of the public.

4TH TV REPORTER: I think what the first TV reporter says is true, but I'm not at all sure that it's right.

1ST TV REPORTER: I'm not suggesting that it's right, I'm trying to suggest that it is our daily standard.

4TH TV REPORTER: Well, it may be our daily standard, but if it is then we are really passing the buck. We are saying that we will not make this decision on the basis of what we think is right. We will make it on the basis of what we think the public will think. And as one who has been battered by, as have many others, the demands for good news for a change, then I think that we have to think about that very seriously . . .

MR. NESSON: But at any rate . . .

4TH TV REPORTER: . . . as to whether we will give them what they think they will want.

MR. NESSON: Do you all buy this sliding scale? Is there not an editor here who would say national security be damned, I'm going to print it if it's good news.

4TH TV REPORTER: If it's what?

MR. NESSON: I'm going to print it if it's news.

4TH TV REPORTER: The editor would say, "What is the national security?" He would try to define that.

MR. NESSON: That's what I'm asking, is there any editor here who wouldn't ask that question? Is there any editor here who would say, "I will make a judgment as to whether material I'm considering bears on an issue of public importance in a way that's significant to the democratic process of the country. And if the answer is yes, it prints. And let them worry about national security, that's not my job." Is there any editor here that would go for that?

2ND EDITOR: Well, if it's important enough, yes. I mean, again, there are even gradations among that. Hypothetically there could be such a case. I think the concentration camp example is such an example.

1ST EDITOR: The Pentagon Papers case was such an example, wasn't it?

MR NESSON: Well, I don't know, what I'm trying to ask is this: Is there anyone who would say, "As soon as I as a newspaper editor, get into the business of making judgments myself, balancing news value against its interest in national security, I'm playing censor, I'm playing God. That's not my job as an editor." Is there anyone who thinks that's right?

2ND REPORTER: One of the things that troubles me about much of this is I think a lot of us on my side of the table, the news media side of the table, are forgetting the essential anarchic tradition that underlies the First Amendment. In judicial opinions we have a tendency to speak of it as robustness of publicity and openness in society. But there is a fundamental hostility between order and public information. And when our lawyer here raises the question about whether or not the press ought to be sensitive about when we disobey the law, I'm of course troubled by that as a citizen. But as a journalist there are times when my strongest sense is that the First Amendment is a mandate for an anarchic indifference to the felt needs of order, regularity, and continuity. In other words, we ought to kick over the bucket every now and then in our side of it, and maybe a Pentagon Papers is a spectacular form of kicking over the bucket. Because there we said—one presumes we said at some point—if it gets to a crunch between our interest in publishing and a question of protection of the national security, let someone else worry about it. And when we get to one of these other cases later in our conference about breaching grand jury secrecy, you're going to see this tension between anarchic traditions of an open press and the protective order even more vividly than you do here.

MR. NESSON: Is that a yes or a no?

2ND REPORTER: This is a yes, qualified.

1ST EDITOR: Aren't you saying, should editors be responsible or not?

MR. NESSON: I'm asking . . .

1ST EDITOR: Then the answer is that editors must be responsible . . .

MR. NESSON: What is the editor's concept of a free press?

1ST EDITOR: A free press is a responsible press.

MR. NESSON: And responsibility takes into account the national security.

1ST EDITOR: Yes, it does. Otherwise how are you going to answer Justice (Potter) Stewart when he turned to (Alexander M.) Bickel or (William R.) Glendon in the Pentagon Papers case and said, "What if I take this back in chambers"—and they had mountains of documents sealed, and they hadn't read them—"and find that the publication of this material will cost the lives of . . ." How do you answer that? And the question was asked by editors before Justice Stewart asked it, and I was appalled at his task of reading 7,000 pages, making a decision in 24 hours, because I felt it was impossible. But you've got to ask those questions and thousands like them.

MR. NESSON: Well, now, there's a little difference though. The difference is he's asking questions, and I'm posing it, do you have to ask the question?

1ST EDITOR: Yes, I have to ask the question and furthermore I've got to answer it to my satisfaction.

MR. NESSON: And is the question you ask going to be the same question he asks?

1ST EDITOR: Well, I would hope that I'd ask more.

MR. NESSON: He asks, "Will this cause direct immediate, irreparable harm to our nation or its peoples." Is that the question you ask?

1ST EDITOR: Well, yes, I ask it in some form or other.

MR. NESSON: What does that mean to you?

1ST EDITOR: That I struggle with the question of responsibility.

MR. NESSON: All right, fine, fine, fine. But what is a direct and immediate and irreparable harm?

1ST EDITOR: Well, I don't know the answers to those, but we're back . . .

MR. NESSON: But you'd know it if you'd see it.

1ST EDITOR: I think so. Yes.

2ND PROSECUTOR: What about death to an individual?

MR. NESSON: Yes, what about death to an individual?

1ST EDITOR: Well, that's one of the standards.

MR. NESSON: Is that enough, just one death?

2ND PROSECUTOR: Well, there was a kidnapping case in New York. The police asked the press there, and there were a number of papers at that time in New York, to hold that information to save the child's life. One newspaper breached the agreement, printed it, and the kid died. The kid died, and the other newspapers castigated the one newspaper that breached the agreement. There was tremendous revulsion in the public that the idea that a newspaper would breach that agreement that might have been the cause of the death of that child, that infant. I think that's an important consideration for a newspaper editor, and I think he would consider it.

1ST EDITOR: It's more complicated than that, because you, I think, end up by asking yourself whose death? The death of whom?

MR. NESSON: He's going to be our double agent over in Hungary.

1ST EDITOR: Or the death of Ilsa Koch is one thing, and the death of this child is another. The death of the CIA's finance minister does come into it, whether you want it to or not.

MR. NESSON: Well, let's move this thing into court. Let's suppose that this newspaper decides they're going to print these documents. The director of CIA sat down with the editor, he's given him stuff about how people are going to die, he's given him some stuff about how important the spy network is. And for some reason the editor is just not convinced, at which point the CIA director says I'm going to court. And he hires a distinguished lawyer to represent him, and the lawyer goes into court. Where is the second judge?

2ND JUDGE: I suspect our distinguished lawyer would first say, "I want it understood I'm not handling this on a contingent basis."

(Laughter)

MR. NESSON (Addresses 2nd Lawyer): You represent the CIA, and you're going to try to stop the publication of this material. You appear before the judge here. What do you say to him? Make your argument.

2ND LAWYER: First, I think I would have talked over with my client essentially the same thing that he would have talked over with the editor before that. I think there would be many parts of this information that I would make no effort to ask the court to restrain. I would really narrow it down to the problems that you have been talking about. I would narrow it down to the information contained in the Lord's document which presumably would expose the particular people in a network that was providing useful information to the United States. And I think I would tell my client that he was going to have to put in a good deal more information to attempt to establish that than a few simple affidavits which are conclusory. I think you've probably got to give the judge more information than is contained in the Lord's paper itself. I think he's going to have to expose all of that, he's obviously going to have to expose all of that to defense counsel if he doesn't. I think there's some chance of prevailing if he goes into sufficient detail to establish the loss of life, the loss of information, and you have to show what he'd been getting, how useful the potential of it was, and . . .

MR. NESSON (Tells the 2nd Lawyer): Do you start off by notifying the first lawyer, who's representing the newspaper, that you're intending to sue? Do you call him up on the phone and say, "We're about to file papers, we'll have them ready in three hours"?

2ND LAWYER: Yes, I would.

MR. NESSON: And what do you do, Mr. Defense Lawyer, when he calls you up with that?

1ST LAWYER (FOR THE DEFENSE): I'd try to find out what the case is all about.

MR. NESSON: You call the editor.

1ST LAWYER: I call the editor.

MR. NESSON: And the editor says we want to publish this stuff, the hell with the CIA. And he says how long have we got.

1ST LAWYER: Well, he's got as long as his next deadline to make the decision as to whether he wants to publish it or not. If the CIA lawyer goes to court and gets a temporary, ex parte temporary restraining order, I would then go to court and argue under *Near v. Minnesota* that . . .

MR. NESSON: Hold on, we haven't gotten anywhere near court yet. We haven't even got any papers filed yet. We've got three hours before he's going to make it down to the clerk's office. And he's got a print deadline which says he can hit the streets in two.

2ND LAWYER (FOR THE CIA): But I would have told him it's going in for TRO because under the federal rules I have to tell him I'm doing it for TRO or I won't get it.

MR. NESSON: And I want to know what the defense counsel is going to tell the editor and what the editor is going to do.

1ST LAWYER: I think what I would advise the editor is two things. I would say that in all probability the chances of getting a temporary restraining order, or at least a preliminary injunction, were not good, for the simple reason that under the doctrine of *Near v. Minnesota* prior restraints are looked upon with, shall we say, some disfavor by the Supreme Court, referring him to the Pentagon Papers case. And then I would think that the CIA's lawyer is a very, very resourceful individual and probably would take the Marchetti case and try to fashion relief out of that on the theory that the writer of this document had so breached his oath of secrecy to the CIA . . . [*Alfred A. Knopf, Inc. v. Colby,* 509 F.2d 1362 (4th Cir. 1975).]

MR. NESSON: Hold on, will you? I'm the editor and I've got two hours to hit the deadline. I've got a lot of work to do. Don't bother me with all this stuff. Should I print it or shouldn't I? I want to print it. Can I print it?

1ST LAWYER: Well, if he wanted my advice, I would have to spell out what I thought the law to be. The decision as to whether to print or not is up to him. I would add one conditional factor, and that is the question of whether or not, upon my being notified by the CIA lawyer that he is going to court, as to whether the judge might consider some type of a contempt citation against the newspaper because they proceeded to publish, even though the papers had not in fact been filed. I think, too, on the basis of the law as I understand it, I would advise my client that absent any order that had been entered that there would be no reasonable chance that the newspaper—or that he personally— would be held in contempt. Now, in view of saying, "What do you think?" I think I would say, "It's got to be your decision, from a personal standpoint." I think, in view of the potential danger here, I would forego publication, but that, sir, is the decision of the newspaper and not of a lawyer.

2ND LAWYER: Would you advise him as to the consequences if he did publish?

1ST LAWYER: Yes.

2ND LAWYER: I would agree with you. There's always a limited, very limited, chance even on these facts that you're going to get a preliminary injunction, but I would think on these facts you have a pretty good chance of a criminal prosecution thereafter.

MR. NESSON (Turns to the 1st Editor): On the basis of what you know, educated by the Pentagon Papers case, and starting from the hypothesis that you want to print this stuff, when you get word that a lawsuit's in the wind, does that speed you up or slow you down?

1ST EDITOR: It makes my heart go faster.

(Laughter)

MR. NESSON: You could get it on the street before he hits the clerk's office. Are you going to race him to the courthouse?

1ST EDITOR: In this case? No, I'm not going to, but you postulated that I am, and the only thing that worries me here is the prior restraint thing which I find totally repugnant. But I would be asking my counsel, can we fix it so that the publisher goes to jail rather than the reporter or the editor or . . . (Laughter) . . . who's going to jail and for how long. I would like to have a fair discussion of my chances in that suit.

MR. NESSON: Suppose he were to tell you that he thought that you could publish it, as long as you beat him to the courthouse, that you publish it without serious liability.

1ST EDITOR: This particular case?

MR. NESSON: Yes.

(Simultaneous remarks)

1ST EDITOR: Well, I don't like this case. (Laughter) I'm sorry. I wish you'd got me into a position . . .

1ST GOV'T. OFFICIAL: The assumption is you don't believe the director of the CIA.

MR. NESSON: I would like to get a case to court, and in order to do that I'm going to ask you to assume that when our third editor goes and checks to verify the story, what he finds out is that in fact there's a very substantial likelihood that this whole spy network is a phony. At least it has turned double, that somebody in the CIA would like to see it go, and that in your judgment it's an important element of the story to show what it was that led the CIA down the path of getting into domestic intelligence.

1ST EDITOR: And I was satisfied that ethically we were in a sound position . . .

MR. NESSON: Yes, I want to know if . . .

1ST EDITOR: . . . and acting responsibly . . .

MR. NESSON: Not ethically . . .

1ST EDITOR: Responsibly . . .

MR. NESSON: Legally . . .

1ST LAWYER: That's where I have a problem with much of the discussion here today. The difference between the ethics of the newspaper and the journalistic trade as distinguished from the obligations a lawyer has to advise that the law imposes. This is so because there are many instances, I believe, when the two may, in fact, conflict.

1ST EDITOR: Okay, but for the purposes of argument we are sure of our facts. Our legal position looks good to us, according to our counsel, and our chances of avoiding getting criminally prosecuted are good. Obviously, I would print it.

MR. NESSON: Let me ask our fourth editor the question I'm really driving at with the first editor: To what extent are you going to respect impending court process if you're given the option of acting in a way that will foreclose the CIA lawyer getting to court before you hit the streets? To what extent are you willing, as an editor, to say in this circumstance, well, since they want to go to court, I guess that's the right place for it to be decided.

4TH EDITOR: If I got my back up on the issue of prior restraint, and feeling as strongly as the first editor does about it, and I do, and had the resources and backing of my publisher, I think I'd go with it.

MR. NESSON (Turns to 1st Columnist)

1ST COLUMNIST: I'd go with it.

MR. NESSON: You'd beat him if you could.

1ST COLUMNIST: Yes.

MR. NESSON: In fact, you've got worries without even letting the director of the CIA know that you've got the stuff in the first place.

1ST COLUMNIST: No, I have no worries about that.

MR. NESSON: Even knowing that maybe what the CIA director will tell his lawyer to do is . . . Forget about calling the defense counsel. I'll call him ten minutes before you get the papers ready to go, rather than three hours.

1ST EDITOR: Oh, that's subterfuge. You'd have to call him, professionally, to get his response and to listen to his arguments.

4TH EDITOR: I thought we'd gone through that before.

1ST EDITOR: Well, I thought we had too, but you suddenly suggested that . . .

MR. NESSON: Yes, but you're going to call him, and then, when he takes the steps that he's got available to him, you're going to try and beat him with it.

1ST EDITOR: Yes. O.K.

MR. NESSON: In other words, you have a professional responsibility then to call him but no professional responsibility to honor the legal process when it begins to get into motion?

1ST EDITOR: Well, of course, we've got that.

MR. NESSON: But if you can beat him to the courthouse, beat him.

1ST EDITOR: Yes.

1ST COLUMNIST: Well, your lawyer has told you that the legal process isn't that cut and dried.

1ST EDITOR: In the Pentagon Papers those facts did obtain, really. The appellate court was in fact sitting while the second story was going through the composing room, and the plates were being put on the press, and they were still sitting when the normal press started, and the newspaper waited five minutes just to be clean with Jesus and then went. And then they handed down the decision, saying you can't—you've got to stop.

MR. NESSON: So that any lawyer here and any government personnel here, thinking of instituting suit, could be on fair notice. The suit . . .

VOICE: They're going to get that thing filed.

1ST EDITOR: The suit of prior restraint.

4TH EDITOR: That's the issue, prior restraint.

MR. NESSON (Turns to the 2nd Lawyer): All right, make your argument to the judge. You beat him to the courthouse.

2ND LAWYER: I beat him to the courthouse?

MR. NESSON: You got there. He hasn't printed it yet.

2ND LAWYER: I would tell the judge that if he doesn't issue a temporary restraining order on this, we'd have an immediate appearance on a preliminary injunction whenever the other counsel shows up.

MR. NESSON: Judge?

2ND LAWYER: I'd ask for it.

2ND JUDGE: Well, I'm inclined to think he might get his TRO. I don't think it would last very long, in fact.

MR. NESSON: What does he have to show you to get the TRO?

2ND JUDGE: I think he has to show me what Justice Brennan spoke about in the Pentagon Papers case. [In the Pentagon Papers case Justice Brennan declared, "Thus, any governmental allegation and proof that publication must inevitably, directly, and immediately cause the occurrence of an event kindred to imperiling the safety of a transport already at sea can support even the issuance of an interim restraining order." 403 U.S. at 726-727.]

MR. NESSON: He runs in; he's got a complaint two pages long written in a real hurry.

2ND JUDGE: You're just talking about the story now. You're not talking about the . . .

MR. NESSON: He wants to enjoin them. He wants to stop them from printing whatever part of it is he wants to stop from printing.

2ND JUDGE: Well, I'm not sure. It makes a difference now whether he's talking about printing the CIA document itself or whether he's printing a story.

MR. NESSON: Suppose the CIA document . . .

2ND LAWYER: I would come in with the CIA document, and I would come in with an affidavit from the CIA director, which might be rather brief, if we're working that fast now.

2ND JUDGE: It might depend on what circuit I'm in. For example, if I'm in the Fourth Circuit, I'd have to assume the classification was reasonable. I would probably give him his TRO. I think I'd be bound to because I have before me only the affidavit that this affects national defense, and the lives of these people. But I'd give him his preliminary hearing the next morning, and I'd probably dissolve it because by that time I would have expected the director of the CIA, if it really was factual, to get his people the hell out of wherever they are.

MR. NESSON: Okay. So you're going to grant a short TRO.

1ST GOV'T. OFFICIAL: In one day?

MR. NESSON: Hold on. Let's get to that in a minute. We just got a TRO, right?

2ND JUDGE: Right.

MR. NESSON: We got it on the basis of a complaint and a short affidavit from the director of the CIA saying that this document is classified and relates to national security.

2ND JUDGE: Yes.

MR. NESSON: Was the defense counsel present?

2ND JUDGE: Now see, do you want to put me on the United States Supreme Court?

MR. NESSON: No, no, no, no, no.

(Laughter)

2ND JUDGE: No, no. But suppose I'm on the Fourth Circuit, and . . .

MR. NESSON: And your understanding is . . .

2ND JUDGE: Judge Haynsworth wrote the Marchetti case, and I think that I would have to assume that the classification has its regularity, it's an appropriate one, until I can examine it *in camera* if need be.

MR. NESSON: Suppose you were in the D.C. Circuit. What's your own judgment of what the proper thing to do would be?

2ND JUDGE: Well, I think I'd probably be safer in turning down the restraining order in the D.C. Circuit than I would be in the Fourth Circuit, and I don't mean that critically at all.

MR. NESSON: But your judgment would be not to issue it unless you were constrained by precedent?

2ND JUDGE: No, I can't honestly say that because I keep coming back to Mr. Justice Brennan's statement about the transport at sea, there are things that require prior restraint, and I do despise the words prior restraint. If I had my way, I would use Mr. Justice Black's situation: print and be damned. But I'm a district judge, and I've been indoctrinated, and I'm duty-bound to follow my circuit. And I think my circuit would expect me to issue the TRO.

MR. NESSON: TRO, *ex parte.*

2ND JUDGE: *Ex parte,* well, most of them are.

MR. NESSON: Right. On the basis of a short affidavit from the director of the CIA.

2ND LAWYER: And I have my statement that I have notified counsel on the other side.

2ND JUDGE: Well, you'd have to do that or show why you hadn't. But I'd sure give them a quick hearing on it.

MR. NESSON (Turns to 3rd Judge): Judge, is that what he should do?

3RD JUDGE: I just want to interject here that Marchetti seems to me not to relate to this, not in the least. This was a case in which the CIA sought to enjoin its former agent, who sought to release stuff that he had agreed under oath not to release. It's like a trade secret. We've all known for years that if, under the confidential employment relationships, someone requires information which is a trade secret, he has a right of free speech, but he may not violate that agreement. And the prior restraint may issue. This is the same kind of thing as a trade secret. There's no violation of that kind of agreement to be enjoined here. This is like the New York *Times* case, and whether this isn't really top-secret stuff or not, it has nothing to do with the issuance of a TRO. You would have to approach this under the standards of the New York *Times.*

MR. NESSON: In other words, what you're saying is it doesn't make any difference whether this thing is classified or not.

3RD JUDGE: No, it's a New York *Times* case. I've seen it is, and rightly so. But the question is whether it so relates to national defense under the rule stated by Mr. Justices Stewart and White—it should be enjoined because we don't know what it was that was there, because they didn't tell us, but we know that there's some kind of information which so relates to national defense that it may be enjoined. But I don't know to what extent it might be adopted, if this would be handled so. [In the Pentagon Papers case, Mr. Justice Stewart and Mr. Justice White indicated that prior restraints were unconstitutional unless publication would result in direct, immediate, and irreparable damage to the United States. 403 U.S. at 727-740.]

MR. NESSON: But all your judge had was a complaint and a little affidavit from the director of the CIA.

3RD JUDGE: Well, if I were the trial judge, I would issue a TRO and have a prompt hearing too, but in the end I don't think this is the case for prior restraints.

MR. NESSON: Well, we've got the TRO, and you agree with the judge of the lower court on that.

3RD JUDGE: Yes.

MR. NESSON (Calls on 1st Judge): Judge? Would you issue the TRO?

1ST JUDGE: Well, it's very clear that not only after the New York *Times* case but earlier, a TRO prior restraint was only justified in the most extraordinary case, but I'm looking at the New York *Times* opinion here.

MR. NESSON: Which opinion?

(Laughter)

1ST JUDGE: Brennan's, right now. And Justice Brennan said, "Certainly, it is difficult to fault the several courts below for seeking to assure that the issues here involved were preserved for ultimate review by this court." And then Justice White, with whom Justice Stewart concurred: "I do not say that in no circumstances would the First Amendment permit an injunction against publishing information about government plans or operations." Well . . .

MR. NESSON: Would you go back to Justice Brennan there, please, for a minute? Would you read the next sentence?

1ST JUDGE: "Even if it be assumed that some of the interim restraint were proper in the two cases before us, that assumption has no bearing upon the propriety of similar judicial action in the future."

MR. NESSON: What about that one? How come you took the first sentence and left that one out?

1ST JUDGE: Because it's on a different page. (Laughter and applause) What I get from Brennan's opinion and the others is that in some cases there must be time for reflection and examination of the documents. Now I think I said previously that this case was a far more damaging case in the national security interest or had less to justify publication than the Pentagon Papers case. I think this would be close to the situation where at least the District Court should take a look at all the information. I think I would go along with the District Judge and take a look and make a record and examine the documents *in camera*. But then, depending . . .

MR. NESSON: Before you issued the TRO or after?

1ST JUDGE: No, I think that a short TRO with an immediate hearing would be called for.

MR. NESSON: That's okay. (Calls on 4th Judge): How about you?

4TH JUDGE: Yes, I think, for the reasons identified by the other judges . . .

MR. NESSON: So we're uniform. A TRO issues in this case, on the basis of a complaint and a short affidavit.

4TH JUDGE: May I just say that I think it's only an indication that you need a reflective judgment by the court rather than a nonjudgment by the court. All a TRO does is give you time to think about the question.

2ND REPORTER: It subverts the press interest absolutely.

4TH JUDGE: It suspends it for a very short period of time.

2ND REPORTER: And suspension is the equivalent of subversion.

4TH JUDGE: That may be. But you get a delayed deadline on the story, and if that's a subversion, that's it, but . . .

2ND LAWYER: Now we get two stories rather than one.

4TH JUDGE: If you get . . .

2ND LAWYER: If you left him enough to print the first time . . .

4TH JUDGE: I wasn't certain, by the way, that the CIA lawyer did have to notify counsel for the newspaper before he went for the TRO.

2ND JUDGE: He has to file an affidavit, doesn't he, Judge, as to why he didn't notify . . .

4TH JUDGE: Yes, I think he has to do that, but I think he could say that it was possible for the counsel for the newspaper to tell the editor that he would print before he could get to the judge, and in this particular case he couldn't take that risk. So I'm not at all certain that he has to notify the counsel of the newspaper rather than have an escape for that, but it all ties in with the idea that, if the courts are to be brought in at all, they must be brought in reflectively. There's no point in bringing them in without reflection. And now, as long as you happened to ask me to say something, I want to take issue with some points that have been made up to now about what I understood people to say was the divergence between ethical values and legal rule. I think it was one of the lawyers who said that the ethics are in opposition to the law because the law might say you can print because there's no contempt, but the ethics might indicate otherwise. I think the fundamental point about law is that it has a different, a narrower, set of values than those that are comprehended by ethics, good taste, volunteerism, judgment, manners, and all the things that people do in their lives and all the standards of conduct that people have in their lives. What the law does is to say, for a particular band of these, we have not only the standards that apply voluntarily because of breach of taste or breach of ethics, but we have compulsions. There may be damages. There may be prosecution. There may be contempt, and all that. So it's not at all inconsistent in my mind for the ethics to tell an editor not to publish and for a lawyer to say that the law wouldn't punish you if you did, because the law just simply has a narrower band of values that it indicates.

MR. NESSON: We have one thing that does seem to be inconsistent, at least with what some reporters here are saying, namely, we have every judge in the room issuing a temporary restraining order, prior restraint against the press.

4TH JUDGE: Well, because the doctrine of prior restraint is, like so many of the legal rules, not an absolute. It has limits. Very few legal rules are absolutes that apply in all circumstances at all times and in all ways. Cardozo has a piece on that, that all legal rules have limits, just as H_2O is a liquid but within limits of 32 degrees to 212 degrees. If the question is whether it is absolute so that a court can't even consider whether this is a case for one of the exceptions to the absolute, then the rule is not without exceptions, and somebody must decide whether it is within the exceptions. That is, a court must decide it.

2ND REPORTER: What?

4TH JUDGE: At the moment the Supreme Court decision indicates that a court makes the ultimate decision.

1ST TV REPORTER (Asks 4th Judge): Is it temporary restraint, not prior?

4TH JUDGE: It is prior. What I'm saying is that the doctrine that prohibits prior restraint on the newspapers is not an absolute doctrine. It is a 99 and 44/100ths percent doctrine. But in order to determine whether the 56/100ths percent applies under the law as we have it or the society as we have it, judgment must be made by a court. I take it that under the society as we have it, it must be a reflective judgment and not a nonsense judgement of the throwing of the dice like in Rabelais, and that therefore there has to be a time to look at the papers and have the counsel in to explain the situation.

1ST TV REPORTER: So you must restrain to give you time to decide if you can restrain?

4TH JUDGE: You must restrain for a day to give you time to decide whether you will restrain for a longer period of time.

MR. NESSON (Asks 3rd Lawyer): Is that true?

3RD LAWYER: I would be interested in hearing from the judges why they wouldn't ask for a little bit more from the director of the CIA than a short affidavit saying that it would harm national defense, which is, of course, precisely the affidavit that was presented in the Pentagon Papers case.

MR. NESSON: How about that?

3RD LAWYER: The teaching of Justice Brennan's opinion would be that at least something more than that was required to get any prior restraint.

4TH JUDGE: Well, I think that if the affidavit were alone, all you had was the two pages, that might be a problem. But I would suppose the CIA lawyer would provide the document at least *in camera,* and I don't have any trouble in reading this document with a two-page affidavit from the director. It seems there are very substantial possibilities of the loss of life and having an effect on a very important national interest. Even with, as in this case, the director saying, "These are the only six sentences you get, I can't give you another word. I can't tell you another thing about this case, as in the affidavit here, you have my affidavit of five sentences or whatever it is, which is quoted in the case."

4TH JUDGE: All right. If the CIA lawyer would do that, I would get a new lawyer.

(Simultaneous remarks, laughter)

4TH LAWYER: Would that make a difference to you? I can't tell you any more because it's so dangerous to reveal anything. Those are the facts in this affidavit.

4TH JUDGE: Well, but, pardon me, I didn't understand from six that there's an affidavit without any indication of the document. Is that the . . .

MR. NESSON: What is the standard that you use, Judge? Are you saying, as I thought I heard our second judge say, if I—forget about looking at the document—need a day to get my thoughts together, I need a day even to look up and find Judge Brennan's opinion in which he says that the basic error in the case was the issuance of the temporary relief in the first place. I've got to have a day. You seem to be saying, well, no, before I issue the TRO, I've got to look at the document. I've got to make my own judgment as to whether they can prove the case, namely, irreparable, immediate harm.

(Simultaneous remarks)

4TH JUDGE: Well, I think I would not take a document that had only five lines saying this is a case where national security is involved, even from the director of the CIA, and had absolutely nothing more than that. I would be very skeptical of that, if the presumption of regularity to which the second judge referred went that far. I'd suppose there would be a little more than that, than a mere one-sentence statement saying the national interest was involved.

MR. NESSON: Here's what it says: This document is classified top secret, Lord's. Now the Lord's classification is itself a secret classification, so high that there's very little classified that way. Even in their legal classification, there's no provision for it. It's altogether special. Anything having to do with subversive spies, double agents, is so sensitive that we're reluctant even to show it to you.

4TH JUDGE: He says that it's all about subversives and spies and double agents?

MR. NESSON: Right.

4TH JUDGE: That's involved in this thing?

MR. NESSON: Right. And we think that they've got a document. We don't know for sure.

4TH JUDGE: Well, it may be that that's more than five lines saying that this is a violation of national interest, and I think it's good enough for the TRO. But may I just say that I'm not sure, although the legal doctrines are different from the ethical doctrines because of their span, that the intellectual analysis and the ethical analysis, the legal analysis, are different in the sense that everybody is measuring some trade-offs. Everybody is measuring the trade-off of prior restraint as a good of society. Everybody is measuring the danger. Everybody is measuring the justification for the story, and I don't care who you are and what point in the picture you come into it, whether you're the newspaper reporter who gets the story in the first place or the editor with whom he consults, or the publisher of the paper, or the counsel, or the judge, the intellectual processes have got to start with these trade-offs. You're measuring what's the good, what's the harm, and there's absolutely no way to avoid these. You may have different experiences.

MR. NESSON: Yes, but we've got a way to avoid it. Judge Brennan suggested it. Justice Brennan says that before you issue any temporary restraints the government has got to have met the burden as set out in the Pentagon Papers, namely, a demonstration to you, satisfactory to you, that in fact publication would cause immediate, irreparable injury to the nation or its people.

4TH JUDGE: Well, I submit that Justice Brennan's standard, especially in the context of the Stewart-White centrist position, is met for this purpose on the first day and may or may not be met on the second day. I think you have a very different question, whether you're talking about the first day or the second day.

MR. NESSON: In other words, a little prior restraint is okay.

(Laughter)

MR. NESSON: Judge?

2ND JUDGE: What you're missing, or what's missing here, if I may say it, is that courts are not 9:00 to 5:00 institutions. A temporary restraining order is exactly that. I have heard matters at 4:00 o'clock in the morning, and this is so important that I have no doubt that by 4:00 o'clock in the morning, if need be, the CIA would have to come in and satisfy me that it did come within the rule of the . . .

MR. NESSON: All right. So you're going to have a real effect, but you're going to issue that temporary restraining order. You're going to issue it on your theory, under a presumption of regularity for government acts, to wit, the classification of a document "top secret," and top secret means disclosure would substantially upset major intelligence operations, whatever the lingo was, right?

2ND JUDGE: I think I would. I'd want to have . . .

MR. NESSON: And you're required to presume the regularity of that classification?

2ND JUDGE: But the hearing would be so prompt, it would be ridiculous. I've heard them in my pajamas before.

(Laughter)

3RD TV REPORTER: But wouldn't that be appealable?

MR. NESSON: Let's hold on just a second.

2ND JUDGE: They don't touch temporary restraining orders. Preliminary injunctions, yes.

MR. NESSON (Calls on 3rd (appellate) Judge): Judge, you don't agree with his reading of your presumption. Right?

3RD JUDGE: Well, I would not, in the context of this case—it's a rule of substance to issue a TRO under the New York *Times* case. It seems to me the judge would have to be shown that it actually did have this very substantial adverse impact on the national defense.

MR. NESSON: Even before issuing the TRO?

3RD JUDGE: Well, a showing that at least this may be that kind of a case.

MR. NESSON: And you wouldn't presume that because it was classified top secret?

3RD JUDGE: No, I would not presume it.

MR. NESSON: Why the presumption in one case and not in the other? What I'd really like to ask you is why the presumption in any case? And the fact of the matter is that toilet paper is classified confidential. Everything is classified something. Why is there a presumption of regularity?

3RD JUDGE: I don't go along with that. I don't understand what you mean.

MR. NESSON: Let me ask someone else.

3RD JUDGE: About toilet paper now?

(Laughter)

MR. NESSON: Well, yes, I'm just having some fun.

3RD JUDGE: But this . . .

MR. NESSON: However, there have been Navy menus classified.

(Laughter and simultaneous remarks)

MR. NESSON: Let me put it this way to you, Judge. Why is it that every district judge who has had to deal in depth with classification problems—that is, who've had witnesses called before them and examined classifications—has come out of the experience somewhat less respectful, let's say, of the classification system?

3RD JUDGE: That's why I think you've got to look at the facts of a particular case, when you come down to issuing a prior restraint, which should be done only in very, very extreme cases. I think one would have to know the actual facts, and at least on the basis of what you know at the time the CIA lawyer comes in you'd have a basis for a judgment after a hearing made by afternoon. This will turn out to be a kind of case in which an injunction is issued under Mr. Justice Stewart's New York *Times* opinion. In other words, you've got to know what the facts are and the fact that if they suddenly came in and said this is top secret. You don't know what it is, no TRO.

1ST GOV'T. OFFICIAL: Can I add to the situation which does sometimes arise that the Hungarians may suspect that they have a spy among them, but that the publication and rubbing their noses in it will probably cause them to break off relations with the United States and substantially affect the present detente structure with the Soviet Union.

MR. NESSON: I see. In other words, they know the information.

1ST GOV'T. OFFICIAL: They may know—they may suspect. But I'm getting back to the U-2 case with President Eisenhower.

MR. NESSON (Calls on 2nd Columnist): Do you want to say something now?

2ND COLUMNIST: Oh, I was just going to say that there's a certain unreality, it seems to me, here—everybody talking about how narrow and careful the CIA director will be in his affidavit; his lawyer says how he will insist on only the very limited application. In fact in the Marchetti case the CIA originally came in without notice and got a restraint against hundreds of items, most of which, on examination months later, turned out to be so ludicrous that even the CIA dropped them. In the Pentagon Papers case the government came in with claims that the country would fall and so on, and one or two judges along the way, not the District judges, but Court of Appeals judges who hadn't had the experience of seeing the government officials cross-examined on those claims. Anyway the claims were absurd. So I think we shouldn't accept this notion that there are only going to be little, narrow . . .

MR. NESSON (Calls on 3rd Reporter)

3RD REPORTER: I think one of the basic differences between the way we look at things and judges look at things is to hear judges repeating a phrase which I as a newspaperman first attribute to L. Patrick Gray: the presumption of regularity. Well, we presume irregularity. And, you know, I see no reason to trust intrinsically classifications or damn near anything else the government does.

MR. NESSON: And they see no reason why you can't put up with a day or two of prior restraint. Why can't you?

3RD REPORTER: Well, because I think, if I put up with a day or two of prior restraint, I may eventually get a permanent restraint.

MR. NESSON: Uh-huh! (Turns to 2nd Reporter): Why can't you put up with it?

2ND REPORTER: I can't put up with prior restraint because my understanding—and that's an understanding upon which I operate practically—is that the First Amendment forbids them.

MR. NESSON: In other words, it's just written in the books.

2ND REPORTER: No.

3RD TV REPORTER: I think prior restraint is contagious, and we've seen it since the Pentagon Papers. We've seen it in the Marchetti case. We've seen it in "Hearts and Minds" out on the West coast. We've seen it, I guess, in the Agee case, and we're seeing more and more of it. If we come back in five years, we won't be able to count the cases of prior restraint.

2ND REPORTER: But that's not the question.

MR. NESSON: So be a little more articulate for me. What's the matter with one day in this case? Is there anything really?

3RD TV REPORTER: It's like being a little bit pregnant. What's happened is the threat of having to go to court and having to go to the Supreme Court, because this case would go to the Supreme Court—that threat now exists. Every time it comes up, the ripples that have been discussed here go out, and they do chill. We don't like that word, some of us, but it does chill the willingness of the press everywhere to print.

4TH EDITOR: You're also adding contempt to an editor's words, once the TRO is issued.

MR. NESSON: That is, once the restraint is issued.

(Simultaneous remarks)

FORMER GOV'T. OFFICIAL: The trouble with using prior restraint as a doctrine, doing as the last speaker has done, is to suggest that any time you exercise an extraordinary governmental power like restraining the publication of any information, you thereby subject that power to subsequent abuse. Then you almost never exercise these kinds of powers. And it seems to me if there is any time in which the prior restraint is legitimately available to a government institution such as a court, then it should be available in this instance where a life is jeopardized if the information is published. The only alternative to prior restraint is subsequent restraint, where it makes no difference at all in terms of what you're trying to protect. There is a distinction that I think one of the judges is getting at—a little bit of prior restraint is all right. What is it that you're trying to protect? Ultimately the right to publish and the right for the public to know this information and subjecting that right to a time limitation doesn't diminish it very much, I don't think, in the long run.

MR. NESSON (Calls on 5th Judge)

5TH JUDGE: I think our fourth judge and those who have spoken subsequent to him have assumed that we're talking about a one-day or two-day period. But if the argument of the fourth judge is correct, you must allow the Court of Appeals and the Supreme Court of the United States an equal time to reflect. And you are really talking about months and not about a day.

MR. NESSON (Calls on 7th Editor)

7TH EDITOR: I heard no discussion at all about the restraint on government from costing lives. It's all been we're going to cost lives. I don't know if that spy network is knocking somebody off, and who worries about that? So I'm a little fuzzy on it.

MR. NESSON: Does that lead you to conclude that they shouldn't be able to hold you up for a day?

7TH EDITOR: Yes, among other things.

MR. NESSON: Why?

7TH EDITOR: Well, because I think it's the public right to know what they're doing, so let the public have a voice in the process.

MR. NESSON: And know today?

7TH EDITOR: Today, yes.

MR. NESSON: What about tomorrow?

7TH EDITOR: As soon as we learn it—tomorrow's not good enough.

MR. NESSON: What's the matter with tomorrow?

7TH EDITOR: We might lose the story.

MR. NESSON (Calls on 5th Lawyer): What's the matter with tomorrow?

5TH LAWYER: Well, the trouble with tomorrow is that the public doesn't have a chance to act on the information.

MR. NESSON: You mean today they don't.

5TH LAWYER: Well, . . . tomorrow. If it's published tomorrow, you'll lose the information forever.

1ST EDITOR: And it's not tomorrow. It's a minimum of 15 days, if not the months that the last judge noted.

1ST TV REPORTER: It's not really the amount of time. There is a dilemma here.

3RD REPORTER: It is the amount of time.

(Simultaneous conversation)

2ND REPORTER: No, it isn't the amount of time. It's the fact that any delay emerged from the government.

1ST TV REPORTER: I don't want to bargain this, that it has to be one day or two days or ten days. Clearly, the one day may become more than one day if there is an appeals process. What I say is it's not the amount of time. What I want to say is that I will not let this become a negotiating session between the law and the press as to how much time is acceptable and how much time is not acceptable. But I don't think that is what is at issue. I just want to add to that. I see a dilemma here, and I understand the dilemma. The courts cannot function without having time for deliberation. The press cannot really function adequately because time is to us also of the essence. But in a contrary manner. That is to say, you need a lot of time, but we can't give you a lot of time. There may be cases where the thing has to be published today to be meaningful. Or it has to be published this minute to be meaningful. There are cases which I could conceive of, at least no more theoretical or hypothetical than some of these cases, where if the government could stop it for 24 hours, they would have accomplished their purpose. That is possible. But the essence is the temporary restraining order, after which they say, publish and be damned; that we don't give a damn because we got those 24 hours that we wanted. Now I see this head-on collision because no court can say that we dropped all legal issues. If you say that you don't have time for that or to consider them, then we cannot consider, and we insist that under a legal order we do have a right to consider. And there is only one thing for the press to say at that point, and it's being increasingly said, and Martin Luther King said it in another connection, and it is called civil disobedience. And that is, we understand, your responsibility. We understand that you're not going to be stampeded into anything. And we have ours. And some time they may be in a head-on collision. And somebody may go to jail for it. But that's how it is.

MR. NESSON (Calls on 2nd Gov't. Official)

2ND GOV'T. OFFICIAL: What you are raising is, I think, something. If you exercise it very often it would be quite counterproductive for the good of the press and its freedom, because you owe your freedom in a sense to the protection of the law.

1ST TV REPORTER: Certainly the freedom of individual reporters.

2ND GOV'T. OFFICIAL: You certainly owe it to the protection of the law, and if it becomes well known that you will only accept the law when it's your way and you will not accept the law when it's not your way, I think you're going to lose a good deal of it. For one thing, it is quite possible to make the criminal sanctions so severe that you will exercise this freedom in defiance of the law extremely rarely, and you are talking about instances of civil disobedience.

1ST TV REPORTER: I don't say this gladly, you understand.

2ND GOV'T. OFFICIAL: No, I understand. I think it's counterproductive to have this idea that we must rush despite the law.

5TH LAWYER: But we're also talking about unconstitutional orders.

2ND GOV'T. OFFICIAL: Well, you don't know that.

MR. NESSON: Well, hang on for a minute. (Calls on 6th Editor)

6TH EDITOR: I think that there are times when time makes such a difference to publishing that you do have to come down on the side of publishing. One case in point was maintaining the momentum in the Pentagon Papers after the *Times* was enjoined. The editors were told by lawyers that they had a lot of problems, that the paper would have a lot of problems, doubly so in the face of the court enjoining the *Times.* The management had to decide right on deadline whether to go that day with the story one day after the *Times* was enjoined, and . . .

MR. NESSON: Or lose it to another newspaper.

6TH EDITOR: No, no, nobody had it.

MR. NESSON: But you mean to tell me that the competitive factor mentioned over here is not a big item of concern?

6TH EDITOR: It was no item of our concern that day because nobody else had it. The concern was the maintenance of the momentum and not letting a day go past without publishing. It was a fine decision which was made quicker than one would like to decide things, and the thought occurred, "Why can't we think about this for a day?" The *Times* worked on it two or three months. And the editor very properly said, "Because we've got to go and we've got to maintain publication of these papers." And the story was published, and I think that was the proper decision.

5TH JUDGE: May I suggest another way of looking at this problem? Supposing the law did not have prior restraint. Would that be so tragic from the point of view of the law—forget the press for the moment? There are all the various criminal and damage potentialities which the law offers. They may be used harshly, but would it not be better to run the risk of having harsh measures of that kind, which the law would frequently use, and then the publisher might for himself decide whether it is so important to print this that we will run the risk of that penalty, but we don't run the risk of a temporary restraining order?

4TH JUDGE: But may I ask why the temporary restraining order makes a difference? What they're doing is running a risk of a contempt citation? The certainty . . .

5TH JUDGE: You're urging that they violate the law.

4TH JUDGE: Well, you are saying that they're taking . . .

5TH JUDGE: No, I'm telling them that if they want to violate the law or run the risk, that is up to them, but I'm not asking them deliberately to violate an actual *ad hoc, ad hominem* order.

MR. NESSON: In fact once that order is issued, can any legal counsel at least advise that it be violated? We're talking criminal contempt, aren't we, now?

1ST EDITOR: Once the TRO is . . .

MR. NESSON: Once the TRO is issued, and you ask your lawyer, "Can I violate it?" (Turns to Editor's Lawyer): Do you have any choice but to say to him, "No, you can't. My ethical obligation under the canons of ethics is to advise you that you can't commit a crime."?

1ST LAWYER: I would advise him that he was required to obey the order of the court.

3RD TV REPORTER: But is that always true? If that's true in the Fifth Circuit, under the Dickinson case [*United States v. Dickinson*, 465 F. 2d 496 (5th Cir. 1972)], but isn't there an argument that in First Amendment cases that it is not a crime—it is not criminal contempt to go ahead and print?

1ST LAWYER: Well, here we're getting into the absolutes again.

3RD TV REPORTER: No, really . . .

1ST LAWYER: No. Let me see if I can explain it. In the first place, once there is a court order outstanding, then there is an obligation to obey that court order. You can be held in contempt to that court order, even though it is subsequently ruled to be unlawful or unconstitutional. That was established with John L. Lewis and the United Mine Workers case.

3RD TV REPORTER: But that was picketing. That was the threat of violent picketing. Now I'd like to get a legal opinion from someone on the other side of that.

4TH TV REPORTER: But the two reporters in Baton Rouge . . .

3RD TV REPORTER: Well, that's what I'm talking about, the Dickinson case. Ask our lawyer over here for a different . . .

3RD LAWYER: It is certainly not clear that it is the law. Our defense counsel may be right, but there is a significant responsible body of legal opinion to the contrary in the face of what one may call a palpably unconstitutional order.

1ST LAWYER: Well, I can only give you my own experience that I had, rather unfortunately from rather extensive experience with criminal contempt cases, and you will find an occasional indication that you don't have to obey an order because it is unconstitutional. But, by and large, those cases are an aberration. I think the law is pretty well settled, at least in my viewpoint. If you violate an order even though it be unconstitutional you are subject to contempt penalties.

MR. NESSON (Calls on Professor Arthur Miller of Harvard Law School)

MR. MILLER: The Supreme Court subsequent to the John L. Lewis decision decided *Walker v. City of Birmingham* which was an antidemonstration order issued by an Alabama State Court and the mine worker principle of obey or suffer the sanction of criminal contempt was invoked despite the First Amendment overtones of that Alabama State Court order. [*Walker v. City of Birmingham*, 388 U.S. 307 (1967) in which the Court held that petitioners could not bypass orderly judicial review of a temporary injunction before disobeying it.]

MR. NESSON: Well, we have a chance in discussing the grand jury problem of looking much closer at this particular difficulty.

3RD TV REPORTER: May I say one thing before we go on here. The case has been cited here. There is a case on the other side, it is a case from the Supreme Court of the State of Washington which was confirmed with an order against publication and it drew a distinction between the *Walker v. Birmingham* case where there was a threat of human life and violence and threat of publication of ideas and in that case it was held that you could violate an order and they did and they were not held liable and I don't think we should give that up [*State v Sperry*, 79 Wash. 2d 69, 1183 P. 2d 608, cert. denied, 404 U.S. 939 (1971)]. The Supreme Court hasn't ruled on it and I hope they rule the other way.

MR. NESSON: Well, let me just state the proposition in an effort to leave it to the next problem. The courts, for instance the Dickinson court, maintain that courts peculiarly should be in a position of having their orders—temporary orders, permanent orders—obeyed until remedies are exhausted by way of appeal. That is, until someone appeals the order and challenges it he's got no business going around and disobeying it. That's the premise on which the judges decided Dickinson. Now, I'm not interested so much here as to what the law is, we'll leave that to you and your lawyers.

3RD TV REPORTER: I'm speaking as a journalist.

MR. NESSON: Fine, I am interested in people's judgment as to what the right rules ought to be and I will be very interested to understand from the judges as to why that particular rule should pertain to judges and for courts and for no other institution. That is, why is it that with all other forms of statutes, regulations, rules, if the rule is invalid and someone breaks it, they take their chances. There is no such rule that says well, true, this statute was unconstitutional but you violated it and you knew it and therefore you go to jail and the next guy will get the benefit of the ruling. That's one for the judges to think over by way of homework. But the problem I would like to take off from for national security purposes is the consequences of that kind of thinking in national security terms. That is, we now have a situation where it is recognized— at least in one circuit—that a contract can bind a government employee not to disclose any classified information, regardless of the validity of classification. That's the contract. Then a true freedom of information act may come in and modify that but in First Amendment terms there is no bar against the government exacting a contract which will bind the employee for all time and all government employees apparently not to disclose. All right, that's proposition number one. Proposition number two, the government has its own exhaustion remedies—that is, they have a classification procedure. It is true that many items are classified which should not be. True there are ways now of challenging classification within the system and testing the validity of the classification. So, proposition number three, what's to stop the government from suggesting a statute to the Congress that says, well, the judges think that they are very privileged in Dickinson; we should have the same privilege. We will make it an offense—a criminal offense—to disclose classified information to any person not authorized to receive it with no test whatsoever of the legitimacy of the classification, unless the fellow disclosing it has first exhausted the government procedure for challenging the classification. Any problem with that statute?

1ST EDITOR: Well, such a statute is proposed.

MR. NESSON: Absolutely. What I want to move you to now is what should the sanctions be on disclosure of classified information, national security information? You have problems with that statute?

2ND JUDGE: I do.

VARIOUS: Boy. Sure.

MR. NESSON: What's your problem, Judge?·

2ND JUDGE: Well, it seems overbroad for one thing. It smacks right into the First Amendment.

MR. NESSON: Now, hold on, Judge. This statute which we're talking about is going to apply to government officials, right? It's going to apply to government officials disclosing classified information, right? Which they have no right under the First Amendment to disclose, right? Because they've signed a contract. Now, what's the matter with a statute that comes along and simply adds to the damage remedy or the injunctive remedy? What kind of damage are you going to get on this contract, add in a little criminal sanction?

2ND JUDGE: Well, it's one thing to deal with the government employee. It's another thing to deal with a newspaper that has the information.

MR. NESSON: I'm dealing with the government employee. That's who this statute applies to. I want to stop leaks at the source. This is a statute which is going to stop all government employees from leaking classified stuff.

1ST EDITOR: Well, it specifically bars as a defense misclassification.

MR. NESSON: That's true. Unless the fellow has exhausted his remedies inside the system.

2ND JUDGE: Can I go back to before I became a judge?

MR. NESSON: Sure.

2ND JUDGE: I wouldn't have any problem with it. I'd tell him go ahead and divulge it.

MR. NESSON: Go ahead and divulge it.

2ND JUDGE: Because I think the First Amendment really says that. There shall be no abridgement.

MR. NESSON (Calls on 3rd (Appellate) Judge): What do you think? We're taking off from Marchetti, which is what S-1 has done, and saying we're going to attach a criminal sanction right alongside your contract. [S-1 is the proposed legislation recodifying Federal criminal law.]

3RD JUDGE: I don't want to take off from Marchetti—it's gone as far as I want to go. If there is a proposal, I don't want to restrict myself in case such a case should come to my court, but I certainly would have grave doubt that we would uphold it if you assume that it foreclosed the defendant's right to question the reasonableness of what was done when this was classified.

MR. NESSON: It doesn't foreclose, Judge. It does just exactly what the courts do with their own orders. It says exhaust your avenues first. You've got to appeal before you can challenge. You can't just go out and simply disobey and leak this stuff. You've got to go to the interdepartmental security classification review board.

3RD JUDGE: But that might take months.

MR. NESSON: And is that a problem for you?

3RD JUDGE: Yes, it is.

MR. NESSON: And, yet, it's not a problem in the court situation where it takes months to go up?

2ND LAWYER: Well, there's a tremendous difference.

MR. NESSON: What's the difference?

2ND LAWYER: Well, the difference is that one group has some interest in that delay and in protecting that in terms of the substance of what they're doing, protecting themselves in their exercise of various executive powers.

MR. NESSON: True.

2ND LAWYER: The court when it issues its TRO or issues its preliminary injunction has no such vested interest in anything. In the TRO it is simply the maintenance of an objective process. They have no interest in the classification process itself.

MR. NESSON: No interest in taking time to fairly deliberate the case?

2ND LAWYER: Oh, they have an interest in that.

MR. NESSON: And, that might take months.

2ND LAWYER: That's a very different interest than the interest of an executive official and wanting time to cover up.

MR. NESSON: It's a difference, I grant you that, but I don't see where it comes.

2ND LAWYER: Well, if it's as big a difference as the one statute being unconstitutional and the other not.

MR. NESSON: Maybe I haven't stated the statute clearly enough. Once the review process is exhausted, that is, once he's gone to the interdepartmental security review board and they've said, "No, this is still classified, properly so," then he can leak it and take his chances. That's the rule.

2ND LAWYER: If the rule in court were that if the government applied for a preliminary injunction, whatever thereafter happened in court, and you could be guaranteed all of the time involved, okay. But, you don't get that. You don't even get a protection of the jurisdiction on appeal, if there's no merit to it.

MR. NESSON (Calls on 2nd Gov't. Official: Surely you'll defend the statute that the executive branch has submitted.

2ND GOV'T. OFFICIAL: I'm not so sure I want to here today, if I can revert to the professorial role. I'm not so sure I would defend it, no.

MR. NESSON: Anybody defend it? No takers?

1ST GOV'T. OFFICIAL: Aren't there a number of statutes somewhat similar that punish the revelation of certain categories of information?

MR. NESSON: For example?

1ST GOV'T. OFFICIAL: Cotton statistics.

MR. NESSON: I'm not familiar with that.

1ST GOV'T. OFFICIAL: There are several dozen categories. For instance, the revelation of an income tax return by an employee of the Internal Revenue Service is a crime.

MR. NESSON: Okay, fine.

2ND GOV'T. OFFICIAL: Let me make a distinction always between political information and commercial information, or some other kind of information.

MR. NESSON: And defense information.

1ST GOV'T. OFFICIAL: Well, there are lots of different categories.

MR. NESSON: Yes, but . . .

1ST LAWYER: That's why it's so difficult to discuss the statute, you don't know precisely what you're talking about when you're talking in terms of classified information. The lowest classification is one thing. If you're talking about highly secret classification dealing with spies or something else . . .

MR. NESSON: The statute talks about all classified information.

1ST LAWYER: Well, then, I think you may very well have a problem. I suppose if I had to I could defend the statute on this basis, and that is that an employee of the government of the United States does not have the right to take documents, whatever their classification, and distribute them outside of normal government channels.

MR. NESSON: Cite Marchetti.

2ND LAWYER: Cite Marchetti, cite the basic concept, if you will, of federal employment. I don't think that because I was employed by the federal government I had the right to take whatever reports I received from J. Edgar Hoover and pass them out to various friends of mine in the newspaper business, to take them home and write a book about it, perhaps, because I had the right to have access to those documents. In other words, the documents came to me. I assume they came to me in my position as an employee of the federal government.

MR. NESSON: And it follows from that that the government should be able to pass a statute imposing a sanction on you to make you do that.

1ST LAWYER: It follows from that automatically.

MR. NESSON: And that's all the statute does. And has done so in many categories.

1ST TV REPORTER: Well, that's not all it does, though.

1ST LAWYER: Now, I've never read this. What else does it do; I mean, besides that?

1ST TV REPORTER: Sanctions.

MR. NESSON: That's it.

1ST EDITOR: Sanctions journalists.

MR. NESSON: No, it does not. Sorry. Let me be clear on the statute so I don't put any misconceptions.

1ST LAWYER: I've never read it, so I'm going by what you say.

MR. NESSON: The statute . . .

1ST EDITOR: . . . punishes the person who gets the information also.

MR. NESSON: No, it does not. The statute specifically excludes the newspapers from punishment. If they're on the receiving end from a government official, they are not subject to the statute. The government official is subject to the statute.

1ST TV REPORTER: That's not my understanding.

1ST EDITOR: No.

5TH REPORTER: There are two different sections in the statute. The section they're talking about does not permit the sanction against the newspaper which receives the information.

MR. NESSON: Right.

5TH REPORTER: But, there is another section of the statute which is called mishandling defense information which says that a newspaper may be criminally liable for any information it publishes which it knows may help a foreign power or hurt the United States.

MR. NESSON: True enough.

5TH REPORTER: It's in two different sections you're talking about.

1ST GOV'T. OFFICIAL: 798 today specifically says that if you publish communications intelligence it is a crime [18 U.S.C. Sec. 798].

MR. NESSON: Well, the issue I want to put to you is not so much grounded in any specific statute. I want to ask you what criminal sanctions should there be on government officials for disclosing classified information.

1ST LAWYER: I don't think you can answer that question in the abstract. I think you've got to look at the type of information you're talking about, because there's such a broad scope.

MR. NESSON: But now, mind you, that's exactly where the issue is, because the law has been that you do look at the information and you wind up having a trial in which all the information gets laid out, where you cross-examine the government experts and they have to justify why the information was kept secret. Of course, a trial, being a public process, gets a little dicey. So the government wants a statute where they don't have to look at the information, where they just go on the stand and say, classified.

1ST LAWYER: All right, let me go back to where we are now, because as someone pointed out, there are, I would guess, at least 20 different statutes on the books today which make it a crime for government employees in a particular agency of government to disclose information. Income tax is one. Cotton is one. There are many. The Federal Home Loan Bank Board has one. There are many such statutes. Now I don't need to pretend from that, ergo, what you now suggest is a good bill. But, if the government has that right, and it's been recognized all these years, I don't see what element you're adding to it in terms of the specifics. In other words, if you're talking about specific information, now, I do have a problem, I suppose, if you're going to talk about criminal sanctions as it applies to release of information about automobile accidents from the FBI as distinguished from spies operating in Hungary.

MR. NESSON: Let me tell you what I think is added to the problem under any of these statutes as proposed, as soon as something appears in the newspapers which is classified information. Take William Beecher's story on Cambodia, which caused such a flurry in order to find out what his source was. As soon as something like that appears, it would follow from these statutes that somebody has committed an offense, right? Somebody leaked that information. Somebody who was in authorized possession of classified information which had not been declassified.

1ST LAWYER: If you could trace it to the government document, yes.

MR. NESSON: Right. And how are we going to trace it? With this statute aren't we just going to call Beecher in front of the grand jury and say, "Who gave it to you?"

1ST LAWYER: That would be true under existing laws. Say you had an IRS employee who leaked your tax return to the Boston *Globe*. I suppose the prosecutor could in fact call the IRS agent before . . .

MR. NESSON: But our editor isn't so worried, I don't think, about protecting his sources on publishing IRS personal revenue returns. He'd be very . . .

VARIOUS: Why not?

(Simultaneous conversation.)

1ST LAWYER: Depending on the facts, he could be named an aider and abettor. Perhaps a coconspirator. Or an accessory after the fact. There are many ways that the criminal law is designed to bring the editor right into the center of the thing.

1ST PROSECUTOR: Nobody was prosecuted in the Nixon tax-return case, though, as a practical matter. Nobody was brought before a grand jury. I think the press would have an interest in not disclosing its source even in that case.

1ST TV REPORTER: As a matter of fact, that IRS agent was fired.

MR. NESSON: Let's ask a government official here. Suppose the Beecher story was published again. Would the government use a legal method to find out the source, namely the convocation of the grand jury and ask legitimate questions, or would the government wiretap in order to find out?

1ST GOV'T. OFFICIAL: The FBI might wiretap.

(Simultaneous conversation.)

FORMER GOV'T. OFFICIAL: I think one of the problems is the method to stop leaks; it won't stop leaks. The abuses that are obvious under this approach seem to me to outweigh any public benefits of trying to stop leaks this way. This is so because they might lead to more extreme investigative techniques in order to find out who was leaking, such as the 17 wiretaps that were aimed at the leaks that involved newsmen and government officials before. They didn't discover any leaks. All you're doing by this kind of statute is encouraging that kind of extreme investigative technique, which is unwise.

1ST TV REPORTER: If they had discovered leaks, would it have been different?

FORMER GOV'T. OFFICIAL: I don't think so, really. But, if you say there is a public interest in stopping leaks of information properly classified, then at least you have an argument for a statute of this nature, if it would achieve that public interest. I just don't think it would. What it will do, on the other hand, is encourage more extreme investigative techniques, which is not in the public interest.

1ST GOV'T. OFFICIAL: But I think the government's own employees would dearly like to have some punishment of someone who actually leaks the name of one of its sources applicable to them. That is one of the serious morale problems in some government agencies these days. Mr. Agee gets away with it, apparently. Mr. Marchetti gets away with it, apparently.

MR. NESSON: Oh, let's be fair. Mr. Agee gets away with it as long as he stays out of the country.

1ST GOV'T. OFFICIAL: Yes, maybe. It's going to be a very dicey problem after he gets back.

3RD TV REPORTER: Do you think the majority of CIA employees, for example, would be in favor of a new statute imposing criminal sanctions on them?

1ST GOV'T. OFFICIAL: Yes. Not the particular one you have in mind. This one. But the one the CIA director prescribed and suggested.

MR. NESSON: Would it follow if that statute was adopted and a leak showed up in the newspaper that the best route of finding out who had leaked it would be to go and ask the reporters?

1ST GOV'T. OFFICIAL: Oh, I think you'd run smack into the press determination to protect their own sources at that point, and I think that the normal reporter would cheerfully go to jail to protect that source.

2ND REPORTER: Cheerfully?

1ST GOV'T. OFFICIAL: Yes, because it makes a good name.

2ND EDITOR: You run smack into another problem, if I may.

MR. NESSON: Please do.

2ND EDITOR: And that is the government's desire to leak when it's useful for it to leak and it does that.

1ST GOV'T. OFFICIAL: That's an authorized leak.

(Simultaneous conversation.)

1ST EDITOR: You can't have it both ways.

VARIOUS VOICES: That's right.

1ST GOV'T. OFFICIAL: No, no, of course, information is released every day.

2ND EDITOR: We're not talking about release. We're talking about a leak by government officials of information that it suits its purposes to have in the press without its name being involved.

1ST EDITOR: Releasing classified information without going through any declassification procedure and without elaborate laws you force us to go through to get it.

1ST GOV'T. OFFICIAL: The question is whether the individual revealing the information has the authority to release it, and there are a number of individuals who do. Obviously, the head of a department has the authority to release materials, it declassifies it.

2ND EDITOR: Well, if something is classified top secret, where does the authority lie to ignore that classification?

1ST GOV'T. OFFICIAL: Not to ignore it. He has the authority which is in the regulations which set this up as to ways of declassifying that information.

1ST EDITOR: Yes, but those ways are not just quietly asking a reporter to lunch and telling him something.

1ST GOV'T. OFFICIAL: Yes, revealing it. He has the authority to reveal it. The director of CIA has appeared before congressional committees and released confidential material. People ask why, and he says it's on his authority.

1ST EDITOR: Is there legal—I don't know the CIA . . .

MR. NESSON: Yes, that's true. The fact is that the CIA director as he walks around can be declassifying as he goes.

1ST EDITOR: We would like to apply for equal rights.

1ST GOV'T OFFICIAL: Actually, there is a very specific list of names of people who have the right to classify and declassify at different levels of classification. And there's a large number of them who have the right to classify at lower levels and correspondingly have the right to declassify at lower ones.

MR. NESSON (Addresses 1st Gov't. Official): I take it many people—at least in the defense establishment, the defense side of national security—would like the power to control the dissemination of information, any information and all information, the release of which could damage the United States.

1ST GOV'T. OFFICIAL: Yes.

MR. NESSON: You would like that? That's what the classification system does.

1ST GOV'T. OFFICIAL: My own particular view is that no department head should have absolute control over that. He or she should be subject to some review.

MR. NESSON: By whom? Somebody else in the executive branch?

1ST GOV'T. OFFICIAL: Well, in the first place, there is a review by the executive branch. Secondly, the recommendation for legislation which has been submitted in the Marchetti case says that in order to prosecute it would have to be demonstrated to a judge *in camera* that classification was reasonable and not arbitrary or capricious.

MR. NESSON: That is, that the disclosure of the information could reasonably cause injury to the United States?

1ST GOV'T. OFFICIAL: No, that classification of it was not an arbitrary and capricious act.

MR. NESSON: That is, it meets the classification standards.

1ST GOV'T. OFFICIAL: No, that it meets the different levels of classification standards.

2ND EDITOR: It is classifiable.

MR. NESSON: All right, now what I want to ask you is this: Where in that entire structure is the basic principle of the First Amendment to be found? We've heard up and down the table everyone saying the principle is one of balance. We have to look at every fact, every circumstance. We have to weigh. We, as newspaper editors, will take into account a balance between this and a balance between that. Where is the balance of public importance in the classification system?

1ST GOV'T. OFFICIAL: In the first place, that in the initial classification there is some public benefit to be gained by keeping it restricted rather than released. Secondly, in the executive branch review of the comparative benefits of keeping it restricted rather than released. And, thirdly, in the judicial review of whether it was an arbitrary and capricious act in restraining it, rather than releasing it in view of the public policy in support of the First Amendment.

MR. NESSON: (Turns to 3rd Judge): That's the way you understood it? That is, do you understand that when you're judging whether something has been properly classified that you are to take into account and make a balance yourself as to whether the public importance of it being disclosed . . .

3RD JUDGE: No, sir.

MR. NESSON: You don't, do you?

3RD JUDGE: No. Now, all I think that the court can do is to look at the information in terms of whether it relates to or is connected with the defense of the country . . .

MR. NESSON: And that is information the unauthorized disclosure of which might reasonably be expected to damage national security.

3RD JUDGE: Yes.

MR. NESSON: Without a mention of the public importance of it being . . .

3RD JUDGE: And there may be reasons that that should be released. But I don't think that's for the court.

1ST EDITOR: Isn't the whole question of executive review of classification just ludicrous? Just ludicrous? I mean, after the Pentagon Papers the executive reclassification of documents announced by the president was put in charge of, you should pardon the expression, Hunt and Colson. It is ludicrous. What are we talking about? Forget it.

MR. NESSON (Calls on 3rd Columnist)

3RD COLUMNIST: We keep talking about the crimes of the press, but we haven't mentioned the crimes of the government. The government, we've heard recently, has committed several crimes. The CIA has actually committed crimes. And, how does the public find out when the government has committed crimes if everything they've committed has been marked top secret. I'm sure that we wouldn't have heard about what happened if the press hadn't revealed that the CIA had been involved in domestic crimes.

MR. NESSON (Calls on 2nd Columnist)

2ND COLUMNIST: I think that's an extremely important point and just to follow up on it, it isn't only the CIA, but I think we rely for our safety in this country today in First Amendment terms very much on government officials who disagree with the policy. And that's how we found out what was happening in Vietnam. That's how we found out about things like the Phoenix Program. [This was a covert U.S. program designed to destroy the Communist infrastructure in South Vietnam.] That's how we found out . . .

1ST GOV'T. OFFICIAL: You found out about the Phoenix Program through testimony from a CIA official.

2ND COLUMNIST: I stand corrected on that. Certainly Vietnam was an example of how government officials who were involved in that war were sickened by it. And, under the notion of S-1, the statute that you've outlined, Prof. Nesson, the decision on whether to declassify, on whether to disclose what's happening in Vietnam, would remain in centralized hands, and we would no longer have that safety of reliance on officials who become sickened at the policy. I think it's a central issue.

3RD TV REPORTER: And what about Watergate?

1ST TV REPORTER: Restated, so much of the orderly process rests on a presumption of regularity. And, demonstrably today, there's been so much goddamn irregularity that how do you expect us to continue on that assumption?

3RD EDITOR: Let us take an example of a case of information leaked that most of us would disagree with, and this is the Otepka case. [Otto Otepka was a State Department employee and militant anti-Communist who leaked information about his fellow government employees during the 1950s.] Otepka's an example of a man who was sickened by government policy who leaks the kind of information that's leaked to the particular publications and the kinds of people I daresay that most of the people in the room here would not agree with. But, under this doctrine of sickening, he was fed up and his cause was taken up subsequently by the right-wing press. Leaking is a two-way street and not everybody who leaks is sickened by the same kind of things that would sicken us around the table.

1ST GOV'T. OFFICIAL: I would say there is another protection for you, and that is what we were referring to earlier, as to whether the prosecutor would actually prosecute. Secondly, whether the jury would actually convict. I think those two factors give considerable weight in support of the First Amendment considerations.

1ST EDITOR: After a substantial expense in order to defend . . .

1ST GOV'T. OFFICIAL: That's the problem of the cost of freedom.

1ST EDITOR: You've left that out of your whole argument. It has been left out of this presentation. As soon as you call your lawyer, the second question you ask him is: "How much is it going to cost to go to the Supreme Court?"

2ND COLUMNIST: The answer is, plenty. Not only the expense, but after the pall of fear has been cast over the government employees who won't want to talk.

2ND EDITOR: Did we agree on free lawyering, then, to solve our problems?

7TH EDITOR: Who determines on their S-1, as you posed it, what is a leak?

MR. NESSON: There would be a trial. It would have to go to the jury.

7TH EDITOR: No. But, who determines in government? What I'm thinking of now is during Air Force budget hearings, when the Navy's trying to get more money, often somebody in the Air Force will leak something that's classified about the Navy for purposes that serve the Air Force. Who would then determine . . .

MR. NESSON: He's committed an offense.

7TH EDITOR: Automatically?

MR. NESSON: That's it under the statute. Then, we've got the prosecutor and the decisions. And, once more—and perhaps this is the place where we could end it for now—this notion that someone on the jury is going to let the fellow off, assumes that the very thing I'm pressing is an issue in the case. That is, that somehow it is an issue for consideration by the jury whether it was in the public interest to release the information. These elements in prosecutorial discretion, which may lead prosecutors not to indict are irrelevant issues in the trial. The only issue will be under existing law, under the proposed law: Was the information such that its release could reasonably be expected to damage the national defense. And, the plus side of it is considered irrelevant.

1ST PROSECUTOR: Excuse me, you asked the question before about an example of a situation where it was assumed that the information was probably classified. An analogy might be the case that arose in the Watergate litigation whereby the prosecutors wanted to put in the general description of the content of the overheard conversations. Judge Sirica ruled that they could do that. An appeal was taken by an intervening party properly under the statute and it went to the Court of Appeals. And I think the Court of Appeals properly said it was unnecessary to get into the content under the statute. The case could be tried under the assumption merely that the man had testified that there had been an intrusion, an unacceptable and illegal intrusion. That was sufficient. The man had testified to it and there was no need to get into the content. So, there's an example of a situation in the law where you don't need to litigate what the content was or whether it was properly classified or what the nature of the overheard conversations were.

MR. NESSON (Calls on Former Broadcaster)

FORMER BROADCASTER: Not for a close, for an opener for later. I like the Otepka question, and I hope it will be pursued. I wish somebody like Roger Robb, who pleaded his case, was here. I would ask all of you who are for this free flow of leaks to remember the early 1950s and the late 1940s when a whole body of men with political persuasions different than some of ours, different from mine, were leaking all the time. The director of the FBI to Roy Cohen and Roy Cohen to John O'Donnell. Newspaper people on the conservative edge being leaked secrets about security risks in government and all kinds of people who have since been revered, being hurt, punished, cast out of government, cast out of the country. I didn't hear the kind of defense of leaks in those days that I hear now.

MR. NESSON: Thank you.

THE CASE

John Peter Burnwood is the chief investigative reporter for the Metropolis *Chronicle,* the leading daily in the populous eastern state of Idyllia. In addition, he does a five-minute "spot" on the local television station's, KROC-TV, evening news based on the content of his daily column. As is true of all good investigative reporters, Burnwood has numerous sources of information through governmental officials, private investigators, credit bureaus, banks, and tipsters. His practice is to use these to the fullest and let the chips fall as they may.

Burnwood currently is covering a Senate election campaign. Because of a schism in the state's dominant political party, there are three major candidates. The first is Alex Aphid, young, aggressive third-term congressman from one of the Metropolis districts. The second is Bob Bumptious, the incumbent senator, a more senior, conservative politician with three terms in the Senate behind him and the current chairman of an influential committee. The third is Carla Cassandra, a former prosecutor who is now a popular, syndicated TV news commentator, the first woman to run for the Senate in the state. She is one of the nation's leading right-to-life advocates, a position that is extremely popular in Idyllia because of its ethnic and religious composition.

The election is five days away. As a windup of Burnwood's month-long coverage, he plans an in-depth profile of each of the three candidates, publishing one a day. There is reason to assume that the other major daily in the state is about to publish its own major series on the election and has assigned its up-and-coming reporter, Ned Nosey, to the story.

One night, an unmarked envelope was delivered to Burnwood. There was no indication as to its source. In it were Xeroxed copies of numerous documents that appeared to be from FBI files. The material pertained to Aphid, Cassandra, and the two candidates for the governorship. There was nothing about Bumptious. Burnwood, who has some familiarity with material of this type from his days covering the Justice Department, has reason to believe it is genuine; he also knows that, if genuine, its release to him either is an intentional leak by the FBI or the result of illicit conduct. Several telephone calls to friends and information sources have revealed nothing conclusive about the documents.

The material on Aphid included a full financial report, which showed Aphid's net worth, outstanding debts, and contained several unexplained "slow-pay" and "no-pay" entries. In addition, there was a three-year-old investigative report on Aphid, containing notes of an interview with one of Aphid's neighbors. These suggest that Aphid conducts frequent, loud parties attended by numerous bearded "hippie" types and that a distinctive, sweet aroma frequently emanates from his apartment. Perhaps the most interesting item pertaining to Aphid was a transcription of notes allegedly made by Dr. Eric Enuresis, a prominent psychiatrist, in the course of treating Aphid. These suggest the possibility of a potentially disabling mental illness. A phone call to Dr. Enuresis yielded nothing other than an invocation of the doctor-patient privilege and an off-hand remark: "This is very strange, I have never had any dealings with the press during my 30 years as a psychiatrist, but you are the second reporter to call today."

Burnwood's column on Aphid contained comments suggesting that the candidate lacked financial responsibility, emotional stability, and led the kind of dissolute life that might not be appropriate for a member of the Senate.

In preparing the profile of Senator Bumptious, Burnwood had another of his contacts, Sheriff Brutus Lascivious Clodde, who is up for reelection next year and has been supported by the *Chronicle* in the past, search the Metropolis police records and, using a local computer terminal, make an inquiry of the FBI's National Crime Information Center. This produced rap sheet entries showing that, as a teenager, Bumptious had been arrested for a hit-and-run vehicular homicide, but was never prosecuted. This disclosure by the sheriff to Burnwood violated both state law and Department of Justice regulations.

Late the night before the Bumptious story was due—very late, in fact—Burnwood stopped at an out-of-the-way watering hole for a nightcap. When he went to the rear of the bar to make a telephone call, he noticed Bumptious in a hidden booth with a strikingly attractive woman 30 years his junior. Bumptious appeared intoxicated, but not sufficiently so to prevent the pair from engaging in amorous activity. Searching his memory, Burnwood recalled that the woman, Wanda Werewolf, had been arrested but not prosecuted for soliciting a year earlier. The scene also was consistent with other reports Burnwood had received about Bumptious' excessive drinking. The following day, Burnwood reported these items to his readers under the headline "Senator Bumptious Involved in Car Death and Linked with Prostitute."

Senator Bumptious immediately brought suit against the city, the state, the FBI, the *Chronicle*, and Burnwood for violating his civil rights by improperly releasing this police data and the defamatory innuendos in the story. Damages against the newspaper and Burnwood in the amount of $250,000 each have been requested and defense of the action will be protracted and costly. Finally, Judge Pettifogger, who was appointed to the bench following years of loyal service to the party, has been asked to direct Burnwood to testify as to his sources for the article. Werewolf also has brought suit for damages.

Burnwood's investigations of Carla Cassandra revealed nothing of an unsavory character. However, the documents purporting to be from the FBI files contained three interesting items. First, a field agent's report in connection with a security clearance of an interview with one of her law professors, Dagby Dolt, indicating that Cassandra had gotten through school by the "skin of her teeth" and either had "little aptitude for law and hard work" or "had spent too much time with men." Second, there was a 25-year-old medical record indicating that at age 15 Carla had had an abortion. And, third, that Cassandra's husband had been convicted of manslaughter for slaying his first wife in a fit of passion and had served five years in prison, that upon his release 14 years ago he had changed his name and moved more than 1,000 miles from his former home to Metropolis to escape his past, that since his arrival in Metropolis he not only has lived a blameless life, but has become a pillar of Metropolis society and a patron of numerous charitable endeavors. Burnwood reported these items in his column on Cassandra without editorial comment.

Questions

1. What is your reaction to Burnwood's investigative activities with regard to Aphid, Bumptious, and Cassandra and the content of his stories about them? If you were the editor of the Metropolis *Chronicle,* would you have printed these three stories? Would you have modified them?

2. Suppose Aphid appears at the newspaper, demands a right to respond to Burnwood's story, and presents the text of that reply, which contains a statement as to why his life-style does not impair his ability to serve as an effective member of the Senate. What should the *Chronicle* do?

3. Is your attitude toward Aphid's right to reply any different if his proposed statements demonstrates that the reports Burnwood received either were bogus or were on another Alex Aphid and that candidate Aphid leads a prim and proper middle-class life-style?

4. Would your response to Questions 2 and 3 be any different if Aphid made the same request to KROC-TV?

5. Suppose Senator Bumptious appears at the newspaper, demands the right to reply to Burnwood's story, and presents the text of that reply, which contains a statement containing facts showing that the vehicular homicide charge was dismissed when it was discovered that Bumptious was not driving at the time of the accident and that he did not know that Werewolf, who he had met in the bar after a long day of campaigning, *might* have been a prostitute? What should the *Chronicle* do? Would your response be any different if Bumptious made the same request to KROC-TV?

6. How should Judge Pettifogger rule regarding the request by Bumptious to order Burnwood to reveal his sources for the story? If ordered to reveal them, what should Burnwood do? In what ways should the legal system take account

of the pressurized environment in which the media operate and the potential effect on the media of expensive and protracted lawsuits?

7. What *should* be the result if Cassandra's husband sues the newspaper or the television station for violation of his right to privacy?

PROCEEDINGS

PROFESSOR ARTHUR MILLER (Harvard Law School): This afternoon on this problem I would prefer if we did not assume, at least did not assume too often, that there's law out there. So I would ask people who are sitting with copies of judicial opinions or advice of counsel or law review articles to put them to one side. As we do in law school we're going to make believe we're in the mythical jurisdiction of Idyllia. And we're going to try to concentrate on what should be the situation rather than what decided cases have told to us. Now, the situation that we've got in this case study is that we're five days away from election; we've got three candidates; and our hero Burnwood wants to do three in-depth profiles of the three candidates. One a day. Suddenly over the transom comes some paper. Now, Burnwood has looked at the papers; he has had experience covering the Department of Justice; they look like FBI documents; Burnwood has made a few telephone calls; he's not sure but he thinks they're real. (Turns to a Reporter): You don't publish, right?

1ST REPORTER: No, sir.

MR. MILLER: Why?

1ST REPORTER: From the appearance here no one makes any effort whatever to check other than apparently the seat-of-the-pants judgment of Mr. Burnwood.

MR. MILLER: You don't publish. They look like FBI documents. Do they tell you things relevant to the senatorial campaign?

1ST REPORTER: Arguably relevant.

MR. MILLER: What do you mean arguably?

1ST REPORTER: Well, only because they seem to be, but . . .

MR. MILLER: Well, I don't understand "arguably" and "seem to be." Is it not newsworthy that one of the major candidates has a potential psychiatric problem, lives in a questionable, that is, nonmiddle class life-style, apparently doesn't pay debts. Isn't that relevant?

1ST REPORTER: It's newsorthy, it's relevant, but not yet publishable.

MR. MILLER: Not yet publishable. What would you do? It's your decision, you are Burnwood, what do you do?

1ST REPORTER: Well, first of all if Burnwood is working for me, Burnwood would have to come forward with more than . . .

MR. MILLER: No, you're Burnwood.

1ST REPORTER: I'm Burnwood.

MR. MILLER: Don't abstract yourself.

111

1ST REPORTER: Okay.

MR. MILLER: You're on the line.

1ST REPORTER: I'm Burnwood. I suspect I'll be looking for work. If I'm Burnwood my first obligation to my reader is to find out whether or not I can give him something for which I can personally and professionally vouch.

MR. MILLER: How do you do that?

1ST REPORTER: Go to your sources, official agencies . . .

MR. MILLER: Which ones, which ones? We're talking about financial data, we are talking about life-style, we are talking about psychiatric data. You've gone to the psychiatrist. Keep that in mind. He invokes the privilege, he says doctor-patient privilege. Doesn't that tell you something?

1ST REPORTER: Well, it tends toward some confirmation, yes.

MR. MILLER: Tends towards some confirmation. Right? How come you didn't push the doctor?

1ST REPORTER: I suspect because there was an ecstasy of anxiety to publish, which usually overrides the capacity to check further.

MR. MILLER: In other words you figure if the doctor says doctor-patient privilege you're on the right track. That tells you more, you're saying, than you should actually get from the invocation of the privilege?

1ST REPORTER: Well, all I'm suggesting is that it is not uncommon for a reporter in possession of this kind of information to fear, perhaps substantially, that further checking will perhaps compromise what he has.

MR. MILLER: Are you saying, therefore, that you are playing the holier-than-thou game, that although you wouldn't publish you know damned well that 90 percent of the reporters would take that and push it. The Podunk *Press*, would they push it? How much work are they going to do?

1ST REPORTER: I assume they would not do as much as a newspaper with more resources, yes.

MR. MILLER: I see. Now, does this mean that since we are surrounded by journalistic Brahmins here today that we can play it holier than thou or should we think about what the mass of journalists do? If you don't like the Podunk *Press*, by the way, take the Harvard *Crimson*. I mean, they are a press.

1ST REPORTER: Or *Rolling Stone.*

MR. MILLER: Or *Rolling Stone.*

1ST REPORTER: I don't think the standards vary though. They don't vary at all.

MR. MILLER: How would you distinguish this case from let's say the Media papers? They came in over the transom. They were published. [Files were stolen from the FBI office in Media, Pennsylvania and released to the press.]

1ST REPORTER: I assume they were published after there was some demonstration of their authenticity.

MR. MILLER: In other words, calling the FBI and saying, "Are these accurate?" Would the FBI answer?

1ST REPORTER: Well, I presume they would.

MR. MILLER (Turns to Former Gov't. Official): Would the FBI answer?

FORMER GOV'T. OFFICIAL: They probably would refuse to answer.

MR. MILLER: Would refuse to answer. (To 1st Reporter): So what would you do then?

1ST REPORTER: Absent any other verification, not publish it.

MR. MILLER: But the Media papers were published. And how do you account for that? The FBI won't confirm . . .

1ST TV REPORTER (To Former Gov't. Official): Are you saying they [the FBI] did not confirm the authenticity of the Media papers?

FORMER GOV'T. OFFICIAL: No, they ultimately did. The question as I understood it, in the same situation, is that these existed and you made an inquiry in the FBI as to the authenticity of the papers. Would they immediately authenticate them? Chances are they'd refuse to say anything.

1ST TV REPORTER: But I think you were misunderstood. That was with regard to this case. But in the Media case it was reported there had been a break-in, the papers had been stolen from the FBI office in Media, and there was every reason to assume that when these papers appeared they were the stolen papers. I don't recall precisely but I don't think it was ever in doubt they were the Media papers.

MR. MILLER: Is there any doubt that once he sees that a psychiatrist is invoking the doctor-patient privilege that these papers have been verified? How much more would you want?

1ST TV REPORTER: Oh, I'd want a lot more. I mean don't assume from my attempt to clear up the record that I'm in any way saying that these have the same authenticity that I think was established for the Media papers. I want a lot more. Even if I thought they were authentic, which I don't think has been established, I don't trust FBI information that much. And the fact that it was authentically FBI doesn't make it authentic to me. So I have a lot of problems with that.

MR. MILLER: What would you do? What would you do to verify it? You're five days from an election.

1ST TV REPORTER: Normally what I would do to verify it is to go to the candidate himself and confront him with it and see to what extent he's willing to confirm any part of it.

MR. MILLER: And if he has no comment?

1ST TV REPORTER: And if he has no comment then I have enormous difficulties. If your question is to get at whether absent some other confirmation I would publish it, the answer is no.

MR. MILLER: I'm trying to get at a definition, a standard that the news-paper people or the media people are willing to live by in terms of this thing called verification. What's the go point? I'm not satisfied with it. I want a lot more. I'd go to the candidate, fine. The candidate says "No comment." Go to the FBI. The FBI won't confirm it at this point. What else would you do?

1ST TV REPORTER: Go to some of his friends, go to . . .

MR. MILLER: His friends.

1ST TV REPORTER: And go to other people who may know.

MR. MILLER: And how about the credit bureau. Would you go to a credit bureau?

1ST TV REPORTER: For the financial information?

MR. MILLER: Yes.

1ST TV REPORTER: Yes, perhaps forlornly he would.

MR. MILLER: Excuse me?

1ST REPORTER: Forlornly. They would not like to respond.

MR. MILLER: Why not?

1ST REPORTER: Because they have habits of confidentiality, which they are selling.

MR. MILLER: Well, you're willing to pay the fee. Buck and a quarter, buck and a half for a financial report. What's that?

1ST REPORTER: The newspaper would not be able to buy this kind of information through a credit reference, specifically of another person, at least as I understand standard credit bureau . . .

MR. MILLER: And suppose the neighbors say yeah, he has a lot of marijuana parties over there? Yep, lots of bearded types come in, real flakey characters, in and out all the time, every day.

1ST REPORTER: Well, we have to be very careful that we're sure that we're all agreed about what's to publish. I'm not sure the fact that people of one particular sartorial preference who come to his house is necessarily relevant news.

MR. MILLER: How about the psychiatric condition?

1ST TV REPORTER: That's touchy. The question is whether this is a profile. This is not a news story. It's a profile of a fellow. If you're writing a profile of a fellow, is it not relevant to a profile that he has friends among some one kind of people? Is that not an interesting little sidelight in the profile?

1ST REPORTER: Well, it's an interesting sidelight if you assume, which I don't assume, that the style of clothing that one chooses to wear necessarily represents his character. I would want to know a good deal more about those people than that there was a commonality of clothing preference.

MR. MILLER: You're writing a profile of a guy and you know what kind of friends he has. Is it not an element of a profile?

1ST REPORTER: I don't know that it adds a great deal. Suppose an alternative circumstance is that all of the people who came there wore blue sweaters. I think the fact that everybody wore blue sweaters might mean something.

1ST TV REPORTER: In writing a profile of a candidate who has a preference for wearing blue sweaters, wouldn't he say he shows a strange preference for people in blue sweaters?

1ST REPORTER: One thing that bothers me, if I may, professor, is I hope you don't proceed on the assumption of the fact that because the election is only five days away it changes the rules.

MR. MILLER: Why shouldn't it?

1ST REPORTER: Because you cannot, however exigent the circumstances, offer to your reader in a season of political choice that which you would not offer at another time even if it would not arguably, demonstrably change the . . .

MR. MILLER: You are telling me that your standard to go is absolutely flat and neutral without regard to timing, without regard to the fact that Ned Nosey—Ned Nosey who wants John Peter Burnwood's status in the State of Idyllia—is breathing down your neck. Am I to assume you have no notions, no sensitivities, no sense of ambition, no ego?

1ST REPORTER: Perhaps overriding all of that is what for lots of us passes for a calling. And in fulfilling that calling I . . .

MR. MILLER: A higher duty it was called this morning, and a higher duty is what?

1ST REPORTER: The higher duty is not to publish that which cannot justify telling to your neighbor.

MR. MILLER: I see. And thus far you have told me you'd want a lot more verification.

1ST REPORTER: A great deal more than this man sought or apparently wanted.

MR. MILLER: Okay. What about Burnwood's technique with regard to Bumptious?

1ST REPORTER: Bumptious is who.

MR. MILLER: Bumptious is the incumbent senator.

1ST REPORTER: Oh, yes, sure.

MR. MILLER: You will note that there's nothing in the transom papers about Bumptious. But our friend Burnwood has gone and gotten some data from the sheriff about Bumptious. What about that?

1ST REPORTER: And then he goes and witnesses Bumptious . . .

MR. MILLER: Yes. Let's take a look at the relationship between Burnwood and Clodde, the sheriff, right now. (A) do you approve of that news-gathering technique? And (B) would you publish it?

1ST REPORTER: The information about Bumptious as a teenager, like the information about Bumptious as a late-night reveller, is not by and of itself relevant to the election campaign.

MR. MILLER: You mean a past arrest is not relevant.

1ST REPORTER: Past arrest, that's right.

MR. MILLER: Not relevant.

1ST REPORTER: By and of itself.

MR. MILLER: So you wouldn't publish it.

1ST REPORTER: No, not on that premise. The fact that the arrest is dated in time raises very serious questions about it.

MR. MILLER: Suppose it was 15 years ago, 10 years ago, 5 years ago?

1ST REPORTER: You're getting closer.

MR. MILLER: Getting closer. Where's the line?

1ST REPORTER: I suspect that if the line is drawn somewhere around Senator Bumptious' public career, you're very close to the white lines.

MR. MILLER: So if it's vehicular homicide after Senator Bumptious came into the public eye it becomes newsworthy?

1ST REPORTER: I've problems with vehicular homicide and its bearing upon his capacity to carry out a public function.

MR. MILLER: Why?

1ST REPORTER: Well, I won't argue vehicular homicide legally. Vehicular homicide may have no bearing on whether or not he is sensitive to the needs of his constituents or his public function.

MR. MILLER: Sensitive to human life. Maybe he was driving like a maniac, hit-and-run, law-and-order. Aren't they all relevant to a candidate who actually is a sitting senator?

1ST REPORTER: Not necessarily.

MR. MILLER: Not necessarily. (Turns to 2nd Reporter): How do you feel about it?

2ND REPORTER: Well, we are talking about an arrest. I think in this case, and it seems to me that as a general principle I would shy away from publishing an arrest unless a conviction follows or unless I could ascertain enough facts to make me feel that there's an awful lot of substance to the arrest.

MR. MILLER: In other words you'd want more data about the arrest.

2ND REPORTER: Yes, and what happened to him subsequently, especially given the period of time lapse including something else that happened . . .

MR. MILLER: What about the technique used to get the arrest data here?

2ND REPORTER: Well, that bothers me because I don't approve of the National Crime Information Center [NCIC], nor do I want to have anything . . . [The National Crime Information Center of the FBI serves as a data bank for crime information.]

MR. MILLER: You just don't want to have anything to do with it?

2ND REPORTER: I would prefer that it did not exist—now this is difficult to argue—to the extent that reporters rely upon it through sheriffs and bolster its existence. That would disturb me.

MR. MILLER: Suppose it were a local file. Let's drop the NCIC for a minute. Suppose it was right there in Clodde's own files? You go up to Clodde and say, "Hi, sheriff, what's new? Got anything for me about the senator?" He says, "How about this?"

2ND REPORTER: I have no problem with that.

MR. MILLER: No problem, no problem. Anybody have any problem?

1ST EDITOR: I have a problem with that.

MR. MILLER: What's that?

1ST EDITOR: In the first place, I think the news story here is the story of what Sheriff Clodde is doing, and I think for a reporter to take that from someone who's running for office himself, evidently, is to use his authority and his resources of office to kind of dump this thing on someone else, and not to figure out a way to make him go public with what he's doing. It creates a story that ought not to be printed.

MR. MILLER: Now you're saying that the story is that the sheriff is violating his trust, right?

1ST EDITOR: Yes, in kind of a sneaky way.

MR. MILLER: Yes, because the sheriff knows that next year he's going to need the *Chronicle's* support, right?

1ST EDITOR: Maybe he needs it now. We don't know quite what he's doing.

MR. MILLER: Suppose there's no such motivation, suppose the sheriff is an appointed official and just at a cocktail party says to Burnwood, "By the way, I happened to be rummaging through the files, tickling the ivories on the old computer today, and look what I came up with."

1ST EDITOR: I would still try to get the reporter, or if I were the reporter I would try to get that part of the story on the record. If it came to court I suppose I would go too uncharily to jail not to be forced to say who the source was. But I think that the source of that story is part of the story.

MR. MILLER: But you publish the story.

1ST EDITOR: Not necessarily, no. I don't think I would.

MR. MILLER: Why not? You say there's a story there but you seem to say the story is about a defaulting sheriff. You don't think you'd publish anything about Bumptious' prior brush with the law.

1ST EDITOR: On the basis of that, no.

MR. MILLER: No. What if it were a five-year-old arrest record? Or one-year-old arrest record?

1ST EDITOR: Well, the first thing I would do would be to go to Bumptious.

MR. MILLER: O.K. He says it's true, I killed somebody with my car. They didn't prosecute me because, well, maybe it was because I was a senator, maybe it was because they didn't really have an air-tight case, maybe because it was obscure, but there is no doubt I hit somebody in the dead of night.

1ST EDITOR: I'd print it.

MR. MILLER: You'd print it.

1ST EDITOR: What's wrong with that? He said it.

MR. MILLER: I see. But you wouldn't print it out of the machine, you wouldn't print it on the basis of what the sheriff told you. What about the fact that you are participating in a crime in receiving the information? The release of that kind of data stipulated in the problem is a crime, is a state crime.

1ST EDITOR: I didn't realize it's a crime for me to receive . . .

MR. MILLER: It's a crime for the sheriff to disclose, it's a crime for you to receive. That's true now in a number of states. If you think back about this morning's conversation about proposed S-1 and some of the examples given, release statutes which make it a crime to release, a growing body of statutes deals with criminal justice information. It's still pending in the Congress to do that for FBI or NCIC data.

1ST EDITOR: Okay, let me ask you because this exchange of information is a little murky. You suggested a moment ago that the reporter went up to the sheriff and said: "Hi, kid, have you got anything for me?"

MR. MILLER: Yes.

1ST EDITOR: The sheriff said, "Well it just so happens." Is that the way . . .

MR. MILLER: Well, take it that way or take it that it's more affirmative than that. Either the sheriff voluntarily bestows it on Burnwood or Burnwood said, "What's new, you got anything for me?" Well, Burnwood says, "You know, the Senate election's five days away, have you got anything on these three candidates, sheriff?"

1ST EDITOR: Those are different, those are different, I think. Do I know at the time that I am asking for this . . .

MR. MILLER: That you're violating laws?

1ST EDITOR: Yes.

MR. MILLER: Well, I suppose you should, shouldn't you? I mean, if you are a well-schooled reporter in a serious newspaper, supposedly that has been told to you as part of your operating instructions.

1ST EDITOR: And he says to me I've got some stuff out of this . . .

MR. MILLER: This is a violation for you as well as the sheriff.

1ST EDITOR: And it's a violation for me?

MR. MILLER: For both. Do you say no, you wouldn't do it.

1ST EDITOR: He says to me, "Do you want to buy these post cards?"

MR. MILLER: Yes.

1ST EDITOR: Then I say no.

MR. MILLER: No. Is there anybody around the table who would either solicit this kind of data or simply receive it?

2ND TV REPORTER: Well, first of all I don't think the statement of the law is correct here. I know you didn't want us to go into that, but there's a mystique of the computer that's very unfortunate these days. Those of us who started out as police reporters know that it's considered perfectly all right—or was—to get arrest records. And no one ever questioned that until this bugaboo of the NCIC came upon us. The civil libertarian's point of view was supposed to be, oh, my God, we can't take anything out of that. In fact what has now happened is that matters of public record which we would all print in the past if we got it off a little card at the local grubby police station suddenly becomes unusable when we get it off of a console.

MR. MILLER: So what's your disagreement with the law.

2ND TV REPORTER: I think that's very confusing.

MR. MILLER: I invite you to read Chapter 805 of the laws of Massachusetts for the year 1972 and you will see in no uncertain terms that any law enforcement agent who releases arrest data is guilty of a crime; anyone who receives arrest data is guilty of a crime. And it doesn't mention the computer once in the statute.

(2nd Editor speaks up incredulously): You mean an arrest record is not a public record?

MR. MILLER: That's right.

2ND EDITOR: That's incredible.

MR. MILLER: That's incredible. Why is it so incredible?

2ND EDITOR: The police book is a public record. It's not in Massachusetts?

MR. MILLER: In Massachusetts it is known as criminal offender record information and it is declared confidential except under certain circumstances. That's an outrage, right?

2ND EDITOR: Absolutely.

MR. MILLER: You just don't believe in privacy, huh?

2ND EDITOR: Not when somebody's arrested. An arrest is a public act.

MR. MILLER: Is it? Says who?

2ND EDITOR: If I'm arrested I want people to know about it.

(Laughter)

MR. MILLER: You want people to know. That's right. that's right, that's right. You can go to the corner and scream, I've been arrested, you can make it as public as you want. But I don't want it known, I don't want my dean to know I have been arrested.

1ST JUDGE: In the District of Columbia there is a statute that requires that every arrest be entered in the blotter because that was passed at a time when they wanted to make sure that people were not being detained without having been entered in the blotter. Therefore the statute says if a policeman arrests you it must be entered in the blotter at the local precinct station.

MR. MILLER: Yes.

1ST JUDGE: I draw a distinction between that and central indexing which makes it known to others but at least there is some historic record of a historic fact.

MR. MILLER: That's right. And even in some of the states that have these statutes, the blotter is still available. But the blotter for five years ago is not going to be usable to a policeman now. I mean it's like taking a fishing expedition over five years of blotters. What you want and what you thought you could get and what you still can get in most states is that you can walk into the centralized system—it doesn't make a damned bit of difference whether it's a computerized or a manual system—and get the rap sheet. Say, you've got a name, Bob Bumptious. Yes, arrested June 23rd, '44, charged felony, et cetera, et cetera. Well, unfortunately—and I think this is one of the conflicts between law and media—society is starting to edge toward the privacy side. Society is starting to put some weight on the proposition that certain things that you characterize as public information because it's in your blood to characterize it as public information—you've been doing it for years—maybe no longer should be public information. Now, the question is what is a reporter going to do when that reporter bumps up against such a statute? What will you do? You're now educated, your consciousness has been raised. You still don't like it but what are you going to do? You've just been sent to the Boston *Globe,* God help you, what are you going to do.

2ND EDITOR: Well, I'm not going to invite anybody to break the law.

MR. MILLER: You're not going to invite.

2ND EDITOR: That's right, so I wouldn't ask for it. Under those conditions I'd have to go on a fishing expedition through the old blotters.

MR. MILLER: You'll sit there and go through five years looking up Bumptious.

2ND EDITOR: 10, 15, whatever.

MR. MILLER: Is there anyone here who would go after the file?

3RD EDITOR: Go after the law.

MR. MILLER: What do you mean, go after the law?

3RD EDITOR: Call my lawyer.

MR. MILLER: Call your lawyer? You must have that printed on a card.

3RD EDITOR: And the backside says too expensive.

MR. MILLER: How would you go after the law?

3RD EDITOR: Why can't you challenge that?

MR. MILLER: How, what would you say?

2ND EDITOR: He's got three days.

MR. MILLER: No, no, no, I mean the principle that it is not a public record. I mean we could not go in and challenge that. I'm really asking if we could not challenge that by saying that we disagree with the law?

4TH EDITOR: You mean could we get a declaratory judgment?

MR. MILLER: In other words, you go in and try to get the statute declared unconstitutional.

3RD EDITOR: Yes.

MR. MILLER (Turns to 1st Lawyer): How do you react on that? Procedurally, how can you do it?

1ST LAWYER: Well, you go into court for a declaratory judgment, maybe saying you had certain information you thought you had a right to print. I wonder, if the reporters were in possession of the information, if it occurred a year ago and it was hit-and-run, vehicular homicide, and nothing ever happened, and there were five days before an election, whether they'd really wait.

MR. MILLER: Do you think they'd go with the story?

1ST LAWYER: Well, another way to challenge is to print it and let somebody . . .

3RD EDITOR: Go with the story as a challenge.

MR. MILLER: In other words if Burnwood hands it up to you and says, "You know, I was just talking to Clodde and Clodde gave me this freebee."

3RD EDITOR: Yes.

MR. MILLER: You'd go with it.

3RD EDITOR: If I wanted to challenge the law. That's the point we're talking about.

MR. MILLER: All right.

3RD EDITOR: If we wanted to make that our case we'd go with it.

3RD REPORTER: Professor, I think the law is basically so stupid that I would inquire of people in the police department whom I thought would not be likely to put themselves and myself in jeopardy if any of the candidates had ever been arrested before.

MR. MILLER: You'd violate the law.

3RD REPORTER: Yes.

MR. MILLER: You'd just violate the law because you think it's stupid. And who the hell are you?

3RD REPORTER: A newspaper reporter.

MR. MILLER: You're a newspaper reporter. Does that make you bigger than a bread box?

3RD REPORTER: Yes, probably.

MR. MILLER: So you're ready to go to jail for it?

3RD REPORTER: Yes, I would take some care in whom I talked to and try to make it less likely that he would go running . . .

MR. MILLER: You'd do it in a subversive manner, is that what you mean?

3RD REPORTER: Carefully.

(Laughter)

MR. MILLER: I see. Man of principle, eh. You think the law is stupid, but you're going to try to subvert it in a way so you won't be caught.

3RD REPORTER: Yes.

MR. MILLER: Because you're a newspaper person.

3RD REPORTER: Because I'm representing the public's right to know whether their incumbent senator . . .

MR. MILLER: Oooh. I see.

3RD REPORTER: . . . has gotten away with vehicular homicide and should have been arrested.

MR. MILLER: I'm sorry, I'm sorry. It's a latter-day case of walking on water. Society has made a decision in passing that statute, hasn't it? Society made the decision that certain aspects of privacy might be more valuable than your status as a newspaper person.

3RD REPORTER: That's right.

MR. MILLER: But you think it's stupid.

3RD REPORTER: Right.

MR. MILLER: And you'd violate it.

3RD REPORTER: Right.

MR. MILLER: How are you different from other violators of the law?

3RD REPORTER: Well, I might . . .

MR. MILLER: An attorney general to take a hypothetical case?

3RD REPORTER: If the attorney general's going to jail I might too.

MR. MILLER: You might too. But you're doing it ostensibly because you think a newspaper person has a right by virtue of that status to break the law.

3RD REPORTER: That kind of a law, yes.

MR. MILLER: "That kind of a law," you spit out. In other words, what is "that kind of a law"? One you disagree with?

3RD REPORTER: Well . . .

MR. MILLER: Any law that prevents you from getting something you want, huh? That inability to outgrow your anal retentive phase. Anything you want you're going to go after because you're a newspaper person.

3RD REPORTER: No, not anything. I'm not going to steal out of somebody's briefcase.

MR. MILLER: Oh, I see, that's a sharp distinction. Like this morning you wouldn't pay for news, right? That was the consensus here. Nobody around this table is going to pay for news, right?

3RD REPORTER: Some would.

MR. MILLER: Some would. But of those who wouldn't pay for news would you invite Clodde to break the law to get information, knowing that in a sense you're paying through your support of Clodde at the next election?

3RD REPORTER: That's an element I wouldn't go to Clodde for.

MR. MILLER: Where would you go?

3RD REPORTER: Oh, I'd find some old source . . .

MR. MILLER: Would you receive it from Clodde, knowing that Clodde has in the back of his mind, "Gee, if I give him a couple of things they'll be nice to me next fall."?

3RD REPORTER: If he volunteers it to me as a reporter who never talks to editors about editorials, yes. I don't think I can . . .

MR. MILLER: You can draw that distinction between paying money, asking for it knowing it's in violation of law, or just passively receiving it . . .

3RD REPORTER: No, I'm not going to pay for it, I'm not going to pay for it . . .

MR. MILLER: I just want to see where the line is. Where's the line, where's the ethical cutting edge? You won't pay, you won't pay. That's dirty pool. You won't ask for it . . .

3RD REPORTER: Yes, I will.

MR. MILLER: You will ask for it?

3RD REPORTER: Not from Clodde under the circumstances you've described, but I'll find an elderly sergeant and get it from him.

MR. MILLER: Oh, I see, elderly sergeants are fair game. Why? Why are they fair game?

3RD REPORTER: Because they are not relying on the political support which you have said my newspaper trades with Clodde.

MR. MILLER: I see, I see, so you will invite a breach of law and participate in a breach of law. (Turns to 2nd Reporter): Would you?

2ND REPORTER: The inviting part bothers me. I'm not so sure I'd go and solicit it from a Clodde knowing what he would have to do in order to get it. If he came to me with the information, though, I think it would be unrealistic to suggest that I should shut my ears to it. Many suggestions were made this morning that you can confirm information after all by other certain sources. You can go back to Bumptious himself. You can ferret it out once you know what you think to be the fact in the matter. And once you've established the details then you're in a position to approach him without feeling guilty about the original tip.

MR. MILLER: Now, what about these Media, Pennsylvania papers we know were garnered in violation of law? They came over the transom, right? Can you distinguish that from either paying for news—dirty pool—or trying to entice Clodde because Clodde figures he's going to get a quid pro quo, namely political support, at the next election. Can you distinguish simply receiving stuff over the transom you know has been stolen?

1ST TV REPORTER: Professor Miller, I'm going to stick my neck out, knowing that it's about to be cut off. But I do think that one should avoid taking merely defensive positions because I think there are things here whose clarification is more important than simply falling back and making hackneyed arguments. I think you have a point, so therefore let me say this very tentatively. I think you raise a quite important issue about privacy. I still think that most of the legitimacy of what we do basically comes from a sense of approval of our audiences, thereby meaning that what we do is public service. And for a great many years public service was equated by journalists with finding out everything we could and telling people everything they wanted to know. I think you are probably right in saying that trends change and one of the newer trends is that people are beginning to worry about being manipulated and about their privacy being invaded. Therefore, it may not be an absolute value any more to find out everything about everything, and damn the consequences. That being so, I think it would behoove us to realize that this is a growing feeling and to recognize it. Therefore, what I come down to as a practical matter—and I'm not saying that I'm happy with it or that it's absolute and I'll rest with it—but as a practical matter it is this: I would not go after or willingly try to obtain either by payment or by cajoling an elderly sergeant or a young captain, or whatever, information which for him would violate the law, at least in the state of Massachusetts, and presumably other states. The situation changes for me when it comes in over the transom. And you're going to subject me to some questioning which will make this sound silly but so be it.

MR. MILLER: Now, now, don't get defensive.

1ST TV REPORTER: The situation changes for me when it comes over the transom in that if it comes over the transom and if you stipulate that there is no question of its authenticity as information, it has become invested with something else. It's information which could come over any transom. It is in a sense, in a very large sense, in a public domain now. Now my question . . .

MR. MILLER: Because somebody's stolen it?

1ST TV REPORTER: Now, the issue that I face, apart from the issue of somebody else's privacy, is the issue of whether I have a personal right to suppress information. How can I unknow what I have come to know? How can I abolish what has come into my consciousness? Now, I may go through a lot of practical procedures to try to confirm it elsewhere, or get it on some other basis. There are things reporters do when they don't want to be faced with the simple results of their own acts and their own conscience, and there are a lot of things they do. But I think I have to recognize that the problem you present is a very real one and would be a problem for me every day. At the moment I would tend to come down on the side of: if it comes to me over the transom, if it comes to me in any way that I could consider to be spontaneous, that I can say in conscience I have not told anybody about any law, I'll look at it and say I don't use it. How many other transoms has this gone over? Is this not eventually going to be published, somehow? Must I not consider it. And having looked at it, which I obviously will do, and if it is information which I consider to be of interest, to try to unknow it would be like trying to uninvent the atom bomb for me.

MR. MILLER: Now, what are you saying?

1ST TV REPORTER: I'm not sure what I'm saying.

MR. MILLER: It comes over your transom, right? You stick your hands in your pockets. No, I didn't take it, I didn't take it. It's here. But you're looking at it.

1ST TV REPORTER: Right.

MR. MILLER: You're looking at it. Hum, interesting stuff. Then you go through this process. I've seen it.

1ST TV REPORTER: Right.

MR. MILLER: I have no capacity, unlike the computer, to do a data dump. It's there; I know it.

1ST TV REPORTER: Right.

MR. MILLER: In the real world we can assume if somebody has stolen this, like the Media papers, it's probably gone over another transom.

1ST TV REPORTER: Right.

MR. MILLER: A dozen transoms, "N" transoms.

1ST TV REPORTER: Right.

MR. MILLER: Somebody's going to publish it.

1ST TV REPORTER: Right.

MR. MILLER: Therefore my ethics are now reduced to the lowest common denominator with regard to the "N" transoms in the United States. I will publish because somebody else will publish.

1ST TV REPORTER: Not purely for competitive reasons.

MR. MILLER: I didn't say competitive.

1ST TV REPORTER: I'm willing to make a lot of confessions about my thinking here. Part of it is obviously competitive. But a part of it is also what I have said about it is somehow entering some large thing called the public domain by the fact that it's been spontaneously put out that way. I don't say there's a legal theory, either, but it is a theory of personality.

5TH EDITOR: There's another element to this moral dilemma, leaving aside the legal theory. Suppose someone came into your office in the McGovern campaign and said, "I'm True Davis and I know a lot about Tom Eagleton that you ought to know about. This guy's not fit to be vice-president." And he dumps a bunch of stuff on speeding violations, maybe drunken driving, psychiatric care, and walks out. And it's left to you to pursue it. There's no damned way that you can prove this. There's nothing in the records. You can't get to his doctor because of the patient relationship. You don't print it. McGovern is elected, he's assassinated. Tom Eagleton is now president of the United States with a black box. Now, from a journalists's point of view, that which bears on fitness for public office carries you right to the edge of fair comment, fairness doctrine and so forth, in all these three cases here. You're fairly secure that you're not liable for libel with a political figure. You're probably secure in the knowledge that you can label it comment and get away with a lot more than you would in your news columns. The question still remains.

MR. MILLER: It's inside you, right? The law isn't telling you a damned thing.

5TH EDITOR: That's right, and it can't.

MR. MILLER: Now, you tell me how you draw that line. Are you going to publish anything that comes over the transom, are you only going to publish that which might put an unfit person or keep an unfit person away from the black box?

5TH EDITOR: Well, in the case of Carla Cassandra . . .

MR. MILLER: Stick with Bumptious. Bumptious is a midpoint, he's just a senator.

5TH EDITOR: He's also an office-holder.

MR. MILLER: Well, what about Aphid. Let me move even away from Bumptious. Aphid.

3RD EDITOR: Go back to Bumptious for a minute.

MR. MILLER: Yes.

5TH EDITOR: As a teenager in a vehicular homicide, all right, probably not be noteworthy or newsworthy.

3RD EDITOR: If he were a sitting senator and was in the kind of accident you described, that would not be a secret at this time for Clodde to tell anybody. I do not see how a sitting senator could not have that information leak out, get out, or be out and be in the file.

MR. MILLER: Therefore it should be fair game.

5TH EDITOR: Right.

3RD EDITOR: Well, I mean, what you're doing is repeating what you've already published.

MR. MILLER: Now, how does that help you with Aphid's psychiatric—potential psychiatric—problem? Which takes you away from the Eagleton thing, which is obviously what it's modeled on. It's not a president, it's not a vice-president, it's not a history of psychiatric care. It's a potential. He's been to a psychiatrist, but at this point it's potential.

3RD EDITOR: I'd have to know a lot more about his problems. If I couldn't find out I'm not sure I'd publish it.

MR. MILLER: (Turns to 5th Editor): Would you publish?

5TH EDITOR: When I first read the case, the pencil note I jotted down was he obviously has to be equally nasty to all three of them. And in these circumstances, if it were a matter of record and he set out in the three commentaries to be equally nasty, I suppose rather than . . .

3RD EDITOR: Why does he have to be equally nasty? Is that the fairness doctrine?

5TH EDITOR: Well, I think no. I think it should be Burnwood's fairness doctrine, I mean the fairness doctrine . . .

3RD EDITOR: No, I disagree.

5TH EDITOR: It's what you make it for yourself, isn't it?

3RD EDITOR: No. First of all, I don't think you should start out being nasty.

5TH EDITOR: Reading this document, that was my reaction. Burnwood is the guy with the record of letting the chips fall as they may. He obviously for years has had an editor who has let the chips fall where they may.

MR. MILLER: Well, let's not focus on it, let's see if we can get an articulation of how either a reporter or an editor makes the decision to go with transom-type data.

3RD EDITOR: It matters what it contains, and how much of it you can verify from other sources.

5TH EDITOR: And who the individual is and how old it is.

3RD EDITOR: How old the information is, how relevant it is to the current issues that involve that particular person at that particular moment.

MR. MILLER: And you sit around in the editorial room discussing that. You have one of these, huh?

3RD EDITOR: No, you usually do more than that. Running guerrilla gun battles all over the floor, then wrestling with these issues. And lots of anguish and lots of memories of what you did in other cases somewhat like it, each a little bit different. And then finally you come to a decision. You may even impose temporary restraint on yourself and wait a day.

MR. MILLER: You may, five days before the election, with three stories to go?

3RD EDITOR: Well, I disagree with three stories to go.

MR. MILLER: Okay, let's talk about real life. It's 6:00 o'clock, you've got an hour and 29 minutes to close, what do you do?

3RD EDITOR: Punt.

MR. MILLER: Punt. What does that mean? You wait a day.

3RD EDITOR: No, you . . .

MR. MILLER: There's no more days.

3RD EDITOR: No more days?

MR. MILLER: Ned Nosey is out there, you can smell him.

3RD EDITOR: As an editor, if I'm not convinced then the rule is simple: when in doubt, leave it out.

MR. MILLER: When in doubt, leave it out.

3RD EDITOR: Right.

MR. MILLER: And how do you define doubt?

3RD EDITOR: It's genetic.

MR. MILLER: How much does the fact that the opposition may have the story bear on it?

3RD EDITOR: Not that much.

MR. MILLER: Not that much.

3RD EDITOR: Not as much as you'd like to imply.

MR. MILLER: Oh, me implying. I'm just a moderator. You would have the group believe the competition is meaningless, it's once again a higher duty.

3RD EDITOR: No, I didn't say meaningless, I said not as much that you're implying.

MR. MILLER: How much?

3RD EDITOR: If we were not sure of our information, we would not publish it.

6TH EDITOR: You left Eagleton out. They left Eagleton out.

MR. MILLER: Yes. Why did you do that?

3RD EDITOR: For the reason that we were not satisfied.

MR. MILLER: But after it was published in the midwest?

3RD EDITOR: The drunk driving thing we didn't cover at all.

3RD REPORTER: Did you kill Anderson's columns?

3RD EDITOR: It never appeared in Anderson's columns.

MR. MILLER: Really.

3RD EDITOR: It was the radio.

MR. MILLER: Well, there is that case in New York. As I recall, I think it was the *Times* going with a story from grand jury minutes about a judge being linked to the Mafia. One person saying to another that we can reach Judge X. The *Times* initially decided not to go with the name of the judge, but on the 6:00 o'clock news the judge's name emerged and the *Times* went back and put the judge's name in the headline. Do you think that's responsible? (Looks at 7th Editor): Why, you're shaking your head.

7TH EDITOR: Public knowledge.

MR. MILLER: I see. So again it's this phenomenon, that if you can get someone lower down the caste totem pole to do your dirty work . . .

7TH EDITOR: Oh, come on, you're attributing a motive to it that I didn't have.

MR. MILLER: Well, how come you . . .

7TH EDITOR: It's out, it's out.

MR. MILLER: Oh, it's out.

7TH EDITOR: It's suddenly in the public domain. Who are you kidding by not running it.

MR. MILLER: Do you think that the papers and the broadcast groups at the top of the totem pole have a duty to raise the consciousness of those below them? To keep the Harvard *Crimson* from publishing things without the kind of verification procedures that others here talk about? I mean, if we're making policy for the nation with regard to the interaction of law and media, do we pit the standards at your level, or at the Harvard *Crimson's* level, or at a median between the two?

7TH EDITOR: None of us is in a position to speak for more than his own group, his own newspaper. There's just a little more trouble to go around than there's time to handle, and the Harvard *Crimson* will have to fend for itself.

MR. MILLER: But you may ultimately get tabbed by First Amendment standards and legal principles that reflect what the Harvard *Crimson* is doing. Right. And isn't it to your own interest to educate them?

7TH EDITOR: Yes, it is in my own interest.

MR. MILLER: Are you doing anything about it?

7TH EDITOR: But not by dictatorship.

MR. MILLER: Oh, you just don't have the time.

7TH EDITOR: That's true.

MR. MILLER: It's not my department. Huh? I mean, I only send the rockets up, where they fall down, that's beyond the scope of my responsibility.

7TH EDITOR: Who said we're sending up the rocket in this case.

MR. MILLER: Yes, I admit the metaphor's a little backward but it's poetic, and you get the point, right? Unless you raise the bottom, the law—I mean, if we're talking about how the law should react to media practices—the simple fact of life is that the law may have to react to media practices more shoddy than yours.

1ST REPORTER: It usually does.

MR. MILLER: And usually does. Now, what should the law do about that? Get a differential system? You know, look in a little black book. Oh, Washington *Post, Sun Times,* New York *Times,* they get a category "A" law. Harvard *Crimson,* they get a different law?

2ND TV REPORTER: Are you shuttling back and forth between the question of verification of documents and the propriety of publishing?

MR. MILLER: Right now I'm shuttling back and forth among three things. Verification of documents, news gathering techniques, and the decision to go. And hopefully we can order them a little better. Right now we're just sort of . . .

2ND TV REPORTER: I think if you assume verification, which some of us have in the discussion here, then it sharpens the questions of violations of privacy, and that's where the law is developing, not in verification.

MR. MILLER: Well, I don't know.

2ND TV REPORTER: I was involved in the Media documents and there was no question the FBI didn't challenge it and you talk about documents coming over the transom. That's rather rare, really. It's more often the situation where you know the source and you know why they're being peddled to you. You know what ax is being ground. That goes into the mix of your calculations as to whether they're verifiable, whether they're accurate. And, to a certain extent, whether to go with it. But, if you assume that the document is true, and an active document, then you get to the question of privacy. On the question of Bumptious, I don't agree with some of this. I think I would go with the fact that he was arrested, if that's true, when he was 15 years old. That's something you need to know about.

MR. MILLER: You go with it because you know it's true. You think it's newsworthy?

2ND TV REPORTER: Yes.

MR. MILLER: You think it's newsworthy?

2ND TV REPORTER: Yes.

1ST REPORTER: Even if it's only an accident?

MR. MILLER: Why?

2ND TV REPORTER: Well, because I think there is a difference. I think when a person lays himself on the line as a candidate for Senate of the United States, all of that is the public's business, the public's right to know.

MR. MILLER: Right to know?

2ND TV REPORTER: Right.

MR. MILLER: Even if it's morbid curiosity?

2ND TV REPORTER: No, it's not morbid curiosity when you're running for the Senate of the United States.

MR. MILLER: I see. I see.

(Simultaneous conversation.)

MR. MILLER (Recognizes 1st Gov't. Official)

1ST GOV'T. OFFICIAL: With juvenile delinquents you don't have a right to know. There are provisions in the statutes to protect their names.

2ND TV REPORTER: Well, apparently this is on the record.

MR. MILLER: Yes. I mean, society is increasingly taking the position that with juveniles you're not going to get that data.

PROSECUTOR: He [Bumptious] was never prosecuted.

MR. MILLER: Yes.

PROSECUTOR: I want to find out why.

3RD REPORTER: That's a good story.

MR. MILLER (Addresses 2nd TV Reporter): Well, how about that?

PROSECUTOR: It's stale data.

2ND TV REPORTER: Well, if that's what you go and ask.

PROSECUTOR: Suppose you can't find out?

MR. MILLER: Nobody knows. It was 25 years ago.

1ST REPORTER: No, let's suppose that the matter is completely verified. The guy was arrested for vehicular homicide and was never prosecuted, and you've gone and interviewed everybody. You've looked at the arrest records, and you have it nailed as much as you can nail it. Why in the name of anything does that bear upon Senator Bumptious' capacity to serve . . .

2ND TV REPORTER: In a profile of a public official running for the Senate, that's obviously a part of the story.

1ST REPORTER: I don't think it is at all.

PROSECUTOR: But, as a teen-ager?

2ND TV REPORTER: Yes.

1ST REPORTER: I don't think it is at all.

MR. MILLER: What age do you cut off? You had a senator who cheated on his exams when he was 19.

1ST REPORTER: Cheating on exams? Does that bear upon whether he's a good lawyer? A good senator?

(Simultaneous conversation.)

PROSECUTOR: Cheating on an exam goes to a man's veracity.

VARIOUS VOICES: Hit and run driving doesn't?

MR. MILLER: Hit and run doesn't?

PROSECUTOR: An arrest? You don't even know whether he's guilty, for God's sake.

2ND TV REPORTER: Assuming that you go and talk to him about that and get all the facts.

PROSECUTOR: Suppose he says, "I was arrested, but there was no merit to it. It was an accident." How does that go to his credibility? How does it go to anything? His qualifications, or anything? How does it go to anything?

3RD REPORTER: He ran.

PROSECUTOR: But it's so damn stale.

7TH EDITOR: He ran, didn't he?

MR. MILLER: He ran what?

7TH EDITOR: He ran away.

MR. MILLER: He ran away. Hit and run. He was arrested. Was it ever proven?

(Simultaneous conversation.)

7TH EDITOR: I thought you said he admitted it.

PROSECUTOR: No!

MR. MILLER: No, he says, "I hit somebody." That's all.

7TH EDITOR: And didn't run?

MR. MILLER: No, he doesn't remember. Maybe he was drunk at the time. Or, he says, "I've got no comment."

2ND TV REPORTER: You satisfy yourself as to whether he was involved in a hit and run.

MR. MILLER: He was, but he was not prosecuted.

2ND TV REPORTER: Well, then, you print it.

MR. MILLER: 25 years ago. Don't you believe in Christian redemption? Oh, you believe in journalism?

2ND TV REPORTER: Yes.

MR. MILLER: What does journalism mean?

2ND TV REPORTER: It doesn't involve Christian redemption when a person is running for the United States Senate.

MR. MILLER: Even though it was a 15-year-old homicide?

2ND TV REPORTER: You don't make a big thing out of it, but that's part of his profile.

MR. MILLER: Part of his profile. I notice you keep focusing on profile. Are you suggesting it's not newsworthy? That you wouldn't stick with the position you're publishing news with a 25-year-old arrest, not followed by prosecution or conviction.

2ND TV REPORTER: No, the difference here is if you're doing a spot story and let's say he has taken a conservative law-and-order position.

MR. MILLER: Yes.

2ND TV REPORTER: If you throw in the fact that he was arrested when he was 15 years old, then I think there's a question about it. But if you're doing a profile on the man's life, he's running for public office, it's news. And, you include it.

1ST REPORTER: I don't think it bears upon his candidacy.

2ND TV REPORTER: Yes.

MR. MILLER: What doesn't?

1ST REPORTER: Is there anything about his life? How about his aunt who happens to be mentally deranged? His aunt. That is a fact in his life. All right, he may never have known her.

2ND REPORTER: That's not an accident.

(Simultaneous conversation.)

1ST REPORTER: No, I'm talking about this profile business. This is a person who is not the senator, who is not going to serve, why isn't that just as relevant if a profile is supposed to be compendious?

1ST TV REPORTER: You were the guy who wouldn't publish that he goes out with blue-sweatered people all the time.

1ST REPORTER: Of course I don't want to publish it. I'm arguing against publishing this accident.

MR. MILLER: Let's switch and see how you react in the Cassandra profile to the publication of the fact that her husband is a convicted felon.

2ND TV REPORTER: I'd print that.

MR. MILLER: You'd print that?

2ND TV REPORTER: Yes.

MR. MILLER: On what theory?

2ND TV REPORTER: On the theory that you are doing a profile of the life of someone who is running for public office.

MR. MILLER: But he's not running for public office.

3RD TV REPORTER: But she is, and she married him. That makes it . . .

MR. MILLER: And that's a mark of Cain.

3RD TV REPORTER: No, it's not a mark of Cain. It tells you something about her, though. She married a man who had been involved in a situation like this.

MR. MILLER: You think it's newsworthy? You think the public has a right to know?

2ND TV REPORTER: There's an example here. Mildred Lilly, who was nominated for the Supreme Court, some of us will remember, had some of this sort of information published about her. And, she was not nominated. She was considered, that's all. And it was news, proper news.

3RD TV REPORTER: It is the fact that Cassandra is running for the Senate that has produced the latent information about her husband.

MR. MILLER: And her husband, be damned. He has no rights in this. He's the tail on the dog, so to speak.

3RD TV REPORTER: I'm afraid so, yes.

MR. MILLER: You're afraid so. Why? What gives you that power to take a man who has worked for 15 years to reclaim his life and reestablish himself in a new community and just destroy him.

2ND TV REPORTER: Perhaps his wife doesn't know he had that history. (Simultaneous conversation.)

3RD TV REPORTER: Well, then, perhaps it's even more important. (Simultaneous conversation.)

MR. MILLER: What gives you the right to do that to that man?

3RD TV REPORTER: The fact that he is married to a candidate for the Senate and she has offered herself for public office.

8TH EDITOR: Can you look at the source of this information both to Cassandra and to Aphid, for example, as it is information that's drifted in over the transom.

MR. MILLER: Yes.

8TH EDITOR: Why was it delivered? I think that's a question. Who is trying to gain something by delivering this information? And, I think that affects your decision on whether it runs.

MR. MILLER: Yes, but our 2nd TV Reporter, I think quite properly, has said once you verify it the decision-making and antenna change somewhat. You know that he was a convicted felon. You know the veracity of everything in that document. And, our 3rd TV Reporter says the person be damned. The whole theory of rehabilitative justice be damned. His 15 years' working in the vineyards to rehabilitate himself be damned. He made a mistake marrying someone who 15 years later was going to run for the Senate. Therefore, he's wide open. You agree? Would you publish it?

8TH EDITOR: My feeling is that this information is not really very relevant and that somebody delivered it to you in an effort to manipulate your newspaper.

MR. MILLER: Yes, but once you've verified it, doesn't that fact drop out.

8TH EDITOR: I have given you my answer. I don't think I would print it.

MR. MILLER: In other words, original sin takes over.

1ST EDITOR: You go to them.

MR. MILLER: Hmm?

1ST EDITOR: You go to the couple, the Cassandras, or whatever they're called, and they immediately say, well, the thing is going to come out. So, they say yes. This is true. And, then, in practical life what happens is they make a speech about it on television and she is elected by the biggest majority in history.

(Simultaneous conversation.)

MR. MILLER: Well, that's a nice Hollywood ending.

1ST EDITOR: It is a political ending.

MR. MILLER: It doesn't help us one iota with the moral problem, does it?

1ST EDITOR: When you go to them, it does, I think.

MR. MILLER (Turns now to 4th Reporter)

4TH REPORTER: I think a more important story, or an equally important story, in the material that comes in over the transom is apparently there's good reason to believe it comes from the FBI. If you can prove that it does, then you ought to be writing that the FBI is leaking the material, and why.

MR. MILLER: But if you do that, you find it necessary to talk about Mr. Cassandra and his felonious murder 15 or 20 years ago.

4TH REPORTER: Not necessarily.

MR. MILLER: Now, let's switch the question and say you do publish it. And now, Cassandra's husband brings an action against the paper for invasion of privacy.

PROSECUTOR: He'll lose.

MR. MILLER: He'll lose? Why?

PROSECUTOR: It was a matter of record.

MR. MILLER: What's a matter of record?

PROSECUTOR: The fact that he was guilty of a felony.

MR. MILLER: Is that the key to the right of privacy?

PROSECUTOR: That's what the law is.

MR. MILLER: Whose law is that? I can cite you a dozen cases the other way, but I don't want to cite cases.

PROSECUTOR: The Restatement of Torts [a treatise setting forth the Law of Torts prepared by the American Law Institute] says that's the law.

MR. MILLER: The Restatement of Torts?

1ST REPORTER: Also, in the Cox Broadcasting case. [*Cox Broadcasting Corp. v Cohn,* 43 U.S. 4343 (U.S. March 4, 1975), in which the Supreme Court held that newspapers have a First Amendment right to publish the identities of rape victims once their names appear on public records.]

(Simultaneous conversation.)

MR. MILLER: I don't think the Cox case covers this at all.

1ST REPORTER: It's a matter of record. It's a court record. Unless it was sealed by court order, it is a court record.

MR. MILLER: But you're talking about truth. Truth is no defense to a privacy action.

1ST PROSECUTOR: No, that's not true.

2ND JUDGE: How about what the Supreme Court said about the victim of a rape. Her name's on the record, so they may print it.

MR. MILLER: They may print it from the record. But let us suppose that Cassandra's husband has changed his name.

3RD REPORTER: That's on record, too.

2ND JUDGE: It may be a link.

MR. MILLER: Hmm?

2ND JUDGE: You have to have the link. Prove that, too.

1ST REPORTER: Well, you're searching for legal justifications for printing, so that's the premise that we're on now, right?

MR. MILLER: I'm just trying to decide whether the newspaper should be held in any sort of remedy for destroying 15 years of a man's life.

1ST REPORTER: And, the prosecutor says, I think . . .

MR. MILLER: The prosecutor says that because the fact of conviction is on the court record somewhere that the individual should be immunized.

1ST REPORTER: He can't collect, but that doesn't satisfy the moral question.

MR. MILLER: No, it certainly does not.

1ST REPORTER: All right, so the . . .

MR. MILLER: What should the law be on that? One reporter wants it published, another wants to publish. They want to take a man's life and destroy it. And the question is: Should the newspaper be held accountable . . .

3RD EDITOR: Why do you say we're going to destroy him?

(Simultaneous conversation.)

2ND EDITOR: Why do you keep assuming he's going to be destroyed. A fair story would point out the 14 years of good works, also.

MR. MILLER: A fair story would?

2ND EDITOR: Yes.

MR. MILLER: But maybe the neighbors don't want to associate with an ax murderer. I mean, I'm not posing an irrational possibility.

PROSECUTOR: No.

2ND TV REPORTER: Well, they wouldn't want to vote for him either. Maybe they wouldn't want to vote for the wife of an ax murderer, too.

MR. MILLER: Yes

2ND TV REPORTER: They should know that.

MR. MILLER: You think that's relevant to her candidacy?

VARIOUS VOICES: Yes.

VARIOUS VOICES: Sure.

(Simultaneous conversation.)

2ND EDITOR: If they feel that's relevant. I wonder how distant the business or family has to be before the information is not germane to the candidacy.

MR. MILLER (Calls on 3rd TV Reporter): How do you make that decision? How do you exercise your admitted discretion in profiling a candidate, deciding what the distancing has to be between the data and the candidate?

3RD TV REPORTER: Well, I think first of all you determine the distance.

MR. MILLER: How do you do it?

3RD TV REPORTER: Well, a distant cousin who's involved in something or other is perhaps not germane. But I think in a case such as this, where you are assembling a profile of a candidate, to leave out something as important as this is to present an incomplete profile.

MR. MILLER: All right, what about Cassandra's abortion at age 15?

3RD TV REPORTER: That's relevant.

MR. MILLER: That's relevant?

3RD TV REPORTER: There are certain things we don't know about Cassandra.

(Simultaneous conversation.)

3RD TV REPORTER: Cassandra's taking a very strong right-to-life position. Is Cassandra, in the course of her campaign, denouncing those who make use of abortion facilities? If she is doing that, then I suggest that if she herself has had an abortion it is a relevant issue in the campaign and I would print that.

MR. MILLER: You would print it? (Turns now to 4th Reporter): Would you?

4TH REPORTER: No, I wouldn't.

MR. MILLER: Why not?

4TH REPORTER: Because it's a long time ago. You don't know anything about her motives then.

MR. MILLER: Is it any longer ago than Mr. Cassandra's homicide?

4TH REPORTER: I wouldn't print that.

MR. MILLER: How about Bumptious' auto accident?

4TH REPORTER: I would, because he's the candidate.

MR. MILLER: And, she's the candidate.

4TH REPORTER: It's too far back and has no bearing on her . . .

MR. MILLER: What do you mean, no bearing? One of our TV Reporters has said it's got bearing. She's taking a position on right to life, and she's had an abortion.

1ST TV REPORTER: And Bumptious takes a position on no-fault insurance.

3RD TV REPORTER: Look, Cassandra is not accused. Cassandra did not go to an office to inquire about an abortion, she had an abortion. We don't know the extent to which Bumptious was responsible for the vehicular homicide, do we?

MR. MILLER: It's harder data. The abortion is a fact. The vehicular homocide is an allegation.

3RD TV REPORTER: Well, that's rather important.

MR. MILLER: Well, I'm not saying it isn't. I'm not saying it isn't. I want to see what our fourth reporter is going to say is the bottom line. You're not going to publish the fact that a right-to-life candidate had an abortion.

1ST TV REPORTER: Well, of course you are. Come off it. I mean, let's start with the reality. Don't let him back you into this corner. Of course you're going to publish it.

4TH REPORTER: No, not if I get it five days before the election.

1ST TV REPORTER: You explain it later. Come on.

MR. MILLER: Five days before the election makes a difference?

4TH REPORTER: The thing that's bothered me on this whole thing is that Burnwood was waiting until five days before the election to do all the stuff he should have been doing as soon as he got the information.

7TH EDITOR: What did he write before this?

MR. MILLER: He was on a campaign trail. You know, reporting speeches, and this stuff comes in over the transom. He had no inkling of it.

7TH EDITOR: That isn't the way life works.

MR. MILLER: Well, maybe it is, maybe it isn't. I don't know. You wouldn't publish. (Calls on 5th Reporter): Would you publish?

5TH REPORTER: I certainly would.

MR. MILLER: Why?

5TH REPORTER: Well, first of all, if a woman has had an abortion and she's running as a right-to-life candidate, then she's a terrible hypocrite and the people who are going to vote for her . . .

(Simultaneous conversation.)

MR. MILLER: She was 15 years old.

5TH REPORTER: Well, that's right, but she should come out and say, "Look, I had an abortion when I was 15 and I made a mistake and it was a terrible thing, and that is why I am a right-to-life candidate." That's only one reason I would publish it.

MR. MILLER: So, you want to make her step up to the bar and be honest?

5TH REPORTER: Absolutely.

MR. MILLER: That's your function?

5TH REPORTER: That's right.

MR. MILLER: All right. Suppose . . .

5TH REPORTER: Well, I'm giving a profile on this woman. You're assuming I'm doing a profile on her.

MR. MILLER: Right. Right.

5TH REPORTER: I think that everything that has happened to her is important.

MR. MILLER: Suppose she had an illegitimate child at age 15? Would you publish that?

7TH EDITOR: She couldn't have.

5TH REPORTER: What?

1ST TV REPORTER: She had the abortion.

(Simultaneous conversation.)

5TH REPORTER: If she had an illegitimate child and I knew it for a fact, yes, I would.

MR. MILLER: You would publish it? (Turns again to 4th Reporter): Would you publish that? She had an illegitimate child at age 15. No abortion. She's now a right-to-life candidate.

4TH REPORTER: A lot of it would depend on what she said about it.

MR. MILLER: About what?

4TH REPORTER: About the child, or about the abortion, too.

MR. MILLER: Well, it was put up for adoption and she doesn't even know where it is now.

4TH REPORTER: If she talked about it, yes, I would.

MR. MILLER: You would go to her and ask her about it?

4TH REPORTER: Of course.

MR. MILLER: And if she said, "I have no comment," what would you do?

4TH REPORTER: Then I wouldn't print it.

MR. MILLER: You wouldn't print that? You wouldn't print the abortion? (Turns to 6th Reporter): What about you?

6TH REPORTER: We'd print it. I'd print it.

MR. MILLER: Both?

6TH REPORTER: The child can't be traced, is that part of it?

MR. MILLER: Yes, let's say it's gone.

6TH REPORTER: Okay. I think both things are relevant.

MR. MILLER: Now, let's take a deviation from the Cox case and use the Edelin case. [Dr. Kenneth Edelin was indicted in Boston for killing a fetus.] I trust everybody in the room knows the recent Edelin abortion case in Massachusetts. You're an editor. You've got your people covering the Edelin case. The following thought occurs to you: Gee, wouldn't it be nice to know who the mother was? Would you send a reporter out to find out who the mother was?

6TH REPORTER: I don't think I'd have thought of it because I just don't see the relevancy at all. Why would that even be a good story?

PROSECUTOR: What has that got to do with anything?

6TH REPORTER: That's right.

MR. MILLER: Well, what did it have to do with the Cox case?

7TH EDITOR: She's a minor, among other things.

PROSECUTOR: That's right.

7TH EDITOR: A juvenile, isn't she?

MR. MILLER: Who? Who?

7TH EDITOR: The mother?

WRITER: 17 years old.

MR. MILLER: Who?

WRITER: The mother in the case is a 17 year old . . .

MR. MILLER: So which way does that cut?

WRITER: It cuts very simply that you don't use her name.

MR. MILLER: If she's 25?

WRITER: You might then, if she had something to say as a person.

MR. MILLER: You don't know. Suppose you don't even know what her age is. You don't know anything about her and it just dawns on you, my God, there's mother out there. It's not in the record. It's not like the Cox case. It's not a public record.

WRITER: I might be curious to know the circumstances, but that does not mean you publish it. We've got all sorts of things we don't publish.

MR. MILLER: All right, you go out and find out it's a 17 year old.

WRITER: That's the end.

MR. MILLER: A 25 year old?

WRITER: Does she have any comments she'd like to make? Does she want to be on the record?

MR. MILLER: It's a profile. It's a human-interest story.

WRITER: Just a second. Now, just a second. Don't run so fast.

MR. MILLER: Oh, sorry.

WRITER: Take it easy, let your Socratic track shoes go a little slower for a second. Does she, as a 25-year-old woman, of majority and of her own free will, care to comment on this case? She might.

MR. MILLER: Yes.

WRITER: She might want to say that the thought what Dr. Edelin did was absolutely right. She might choose to say that it was absolutely wrong. She makes that decision.

MR. MILLER: And you'd honor it?

WRITER: Yes, of course.

MR. MILLER: You wouldn't publish her name?

WRITER: Without her knowledge and consent?

MR. MILLER: Yes.

WRITER: No.

MR. MILLER: Well, how come in the Cox case the rape victim's name got published? What kind of responsible journalism was that, then?

(Simultaneous conversation.)

MR. MILLER: Just a question.

2ND TV REPORTER: The boys in that case had claimed that there was consent involved. They'd been out drinking together. She had done this sort of thing before and the death was an accident.

MR. MILLER: So?

2ND TV REPORTER: It was relevant.

MR. MILLER: The name was relevant? Her name? The dead girl's name?

2ND TV REPORTER: They claimed that this girl had a history of doing these things, and they were accused initially of murder as well as rape.

MR. MILLER: Now, what would you do with the Edelin mother?

2ND TV REPORTER: I wouldn't do it. I wouldn't publish her name.

MR. MILLER: You wouldn't go out and look?

2ND TV REPORTER: I would do what the last speaker said.

MR. MILLER: And if it's just a 25-year-old with nothing . . .

2ND TV REPORTER: If she said, "Look, I have no thoughts about this. Leave me out of it." I'd certainly leave her out of it.

MR. MILLER: And, if Cassandra says, "Yes, I had the abortion at age 15, but I was a rape victim, please don't report it," what would you do?

2ND TV REPORTER: The rape victim thing changes everything in Cassandra's case, but if you leave that out, I . . .

3RD REPORTER: Doesn't that depend on just what her right-to-life position is? I mean, if she's against abortions for rape victims?

MR. MILLER: What if the Edelin mother turns out to be Cassandra? And she doesn't want to say anything. She says, "Yes, I'm the Edelin mother, but I've got nothing to say and please don't report it."

3RD TV REPORTER: Which story are you covering?

MR. MILLER: Well, you know . . .

3RD TV REPORTER: In the Edelin story, the identity of the mother is not important.

MR. MILLER: Yes, but your paper's also covering the Cassandra candidacy, right?

3RD TV REPORTER: Well, if Cassandra is currently involved in the Edelin case and is also standing for the United States Senate . . .

(Simultaneous conversation.)

MR. MILLER:But, you see, you're taking the cheap way out. Because what you're really talking about is the mathematical probability.

2ND EDITOR: But when people stand for public office, they voluntarily give up a great deal of their privacy.

MR. MILLER: True, true, true.

2ND EDITOR: Which we've been overlooking for a long time, and that's the difference between her and the Edelin mother.

MR. MILLER: And apparently a number of people here say not only do they give up their privacy, they give up their husband's privacy.

2ND EDITOR: It's quite possible.

MR. MILLER: In other words, we have completely reversed the common-law concept of unity of marriage, which if Cassandra's running, her husband is the . . .

2ND TV REPORTER: With children in all these stories that are run of sons of famous fathers who get in trouble with pot, is it treating them unfairly with regard to other young kids who get caught smoking pot? It's unfortunate that their fathers are senators, or whatever.

MR. MILLER: O.K.

3RD EDITOR: All right, in real time, too, it matters how the candidate uses the spouse or the children in the campaign.

MR. MILLER: In other words, if they become public figures?

3RD EDITOR: Right.

MR. MILLER: Like Joan Kennedy?

3RD EDITOR: Yes. Or Tricia. Or Julie.

MR. MILLER: Let's shift a little bit and pick up a theme that I think we are now moving toward. Let's shift to Bumptious' late-night activities, where Burnwood fortuitously discovers Bumptious in the back room with Wanda Werewolf. (Asks 2nd TV Reporter): Would you publish?

2ND TV REPORTER: Well, I think we're all far more sensitive to this after the Wilbur Mills Tidal Basin episode and I think one reason was the stories that came out about his spending so much money for champagne and that sort of thing. I think a lot of people still wonder where that money came from. And this makes it very relevant. It can make it very relevant.

MR. MILLER: But let's take it in its simplest form. Bumptious in the back room with Wanda Werewolf at 3:30 in the morning in the midst of an embrace.

7TH EDITOR: One time only. You've never seen him with Werewolf before?

MR. MILLER: Never seen him with Werewolf, but as the problem indicates, there have been stories of excessive drinking on Bumptious' part. Do you publish it?

1ST REPORTER: The drinking? No.

(Simultaneous conversation.)

MR. MILLER: Then why was the Mills story published? How do you distinguish . . .

3RD EDITOR: That's a lot different.

MR. MILLER: Tell me. Tell me.

3RD EDITOR: First . . .

MR. MILLER: I want my consciousness raised.

3RD EDITOR: Well, first of all, there was an attempt at a cover-up in that.

PROSECUTOR: He was arrested. It was public.

MR. MILLER: It was public?

3RD EDITOR: It was public.

MR. MILLER: Yes.

PROSECUTOR: It was an arrest. It was on the street. It was in the reflecting pool.

3RD EDITOR: Giving false names.

MR. MILLER: Hmm?

3RD EDITOR: An attempt by the Park Police to cover it up.

1ST REPORTER: You better get off that one quick, professor.

MR. MILLER: Why?

1ST REPORTER: That's a bad one to try and argue privacy.

MR. MILLER: Well, I'm not arguing privacy. I just want to know. I want everybody in the room to think about—particularly the judges—how an editor makes the decision which story gets published and which story doesn't.

1ST REPORTER: That one's too easy.

MR. MILLER: Which one? Mills?

1ST REPORTER: Wilbur Mills is too easy.

PROSECUTOR: And it was bizarre, too.

MR. MILLER: Tell me something about the editorial decision that put the Wilbur Mills story on page 1 that morning and Joan Kennedy's arrest for drunken driving on page 15 that same day?

1ST REPORTER: There might be some here who would argue that Joan Kennedy's arrest ought not to have been in the paper.

MR. MILLER: But Wilbur Mills' should?

1ST REPORTER: Yes, indeed. Absolutely.

MR. MILLER: Why?

1ST REPORTER: Let's assume for the moment that there was no attempt at cover-up, all right? Wilbur Mills' drinking bears upon Wilbur Mills' capacity to perform a public service in a crucially important position.

MR. MILLER: And what if you knew that about other senators or representatives?

1ST REPORTER: Publish it.

MR. MILLER: Publish?

7TH EDITOR: Were they arrested?

MR. MILLER: No, let's say they're not arrested. Let's suppose you know, because your Capitol reporter says, "You know, this is the 15th day in a row that I've gone over to the Hill at 10:30 and Jones has been bombed out of his mind."

PROSECUTOR: That's relevant.

MR. MILLER: You publish it?

PROSECUTOR: Yes, I think that's relevant.

1ST REPORTER: I do, too.

MR. MILLER (Turns to 7th Editor): And you don't know any such case?

7TH EDITOR: Do I know that Jones is bombed out of his mind?

MR. MILLER: Your reporter tells you. Just as your reporter came in with the film at the reflecting pool.

7TH EDITOR: And he goes to Jones and says, "What have you been doing getting stoned out of your mind 15 days in a row?" and he says, "I haven't had a drink for 15 days. I have—something—you, know, I faint every so often. An inner ear infection."

PROSECUTOR: Well, that changes the story.

7TH EDITOR: Which is what one senator used to use as an excuse.

MR. MILLER: But you're evading the question. You know as much about Jones through your reporter as you knew about Mills at the reflecting pool. And I'm not sure that the fact it's out at the reflecting pool is a relevant distinction.

7TH EDITOR: I see. I'd find a way to print that Congressman Jones was on a 15-day toot.

MR. MILLER: You'd print it?

7TH EDITOR: Yes.

MR. MILLER: You'd print. Anybody disagree?

3RD REPORTER: I think we don't. Perhaps we should.

7TH EDITOR: By inference it plainly interfered with the operation of his job and the conduct of his office.

MR. MILLER (Turns to 3rd Reporter): Now, you say we don't.

3RD REPORTER: I think we don't very much.

MR. MILLER: Why don't you?

3RD REPORTER: I don't know. I'd be inclined to.

MR. MILLER: But you don't.

3RD REPORTER: I don't think that the newspapers in Washington as a rule print very much of this except in the most elliptical manner.

MR. MILLER: And why?

7TH EDITOR: Because, more often than not, it does not interfere with the performance of their public job.

MR. MILLER: Do you really believe that?

7TH EDITOR: Yes, I really do.

MR. MILLER: A publicly elected official is bombed at 10:30 in the morning 15 days in a row, and it's not interfering with his public duty?

7TH EDITOR: Well, I said I'd publish that one. But I think it happens less than you think.

MR. MILLER: I don't know how often it happens, or if it happens. I wouldn't say personally I would assume that Wilbur Mills is not an aardvark, that it happens.

2ND EDITOR: Well, there'a a question of proof. The police officers said that Wilbur Mills was drunk on the night he was found . . .

MR. MILLER: Your reporter says 15 days in a row I've seen him bombed out. I can smell his breath.

3RD EDITOR: That's not good enough.

MR. MILLER: What?

2ND EDITOR: Smelling his breath, then, adds another element of truth, and I don't know yet if that's sufficient.

MR. MILLER: But, if a cop . . .

2ND EDITOR: If he denies it . . .

MR. MILLER: But if a cop tells you, you've got a fall guy, right?

2ND EDITOR: Well, you . . .

MR. MILLER: You can attribute it to the cop.

2ND EDITOR: You also had a fight inside of a car and a number of other circumstances that led you to believe it, just as when Carl Albert had the traffic accident when demonstrably drunk. That got published.

PROSECUTOR: Wasn't this an allegation that John Erlichmann made before the Senate committee, that this was suppressed?

MR. MILLER: Why was it suppressed?

PROSECUTOR: He said that. He said it was suppressed, that it was something that people should know.

MR. MILLER: Uh-huh.

3RD REPORTER: Well, I think we don't print it to some extent because we're worrying about, you know, there but for the grace of God go I. Because we're friends of these people, because it's very hard to demonstrate in any categorical way how it affects their duties. We can think it does. But, how do you prove that he listened a little less carefully . . .

MR. MILLER: But I'm your reader. Don't you owe it to me? Don't you owe it to me to tell me that so I know who the hell to vote for next time? Where is this higher duty? To your friends on the Hill?

3RD REPORTER: No. You're asking me why. I'm telling you. I think we ought to print it. I think this is why we don't.

6TH EDITOR: I think we do more than we used to. I mean, different standards prevailed.

MR. MILLER: Uh-huh.

6TH EDITOR: But it is hard to prove that a guy's drunk on the floor unless you can get near him or smell his breath, or do something substantive.

MR. MILLER: And the Mills thing is just convenient. It's all packaged for you?

3RD EDITOR: Well, it's more than that. We don't have a Burnwood on our staff who at 3:30 goes to the Silver Slipper. We're all Harvard educated.

MR. MILLER: You're all at the Harvard Club, then? Well, suppose it's not Wilbur Mills. Suppose Bumptious is the first black candidate for the Senate from Idyllia. He is the shining symbol of the entire black community in the state of Idyllia. 500,000 to 1 million blacks look to him and say, "There's my aspiration symbol."

1ST REPORTER: Bullshit.

MR. MILLER: Hmm?

1ST REPORTER: That's racist.

MR. MILLER: What do you mean it's racist? You go with it?

1ST REPORTER: You cannot make that argument any more than you could make the argument that Adam Clayton Powell was an unqualifiably representative symbol of black aspirations.

MR. MILLER: What are you telling me? Do you go with the story, or do you not go with the story?

1ST REPORTER: I'm telling you, you go with the story.

MR. MILLER: You go with the story?

1ST REPORTER: Of course you do.

MR. MILLER: You would have us believe that the editorial discretion is even-handed. Our third reporter, I think, has suggested, but maybe it's not.

3RD REPORTER: Not on the basis that you've just injected. I think it is there.

MR. MILLER: In other words, you draw no distinction between a nice guy and a bad guy.

3RD REPORTER: I would try not to.

MR. MILLER: You would try not to.

9TH EDITOR: Supposing the FBI tapes in 1964 had not been of Martin Luther King, but had been of Billy Graham. Would we have had to have waited this long? Would those have been published in 1964?

MR. MILLER: If they were Billy Graham?

9TH EDITOR: If they were Billy Graham.

MR. MILLER: Should there be any difference between Martin Luther King and Billy Graham?

9TH EDITOR: No.

MR. MILLER: Should there be any difference between Wilbur Mills and Martin Luther King?

9TH EDITOR: No.

MR. MILLER: Do you think they've been treated equally?

9TH EDITOR: No.

MR. MILLER: Why not?

9TH EDITOR: I think that there has been a difference between the way we go after Senator Bumptious and Senator Lochinvar. And Senator Lochinvar does get the benefit of the doubt.

MR. MILLER: Why?

9TH EDITOR: Because in many times our political opinions jibe with Senator Lochinvar.

MR. MILLER: Is that your higher duty? To your political opinions?

9TH EDITOR: Is it my higher duty? I think it's inequitable.

MR. MILLER: Inequitable. But I take it you would still assert the proposition that you should have total discretion. You should not be second-guessed.

9TH EDITOR: Second-guessed by whom?

MR. MILLER: The courts.

1ST REPORTER: Yes.

9TH EDITOR: Yes.

MR. MILLER: Why? If you are willing to admit that your standard is a little weighted, and, by the way, let us face the fact that we did not have on various points unanimity around the table which also suggests that the editorial discretion and the reportorial techniques are not homogeneous.

2ND EDITOR: Neither are court decisions.

MR. MILLER: Now you've focused the question. As between two lousy institutions, who makes the decisions. In this worst of all possible worlds, what do we do?

1ST REPORTER: Professor, one of the assumptions that seems to underly many of your questions is that necessarily the only remedy is a state remedy. And I think those of us in the news business are inclined always and forever to be suspicious that the first remedy to which one ought to resort is a state remedy.

MR. MILLER: Let's assume that the discretion line is uneven. How are you going to remedy that?

1ST REPORTER: I think you have to take a chance that sometimes it won't be remedied. That's preferable to having a state remedy.

MR. MILLER: Preferably, no remedy is better than a state remedy?

1ST REPORTER: In this field, yes.

MR. MILLER (Turns to 3rd Judge): How do you feel about that?

3RD JUDGE: Well, I'm probably the wrong fellow to ask, professor. I come from a city with a publisher, but no newspapers. But, I really think it's an ethical problem. I'm not sure which one you're on now. I don't have any trouble about Bumptious and his conduct. In spite of appearances, I do know the difference between love and hanky-panky. And, I think hanky-panky in a candidate is news. That people are entitled to know about it.

1ST TV REPORTER: Listen, love is news.

MR. MILLER: I beg your pardon?

1ST TV REPORTER: Love is news.

MR. MILLER: It's good news.

3RD JUDGE: Now, with Cassandra, I have more trouble with that. About her husband. But, yet, I know it was Mr. Justice Stewart who suggested that it was very difficult to determine what is relevant. There is a line of cases, ex-convicts have rehabilitated themselves and they are entitled to privacy. But she is a candidate. And she lives with him. And he is an ex-convict. I think they'd be legally safe in printing.

MR. MILLER: Yes, but what about a very general proposition that we've just heard over here, that despite the uneven quality in the exercise of discretion both in news gathering techniques and the editorial decision to go or not go, no remedy, when there is a deviation from a norm, is better than a state remedy.

3RD JUDGE: I would agree.

8TH EDITOR: Well, let me suggest that there is a remedy, and it doesn't always lie with the courts. A newspaper and the editors and the reporters of a newspaper are on trial every day before their readers.

MR. MILLER: You mean, we just let the marketplace take over?

8TH EDITOR: That's a very effective control.

MR. MILLER: What's that going to do for Cassandra's husband?

8TH EDITOR: I don't know what it's going to do for Cassandra's husband, and as I said, I would have serious doubts about the propriety of printing that piece of information.

MR. MILLER: Well, let's print it. Let's take that as a given. It's printed. What are you going to do for Cassandra's husband. Thirty years from now maybe your circulation will drop two points. What's that going to do for Cassandra's husband?

8TH EDITOR: Well, I would say that you would also have an obligation to let him have his say about this after you've printed it.

MR. MILLER: Give him a right of reply?

8TH EDITOR: Yes.

MR. MILLER: Would you give Aphid a right of reply if you published the data about him and it proved to be totally erroneous?

8TH EDITOR: Yes, you certainly would.

MR. MILLER: He walks in and says, "Damn it, I want a right of reply. I've written this out. 500 words. Here it is. I want it on page 1 tomorrow."

8TH EDITOR: I would not bargain with him in that context.

MR. MILLER: What do you mean bargain?

8TH EDITOR: I certainly wouldn't bargain with him if he came in with his counsel and tried to force us to do it.

MR. MILLER: Why not?

8TH EDITOR: Because I think that's an interference with the First Amendment privileges.

MR. MILLER: He's supposed to come in on bended knee?

8TH EDITOR: No, no.

MR. MILLER: Supplicant. Great white publisher, please. It's an interesting line. If he comes in as a supplicant and asks you to pat his head, you'll do it. But, he says, "Damn it, you hurt me, and here's my lawyer and here's my draft," you won't publish it.

8TH EDITOR: I think he's interfering with the discretion that a newspaper editor ought to have.

MR. MILLER: In other words, not only will you exercise total discretion about what you publish without state interference, but you want total discretion on the right of reply, too.

8TH EDITOR: Unless you want to turn over your newspaper to this kind of pressure.

MR. MILLER: You're really worried about that? I mean, you've got a virility hang-up about it?

8TH EDITOR: All right . . .

MR. MILLER: Is it a real problem, do you think?

8TH EDITOR: I think this is a beginning of a destruction of . . .

MR. MILLER: Oh, the old nose in the tent case, the foot in the door. The floodgates of litigation. The foundations of the republic are crumbling.

8TH EDITOR: You're saying that, I'm not.

MR. MILLER: Well, you're the one who says . . .

8TH EDITOR: You've got to appreciate . . .

MR. MILLER: Look, a lawyer! Kick him out.

8TH EDITOR: You've got the cliches. You should be writing for newspapers.

MR. MILLER: Who's on whose side?

1ST REPORTER: Professor, the presence of counsel is something more than an attitudinal difference in his approach.

MR. MILLER: What is it?

1ST REPORTER: It is not a question between that and whether he comes on bended knee. It makes no difference what his personal attitude is. But when he brings with him an instrument of potential legal force, then you deal with . . .

MR. MILLER: You don't like lawyers, do you?

1ST REPORTER: I don't like lawyers coming into newspapers . . .

MR. MILLER: You don't believe he's got a right to counsel?

1ST REPORTER: He certainly doesn't have any right to have his counsel in there muscling me in my newsroom.

MR. MILLER: In your office?

1ST REPORTER: Of course not.

MR. MILLER: So, under what terms would you give him the right of reply?

1ST REPORTER: I'd say, "After your counsel has gone, let's talk about what it is that you want to say to my newspaper and we'll get a reporter in here and he can take it down."

MR. MILLER: In other words, he's got to beg?

1ST REPORTER: He's got to beg?

MR. MILLER: You're not giving him an inch?

1ST REPORTER: No, we're not forfeiting to him the control over one inch in our newspaper.

MR. MILLER: Forfeiting to him?

1ST REPORTER: That's right.

MR. MILLER: Forfeiting to him. It's we versus them.

1ST REPORTER: And for one very simple reason. We are publishing the newspaper. We are accountable for its contents.

MR. MILLER: But accountable to whom? You just told me you're not accountable to him. You're not accountable to the law. You're not accountable to the state. You're accountable to the marketplace.

1ST REPORTER: If you allow any person to walk in and put something in your newspaper that he decides and then let him walk out again your readers have no recourse to him because he is not subject to their control in the marketplace. And that's where control ought to lie.

PROSECUTOR: Professor Miller, let me ask the first reporter this: Supposing the lawyer comes along in the spirit of conciliation. He's not coming in and demanding in an ultimatum sense, but he's coming along in a spirit of conciliation. He is really the person who is in effect oiling the way for you to allow this man to have a right of reply. I mean, he's not coming in in a threatening manner. Would that make a difference? Just the fact that a man comes in accompanied by a lawyer makes the difference.

1ST REPORTER: If he brought his minister, then it would be different.

PROSECUTOR: Suppose he brought your lawyer. Suppose he came with . . .

1ST EDITOR: What does it matter who he brings? It's the document that matters, whether you should print it or not. I don't care if he comes in a tank. If you can get the tank off the news floor and tell them all to go away, you read what's on that paper, you make your inquiries, and you retain your discretion over whether or not you print it. The presence of the lawyer doesn't oblige you to print the document.

MR. MILLER: It doesn't?

PROSECUTOR: That's my point.

MR. MILLER: Doesn't your attitude sort of go to the reality of the right of reply? I mean, you've got to jump hoops, crawl through walls of fire, and beg, and maybe you'll get a right of reply.

1ST REPORTER: I don't think . . .

MR. MILLER: I'm looking for your accountability. You tell me it's to the readers. I mean, that's hog-wash. To the readers. To the Dick Tracy readers? To the Boston Red Sox box-score readers? I mean, what you're really saying is that the best way you can maintain total editorial discretion (a) on news gathering, (b) on the decision to publish, and (c) on rectifying the situation is by saying, "Well, we're accountable to the great unwashed. If the great unwashed don't like what we're doing, they'll tell us. But, until they tell us, we are king of the hill."

1ST REPORTER: With some allowance for exaggeration that states it quite well.

MR. MILLER: All right, now, what gives you that power? What makes you less accountable, I mean, than me? I've got to be accountable to my students. Or, to a policeman, who's got to be accountable to courts? Or, to elected officials and a whole bunch of other people?

4TH EDITOR: How are you accountable to students any more than newspapers are accountable to the readers?

PROSECUTOR: They evaluate him.

1ST JUDGE: They don't take his course next year.

PROSECUTOR: That's right. They evaluate him . . .

(Simultaneous conversation)

MR. MILLER: They can come in and see their exams.

4TH EDITOR: If you give them a lousy lecture, how do they do it? Afterward you may be dropped from a course. Your accountability is no greater than ours.

MR. MILLER: Oh, I don't want to get involved with my accountability. I have the tenure thing to live through. I've got a much more immediate marketplace in terms of students. I've got student evaluations. I've got a student newspaper that can do unto me what these papers have been doing unto the other people.

4TH EDITOR: We have underground newspapers. We have dissonant voices. We can give you every analogy right down the line.

MR. MILLER: Yes, but you're just not willing to take any level of accountability other than to your readership.

4TH EDITOR: No, we have many other levels of accountability. To our own standards. To our ethics. To . . .

MR. MILLER: To your own standards?

4TH EDITOR: That's right.

MR. MILLER: To your own exercise of discretion?

4TH EDITOR: That's right.

MR. MILLER: Even though it's unequal?

4TH EDITOR: That's right.

MR. MILLER: Even though there is no standard as you go around the table. It's my standard or his standard or her standard or their standard or our standard. What standard?

1ST REPORTER: Well, a nonstate standard.

4TH EDITOR: It's not a Utopia and you make up your mind.

MR. MILLER: There's an anarchy out there.

1ST REPORTER: Yes.

4TH EDITOR: A form of it.

MR. MILLER: And you like it?

(Simultaneous conversation.)

2ND EDITOR: . . . as there is in the law.

3RD REPORTER: Are all law professors equal? Are you and Professor Nesson the same.

MR. MILLER: I haven't got any First Amendment.

1ST REPORTER: I think that's beside the point.

(Simultaneous conversation.)

MR. MILLER: I mean, I don't hide behind the First Amendment and I can't do the kind of damage you people can do.

3RD REPORTER: Oh, I don't know. You could produce bad lawyers.

MR. MILLER: Have been for many years. Now, I'm still looking for accountability.

6TH EDITOR: You had it in the best way you can get it. You don't have one judgment. You have the input of a variety of judgments of editors, plus the publisher as a last recourse in this. In fact, this happens. And this process does get the best input of judgments and rethinking that you can get. You have to assume that we're all trying to do the best we can, which we are. You can't sort of assume that the guy is trying to get justice and isn't going to get heard. Sometimes when they don't get heard, they shouldn't. I'm thinking of the guy who drove us all nuts, who said that we weren't giving the little man enough time to be heard—you know, the equal space and all that. So, finally, we had a meeting in my office because he'd been right through the editors and he'd been harrassing them. We published a whole bunch of his letters. We said he was a lobbyist for big companies, and he wanted more letters in our paper. We said your view has been heard enough and why don't you go down the street to the other papers. He said, "Because you're the one that matters and I have been unjustly treated." They're not always just 100 percent right, these guys pounding at your door. You have to make some judgments and cut them off at some point and do the best you can. Because the alternative is a lousy system, which is to give them space and say, "Here, it's yours. You use it."

MR. MILLER: In other words, you want a presumption for the press of regularity, to use a metaphor I heard this morning.

6TH EDITOR: It's the best of a lot of lousy systems.

MR. MILLER: Is it? Don't we have to look at that? You want a presumption of regularity. This morning some press people at this very table said with regard to the government, there is a presumption of irregularity. And the government should be accountable to the press and to the courts.

6TH EDITOR: The First Amendment gives you the right to be wrong.

MR. MILLER: It gives you the right to be wrong. Maybe so. Maybe so. Cost-free right?

6TH EDITOR: Well, I guess so in the last resort.

MR. MILLER: Really, cost-free.

6TH EDITOR: No, no. As they say, this is a marketplace. They're going to raise hell in other publications and they do.

MR. MILLER: And again, let me go back to a theme; it seems a century ago. Let's give the newspaper the presumption of regularity. Can you honestly say that your model is the norm in your industry?

6TH EDITOR: I can't answer for other people.

MR. MILLER: Trouble is, the other people aren't here today and the question of accountability must take into consideration not only the *Post* and the *Times* and NBC and CBS, which can foot the bill for an ombudsman and can foot the bill for internal control mechanisms and very fancy and marvelously intelligent editors, but the Podunk *Press* and the Harvard *Crimson* and I suspect a numerical majority of media units in the country don't have that kind of resources. (Turns to 2nd Lawyer): What have you got to say?

2ND LAWYER: I still think it's maybe the best of two lousy systems but I'd rather put my faith in the newspaper making the choice.

MR. MILLER: I see. This morning some of the news people were accusing Professor Nesson of being black or white and now you're saying to me there are only two models, right; complete press autonomy, unfettered discretion, hopefully to be exercised according to the model established by our 6th editor, or government control. Are we so barren and sterile of ideas that those are the only two possibilities?

2ND LAWYER: No, but a judge suggested this morning, it seems to me, that the same guy that appointed the Director of CIA appointed the federal district court judge . . .

MR. MILLER: Yes, they're government, aren't they?

2ND LAWYER: . . . and they're both government and if I've got to opt, I'd rather keep the courts out of it.

MR. MILLER: Now tell me, we're all friends here, are you really worried about judges?

2ND LAWYER: Yes.

MR. MILLER: Why?

2ND LAWYER: Because I think they're generally conservative and generally opt for that time to consider and maybe legitimately so, but that doesn't work in a workaday press world.

MR. MILLER: How could they hurt you?

2ND LAWYER: They don't have the mechanics to make the decision and therefore ought to stay out of it.

MR. MILLER: What do you mean by mechanics?

2ND LAWYER: They need the time to make a reasonable decision.

MR. MILLER: And you don't want to give them the time?

2ND LAWYER: You can't and still preserve the First Amendment.

MR. MILLER: You're talking about prior restraint?

2ND LAWYER: Right.

MR. MILLER: Let's turn away from prior restraint. Let's talk about damage liability. Assume with me that somebody blows it and there is an invasion of privacy or what seems to be an invasion of privacy. Notice in the hypothetical case study, I've got Bumptious suing everybody that's walking and Wanda Werewolf suing everybody that's walking. Do you worry about the courts in the context of damage remedies?

2ND LAWYER: Yes.

MR. MILLER: Why? It's no longer the judge's appeal for some time which you don't want to give him, and that's the prior restraint hangup. I want to stay away from that and focus on straight old damage remedies. Why shouldn't you media people be accountable to other human beings? Cassandra's husband; Aphid if there's a total fabrication of the documents and the documents are published; Wanda Werewolf for having been called a prostitute and it was not true. Why shouldn't you be accountable in damages before a court of law?

2ND LAWYER: I'm not arguing that you shouldn't be. You asked me a different question. You asked me if I was worried about the way judges handled it and I think that too many judges pass the cases on to the jury instead of disposing of them on summary judgment.

MR. MILLER: Now who are you worried about, the judge or the jury?

2ND LAWYER: I'm worried about the . . .

MR. MILLER: The jury is your readership. That's your public.

2ND LAWYER: On the contrary, I'm worried about the guy with the Podunk *Press* who doesn't have the lawyer. I'm not worried about the big newspaper that can afford to pay an expensive lawyer.

MR. MILLER: Your point is the cost of legal counsel?

2ND LAWYER: That's one of them, yes.

MR. MILLER: I want to hear the points. Let's hear why the media fear civil liability and damages awarded by courts or courts and juries along normal lincs of negligence or fault or damage? You say one reason is it would cost the news media too much to defend those actions.

2ND LAWYER: That's one major reason.

MR. MILLER: Now, of course everybody else has to defend actions brought against them. Why is the media entitled to have a lighter touch by the legal community?

2ND LAWYER: Because the media, under the First Amendment, has got a specific duty to discharge on behalf of all the public.

MR. MILLER: Of course, if you discharged it at a higher level more carefully and reduced the incidence of negligence or wanton and willful or reckless conduct, the law bills would go down, wouldn't they?

5TH EDITOR: I think the batting average is very good. What more chilling effect than protracted litigation can there be on the press in this country? What greater threat is there today, as a matter of fact? If you agree the press is unique, as the Constitution grants, frivolous suits can be very costly; most suits brought to courts against large newspapers are lost by the plaintiffs but they are time-consuming and aside from the *Times* and the *Post* and the networks and a few magazines you're going to stifle controversial approaches to news—particularly dealing on the fringes of privacy, on the fringes of libel, on the fringes of all of the subjects that we've been discussing.

MR. MILLER: All right, we've now got two factors: the cost of legal services, the potential deterrent effect, the chilling effect, whatever you want to call it. What else is the press, the broadcast media, afraid of in terms of standing up before a court and defending the editorial decision to go against somebody who says, "Hey, you libeled me. Hey, you invaded my privacy."

1ST REPORTER: It is not a matter of a threat because of the inutility, either because of the chilling effect or cost. It is a simple matter of illegitimacy. The courts have no role in that function.

MR. MILLER: Now, from whence cometh this principle?

1ST REPORTER: The First Amendment.

MR. MILLER: The First Amendment? It says so in the First Amendment that courts are illegitimate?

1ST REPORTER: Yes. Congress shall make no law, and by judicial construction that's been applied to the states as well.

MR. MILLER: I see, Congress shall make no law. Congress created the federal courts, therefore, the federal courts are illegitimate under the First Amendment?

1ST REPORTER: In the field of controlling the press, yes.

MR. MILLER: And can you think of any other aspect of American society comparable to that?

1ST REPORTER: No, no, and I can't think of anything more crucial.

MR. MILLER: Anything more crucial.

1ST REPORTER: I think that we are dealing with a problem here of novelty and I take it there is some difficulty in those who don't appreciate the essence of that novelty.

MR. MILLER: All right, so now I hear three arguments. I hear the absolutist position, right?

1ST REPORTER: Yes.

MR. MILLER: Or do I misquote?

1ST REPORTER: No, no, you don't misquote.

MR. MILLER: Absolutist. The world is illegitimate if they purport to second-guess our decisions?

1ST REPORTER: Using the instrument of the state.

MR. MILLER: Using the instrument of the state; that's a good caveat. We'll come back to that. Two, it costs too damn much to defend these suits. Three, the presence of the government coupled with the cost of defense acts as a chilling effect or deterrent on editorial discretion and undermines the First Amendment, right? Anything else?

2ND LAWYER: There is difficulty in handling that kind of thing before a jury, especially when you're dealing with a rich newspaper and a jury which has a tendency to want to cut the head off of the person who brings the bad news.

MR. MILLER: What are you worried about?

2ND LAWYER: That judges won't handle the cases on motions for summary judgments and instead pass . . .

MR. MILLER: In other words, they won't give you the keys to the king-dom quickly enough?

2ND LAWYER: No, they won't apply the laws laid down by the Supreme Court of the United States at all.

MR. MILLER: You're worried about corruption in the judges?

2ND LAWYER: If you're talking about the state judicial system, yes.

MR. MILLER: Oh?

2ND LAWYER: If you've been reading the papers lately you can see why.

MR. MILLER: I teach procedure. I don't even have to read the papers, but you're saying you're not because we're in fast company here. You wouldn't lay that on the federal courts?

2ND LAWYER: No, I wouldn't.

MR. MILLER: You're worried about elected state judges?

2ND LAWYER: Exactly.

MR. MILLER: You're worried, for example, that Judge Pettifogger in our hypothetical case is beholden perhaps to Senator Bumptious for elevation to the next highest bench?

2ND LAWYER: No, more about the electoral process than about the appointment process.

MR. MILLER: Now let's turn it around. I want to hear how the judges react to this.

1ST TV REPORTER: Before you do, one more worry about judges and it does apply to some federal judges and it doesn't have to do with corruption, of course. I have found that judges simply don't understand how the press functions or what some of the press problems are and in the defense of what they consider to be the right to fair trial, right to defense, rights of prosecution as opposed to the First Amendment.

MR. MILLER: You mean these minor or second-class constitutional rights. We all know that if it's in the First Amendment that it's on gold tablets, but fair trial, privacy, of which I gathered from *Roe v. Wade* is also constitutional, that's on sort of dross tablets. [*Roe v. Wade*, 410 U.S. 113 (1973), in which the Court held that the Texas criminal abortion statutes were unconstitutional.]

3RD REPORTER: Silver tablets.

1ST REPORTER: As I was saying . . .

MR. MILLER: Oh sorry, I didn't mean to interrupt you.

1ST TV REPORTER: We have the example of a judge in the District of Columbia who made the cover of *Time* Magazine, a federal district court judge, who sometimes just freely issues protective orders and gag orders, some of which he later comes to regret and occasionally modifies after somebody points out that not only is he interfering with the First Amendment but may even be stepping on the rights of Congress to investigate and so on and then he modifies the order. There is a tendency in what is a very important confrontation between two rights, two important rights—the right to a fair trial and the right to report the news—which sometimes come into friction and tension and which we have to learn to resolve; neither written on gold tablets, both on gold tablets perhaps. But if the judge is the arbiter of these things and decides that what is important for him, first of all, is the right to a fair trial and is in the position to make the decisions as to what these gag orders will be, then I get worried about judges.

MR. MILLER: But don't we have a Mexican standoff here? The press wants to be the dictators with its amendment, the First Amendment, right? But you're not willing to allow the judges to be the dictators with any of the other amendments, particularly when they conflict with your exercise of the First Amendment?

1ST TV REPORTER: I say there is a very important conflict here between two rights.

MR. MILLER: Yes, and at least one reporter, of course, declares his is more primary. It's got number one on it.

3RD EDITOR: That's not a bad concept, doctor.

MR. MILLER: I knew I'd say something you'd like today.

1ST REPORTER: Professor, the Supreme Court has disposed of the question by saying that the First Amendment was a preferred right.

MR. MILLER: Yes, it's preferred all right, absolute.

1ST REPORTER: Absolute.

MR. MILLER: Absolute, preferred equals absolute.

1ST REPORTER: Yes, in this context.

MR. MILLER: Could we have the judges now—equal time, right of reply.

3RD EDITOR: Oh, I thought you were going to pick on them.

MR. MILLER: Me, I don't pick on anyone (Turns to 4th Judge): Judge, you've heard why the press doesn't want to submit anything to the judicial process. How do you react?

4TH JUDGE: Well, I think absolutism in any of these rulings is wrong. On the other hand, on all the fact situations that we have before us this afternoon, I must say that I don't see very many legal problems in the situation now. I don't think that there ought to be very many new laws to bring more matters into the courts. Generally, I would go along with whoever said that no remedy was preferable to a state remedy. I think the legal problems here, logically, would only come after the event and in a suit for damages.

MR. MILLER: But one of our lawyers isn't even willing to go that route. He thinks your process is too costly. He thinks your process is going to deter or chill their exercise of speech. He doesn't trust the jury. He's worried a little bit about the judge.

4TH JUDGE: Corruption?

MR. MILLER: Not corruption, I think he wouldn't put it that way; their conservative viewpoint.

4TH JUDGE: Maybe he didn't hear about those three judges in northern New Jersey whom organized crime had to lay off the other day; state court judges, of course.

MR. MILLER: Then don't you have to face the reporter who says as an absolute matter, no state intrusion—you're illegitimate, even with regard to damage.

4TH JUDGE: No, of course not. The clause in the First Amendment certainly didn't imply that the courts didn't have some say in these matters. But the question is where it comes in and, of course, this is what we've been talking about all day. On the fact situations we have here, I'm thankful that the decisions rest in the hands of the editors not the courts, and for most of this that's exactly where it belongs. Now, I would hope that the editors would exercise some discretion. As most of them around here have indicated, they would on some of these matters and certainly I hope that they're better investigative reporters than this character here who apparently didn't check anything with anybody.

MR. MILLER (Turns to 2nd Judge): Judge, how does a circuit court look at this, from top to bottom? You know, there's a frontal attack on the process going on here. I suppose as a part-time proceduralist, I have some sympathy for the notion that the process is too slow and too costly and sometimes too erratic.

2ND JUDGE: I agree with my colleague, of course, and in the context of these problems I don't see much reason.

MR. MILLER: Let's step away from these problems.

2ND JUDGE: But on an overall basis, there certainly is a role for the courts when the press go to the extreme. They say things within the rather restricted confines of the right to sue for libel and they have been restricted very substantially by the Supreme Court, particularly with a figure in public life or a candidate. A burden of proof has been imposed upon public officials and public figures that is so great that really they don't have much right left. But other people do have some rights and they have not been restricted to the same extent and the Supreme Court is aware of that as in the Gertz case [*Gertz v. Robert*

Welch, Inc., 418 U.S. 523 (1974)]. You remember he was the lawyer from Chicago and he was blasted as being a Red and a Commie and things of that sort and he brought an action. The Supreme Court held that he was entitled to maintain a verdict for his actual harm done. This is not unhealthy as far as I can see. Indeed, it's the only control that I know about to avoid real excesses in the press. I know of no judge who thinks the courts should intervene in the routine kind of things that are involved here. Like my colleague, I would hope that most of this stuff would not get into the press; not until a whole lot more had been done than Burnwood had done. But in the context of the Gertz case, I see no reason in the world why the law shouldn't provide some means to compensate him for the harm done by a lousy newspaper.

MR. MILLER: And your reaction to the reporter's notion that you're totally illegitimate?

2ND JUDGE: I sort of resent that.

MR. MILLER: How are we going to get you two together? Is there any way of getting this fundamentalism. (Asks 5th Judge): Judge?

5TH JUDGE: May I voice some agreement with the reporter? We have talked as though the press were the only ones who claim an absolute privilege, but so do the judges. The judges do not make themselves susceptible to judicial process with respect to their abuses. They enjoy an absolute immunity with respect to what they say. Judges have developed a machinery within their own organization—not as good as it should be, and they still are developing it—with respect to self-discipline by judges who are their own agencies. The difficulty with the claim made by the reporter is that he does not propose that the press shall in some organized way operate so as to discipline its own members. I think there's a very good case to be made for the fact that the press, like the judges, should be immune from ordinary forms of legal liability but only on the condition that they are prepared for themselves to establish a form of voluntary discipline for their own profession.

3RD EDITOR: No, I disagree and I disagree with what you tried to do earlier to impose a standard on the press. I think one of the healthy aspects of the press in this country is that we all are different; the Harvard *Crimson,* the Podunk *Press,* the Washington *Post.* That frightens me as much as anything else you've implied, which is that we subject the media or whatever other phrase you want to a single set of rules, regulation, or discipline. I think it's far healthier from my concept of democracy to have this come out the way it comes out.

FORMER GOV'T. OFFICIAL: I really must disagree with that. I think that what the judge says is very relevant to what's been going on here this afternoon. I think the state, as one of you says, probably shouldn't get involved in these kinds of cases that are outlined in this problem. On the other hand, we have to recognize that the press then has enormous power, almost unchecked, and the standards that the press has really are appalling in some of these instances. For a large, powerful newspaper to say that's not my fault what some other newspaper does, that's not my responsibility, and then to say we should impose no standard, self-imposed standards, on them. I've heard here this afternoon that it's perfectly all right to talk about the pot smoking of a child of a candidate for high office or of any kind of office even though that might ruin that child for life. Now, I think that's an appalling standard and that something ought to be done within the press itself to insure that if that does continue, that at least there be some effort made to check that kind of reporting.

3RD REPORTER: Would the lawyers and judges here seriously argue that the standards which they have written down for their trades are effective? Are these examples that we should emulate?

FORMER GOV'T. OFFICIAL: Well, they're not as ineffective as no standards. There are lawyers who are disbarred.

3RD REPORTER: There are lawyers who are disbarred when they get convicted by the courts.

FORMER GOV'T. OFFICIAL: Well, then the alternative is to do nothing about it.

3RD REPORTER: That I submit is what you have basically done.

FORMER GOV'T. OFFICIAL: No, no.

MR. MILLER: You think the press should do nothing?

3RD REPORTER: I think we have an excellent example that these things don't work when they are organized in that fashion.

2ND GOV'T. OFFICIAL: What things?

3RD REPORTER: These standards, these legal codes of ethics.

MR. MILLER: Don't work?

3RD REPORTER: Right.

2ND TV REPORTER: I think this has been cast in terms of two absolutes and in the real world I don't believe in the absolutist position to the extent that it was stated. I feel that the press certainly should be liable in libel cases when they're not telling the truth. Now, there is a distinction that we've fuzzed up here between the right of privacy and libel cases, and I don't think many of the journalists here would say when we don't get it right and when we are guilty of libel that we should have an absolute privilege there. I don't believe that.

MR. MILLER: But as to privacy, you believe you should have an absolute privilege?

2ND TV REPORTER: Well, privacy is in such an infant stage now, it's so difficult to define. I think the capacity of the right of privacy as a legal tort to chill expression by the media is far greater than libel where there is an absolute standard of truth or falsity. I'll stand on that as a reporter but I do not want to be second-guessed later by a jury as to whether the subject of the story was really a newsworthy person and that I think is a problem.

MR. MILLER: But what about some of the emerging constitutional overtones to privacy?

2ND TV REPORTER: I think it's very troublesome.

MR. MILLER: Very troublesome?

2ND TV REPORTER: Yes.

MR. MILLER: Troublesome in what way? Is something starting to compete with the First Amendment?

2ND TV REPORTER: Yes. That's where we started with the Massachusetts law on arrest records.

MR. MILLER: Yes, now that's just the statute but I'm talking about *Roe v. Wade* or *Griswold v. Connecticut* [*Roe v. Wade*, 410 U.S. 113 (1973); *Griswold v. Connecticut,* 381 U.S. 179 (1965)].

3RD REPORTER: What are those cases?

MR. MILLER: Roe and Wade says that there is a constitutuional right of a woman to have an abortion without being subjected to criminal sanction. Mr. Justice Blackman's opinion seems to be predicated on the recognition of a constitutionally based right of privacy. The dimensions are totally amorphous at this point but they could have that staggering implication. For example, if a woman had a constitutional right to an abortion without being declared a criminal by the state, might she not have a constitutional right to an abortion without that fact being publicized because if it's publicized that will chill her ability to exercise that right. One of you may have been driving at that earlier this afternoon and how does the press react to that? Maybe constitutionally you shouldn't be permitted to publish that fact.

3RD JUDGE: Well, the thought occurs to me that we cover *Roe v. Wade* in Cassandra in this case. At the time *Roe v. Wade* was the law, though we didn't recognize it until the Supreme Court said so. Now Cassandra, when she went through her abortion, that was illegal. That was a criminal act.

MR. MILLER: Well, we don't know.

3RD REPORTER: Maybe she had it done in England.

MR. MILLER: That's right, maybe it was under the law of the state—okay, it might not have been illegal.

3RD JUDGE: It seems to me that what we're really talking about, the newspaper people anyway, is bad judges. Somebody's complaining about judges failing to enter summary judgments when they ought to be. Well, that's a bad judge and that's something we're going to have to live with. I don't think that the newspapers have any special blessing not to confine themselves within the laws enunciated by the United States Supreme Court. They go ahead and print stories and they get sued and if the law says they have to pay damages then they have to pay damages. Now I'm speaking as a lawyer now, as a judge. The gag rules that people are worried about—and somebody mentioned that—I don't believe in gag rules. I think you can have a fair trial without gagging the press. That's the trial judge's responsibility to see that the person gets a fair trial. I'm really not sure what we're talking about is trying to change the law and it ought to be addressed to the nine fellows up on the Hill.

MR. MILLER: Do you have any feeling listening to the proponent of the absolute position that you keep your camel's nose out of his tent and the editor who said, we're not even going to self-regulate? And you say our process has a legitimate function. How can we get you together?

3RD JUDGE: Well, I think it's a necessary function.

3RD EDITOR: Who wants to be together?

MR. MILLER: Oh, you won't even meet with them?

3RD EDITOR: You can have bad judges, you can have bad newspapers. They don't drum the bad judges out.

MR. MILLER: So we've got the worst of all possible worlds, both systems have defects and neither system will tolerate the notion that they should change.

1ST REPORTER: The society can tolerate bad newspapers more than it can bad judges.

MR. MILLER: Really?

1ST REPORTER: Yes.

MR. MILLER: Where does it say that? (Asks 1st Judge): What's your role? Our reporter wants your nose out of his tent.

1ST JUDGE: Well, our absolutist reporter reads the First Amendment more broadly than I think it has been read thus far or should be read. The fact that a constitutional freedom is preferred does not mean it is absolute. It's not even an absolute in the category where it is most absolute—namely, prior restraint, freedom from prior restraint. On the issue of responsibility—which has to be in damage as I don't know of any other way that responsibility can be enforced—I think that the idea of a presumption going with the newspaper is as good as we can get. A strong presumption going with the newspaper that their editorial judgment on what is newsworthy has indeed been correctly exercised. If journalism, both print and broadcast, if they are a fourth branch of government, they are no more immune from some check than the executive branch of government, which is subject to some check in an organized system, usually by declaration or injunction rather than damages. There's no sovereign immunity any more, to speak of, to protect all government officials from any inquiry. I don't think there's to be a sovereign immunity for newspapers.

MR. MILLER: But they say you've got sovereign immunity.

1ST JUDGE: Yes, I think that my colleague's answer is correct that judges have sovereign immunity from damage suits. There's a phrase I once encountered in a law review article which said all persons are presumed to know the law except lawyers, who are presumed to know very little, and judges, who are not presumed to know any at all, because lawyers can rarely be sued and judges can never be sued.

3RD JUDGE: What difference does it make? We're judgment proof anyway.

1ST JUDGE: That's only a latter-day development.

MR. MILLER: But doesn't our reporter friend's point go not simply to the fact that you're immune from suit but that your process is untouchable? They either don't want you at all or they're telling you your process stinks from their perspective because you don't understand what they do from day to day. You'll take too long and you'll cost too much.

1ST JUDGE: Those are problems that are serious and I think that the judges and the law have to accommodate themselves to that and do better because these are very serious defects in the judicial corrective process. This morning I was upset by the idea that just because I said we should take some time for reflection I meant extended time for reflection. I think the judicial process has to be hounded by sessions like these and by other corrective measures to really shape up, but I see a lawyer raising his hand and he will bear me out that in a recent case the court made it possible for the press to present in court what they did need. Unfortunately, the Supreme Court didn't see it that way. I'm not now talking to the time element or the expense element. I have to deal with those separately. But at least our processes make it possible for the press to tell us what they need. I'm not talking about corrupt judges or organized crime judges. But with most judges up and down the land, when someone comes in and explains that he is performing a public function and this is how he does it, most judges may call a particular shot wrong, but they are trying to do the best they can. It's a hard question and we do make mistakes but they're not mistakes of purpose. They are mistakes of judgment such as everybody makes. Judges will fail to accord a presumption of regularity and say this is a matter on which the newspaper has to be given its right. Now, we have to apply a presumption of regularity by giving summary judgments in cases against newspapers and not putting them to the expense of trial. All of our thinking about summary judgments is a wealth of appellate jurisprudence that you should never give summary judgments because somebody might convince some juror— God knows how—that maybe so and so has a right and so forth. It has to be turned around along the lines set forth in some opinions where the press is involved because the conduct of the litigation does have a tariff. It does have a cost which has a deterrent and chilling effect. But I think all of this can be worked out within our scheme. I don't think that that is implacably opposed except on an absolutist philosophy. There are possibilities, there are ways in which the judicial system can shape up, get the newspapers out of the actions faster when they're just trash actions or trivial actions by giving summary judgments to the newspapers and providing some expedition in the limited case of prior restraints. I may be holding out too much hope for what lawyers and judges can do. But I think there are paths that can be developed along these lines that will prevent conflict in most situations. To prevent conflict in all situations is beyond anybody's reach. But to prevent conflict in most situations I think is possible.

MR. MILLER: And I think you'd agree with your colleague that your brethren and your sistern should be prepared to get up at four o'clock in the morning, in their pajamas, and decide cases?

1ST JUDGE: Yes, yes I do. I was sorry that I said one day before, because I think in the particular case two hours would have been enough, and let me give an example of that. Someone was saying about the Supreme Court reading all 12,000 pages of the Pentagon Papers. That's nonsense. All that the Pentagon Papers involved, at least in the first stage, is that the Court said to the government, "Give us your best document that you think can't be published. Let's not worry about all 3,000. Give the Court your pin-up document number one that you think is such that it should not be published, that would be a terrible embarrassment or infringement of national defense, let's start with that." You don't have to read 12,000 pages to get the best or to get the solicitor's view of what is the best and the government couldn't come up with number one. Whoever said this morning that the case we had this morning was less of a reason for an injunction than the Pentagon Papers case I think was off the beam. I think the Pentagon Papers case presented no possibility of a court injunction really. There wasn't any in a history that was as many years old as that. Any reason to stop anything, but this morning's case did present some very hard problems. I was very much troubled by that. If the government's lawyer can't give the judge document number one that has to be stopped—just to start off with and *in camera*—then they're going to lose right away and it doesn't take ten hours. We start in with document number one. Now if document number one really means a lot of people losing their lives, then I do think we have a problem that we have to grapple with. And the newspapers may have to wait the extra time. But that can only be the rarest case where the pin-up document does show a very immediate and substantial interference with national defense.

MR. MILLER (Asks Columnist): How does some of this sound to you?

COLUMNIST: Well, I tend to be more on the judges' side than on the newspaper people's side. I agree with most of what the judge has just said, but I think there is one caution. His statement of the burden of proof is a correct statement of what was done in the District of Columbia circuit in the Pentagon Papers case. It is not a correct statement of what the court of appeals for the Second Circuit did because there Judge Friendly and others made very clear that they thought the trial judge should have read all or most of the Pentagon Papers. They sent the case back for extended hearings and so on. I think newspapers could rightly be very worried that the standard or burden of proof we've just heard would not be generally followed, but that's really this morning's big question. Coming to this one, not only do I agree that the very limited law of libel that remains in this country—limited by comparison with most others—is right, I think it should remain. Remedy and damages should be available for individuals who are not usually the great or the powerful but little people who have been hurt by newspapers. I think it's very important for the press that that should remain. I think the press would be weaker in this country if the document of absolutism did become the law in this country. The press would be in danger of public revulsion and public dislike of a kind that I think would be much more dangerous than the limited responsibility we have in damages now.

MR. MILLER: How do you react to the notion of some mechanism within the journalism profession?

COLUMNIST: Well, once again, I think I tend to divide from what many of my journalist colleagues here have said. I'm for that. I think it's rather a modest reform. The press council works pretty well in England. Of course it can't speak for everybody. It shouldn't speak for everybody, but I think self-discipline is terribly important. I think the ombudsman idea is an extremely significant thing in giving the public confidence in the newspaper profession's concern for its own standards. I'm in general against the external imposition of standards except where the rights of the individual have been damaged as in libel—certainly not in the national security area generally. But I think the notion of self-discipline is very important to either putting through an individual news-paper's operation or a modest kind of press council. I'm not against that.

MR. MILLER (Calls on 6th Reporter): When you started as a reporter, what kind of training did you get?

6TH REPORTER: Four years of undergraduate—you mean in detail?

MR. MILLER: No, no, I mean when you showed up for work the first day, what did they tell you to do? How were you educated at the art of report-ing?

6TH REPORTER: That was a long time ago. They showed me how to operate a speed graphic camera.

MR. MILLER (Calls on 2nd Reporter): How about you?

2ND REPORTER: I was sent out to do a story.

MR. MILLER (Calls on 3rd Reporter)

3RD REPORTER: I had a night city editor who managed to instill a fear of God in me that if I got the middle initial wrong off an arrest record the paper would be bankrupt and I'd never have a job again.

9TH EDITOR: I remember that you could say anything you wanted as long as you attributed it to the police.

(Laughter)

MR. MILLER: Is there any lesson to be learned here?

6TH REPORTER: The training got better when I went to a better paper.

MR. MILLER: In what way did it get better?

6TH REPORTER: Oh, it was much more rigorous when I worked for a much bigger paper than a weekly.

2ND REPORTER: Isn't it fair to suggest that what Professor Miller is getting at, though, is that the kind of training the journalists get by and large is the kind of training you get in every single job in the world: on-the-job training. There is always some sort of gradual process by which you come into contact with more and more experiences which teach you more and more about how to do your job correctly.

MR. MILLER: How to do your job correctly? Now what dimension does that take?

2ND REPORTER: I think that takes the dimension of socialization into the norms of the people you work with.

MR. MILLER: Yes. Now what about these external values that we've been talking about; maybe they shouldn't undercut the First Amendment, but all these things editors sit around and discuss from 6:00 P.M. to 7:29 P.M. every day before they go out and hatchet somebody.

2ND REPORTER: I would like to suggest that it's somewhat hypocritical of news organizations to suggest that they don't want to submit themselves to a standard that applies to all news organizations because there is, as we all know, a remarkable similarity between, say, what appears in the *Post* and the *Times,* which is not accidental. There is a remarkable similarity between what appears in *Time* and *Newsweek,* which is not accidental. In fact, what goes into news publications is tremendously dictated by what goes into other news publications. Professor Miller I think adequately demonstrated a while ago that to some extent the notion that you publish something because somebody else published it reduces the whole profession to the lowest common denominator. I can't quite see why, for example, if you think in your own mind as a newsman that an arrest record—not a conviction record but an arrest record—of a noncandidate is not relevant news, I fail to see how that becomes relevant news just because somebody else printed it. But a lot of that goes on so I think it's perfectly fair to suggest that there really ought to be a professionwide code of ethics, if you will. I would agree, too, that the code of ethics that applies to lawyers is an unfortunate example insofar as it has not worked at all.

PROSECUTOR: Where is the open and robust debate that's supposed to take place as a result of this? We all know that the press seems to have a certain sameness about it in terms of what they report.

MR. MILLER: I think I'm trying to find out whether the press or broadcast media shouldn't broaden their concept of on-the-job training. What are you teaching in journalism school?

JOURNALISM PROF.: I'm glad you asked me that; eight consecutive weeks on the Red Lion case and the Pensions case [*Red Lion Broadcasting Co. v. F.C.C.,* 395 U.S. 367 (1969); *National Broadcasting Company v. F.C.C.,* 516 F 206 1101 (DC, Cir. 1974)]. Now what they'll learn out of that is not only what the Fairness Doctrine is and is supposed to be but because they have cross-examined the producer of that program in the presence of his lawyer by the way, just by accident, and looked at every foot of that film and read the script 20 times, they know all the mistakes that were made in that program, which was quite a good program, but like all journalism, not without its flaws. I would say the unwritten part of the agenda here today is the free passage that journalism gives to journalism, not in news councils, that's another subject for another day, but in what they report. So there's a lot of talk about letting senators and congressmen get away with being drunk—I know a congressman from a western state that I've visited 20 or 30 times, and he has never once been sober and most of the people in this room know whom I'm talking about. Newspapers which say they are now going to report on Wilbur Mills and others who drink and do other things they shouldn't do, should soon start reporting on each other. I cannot think of a time, and I will be corrected gladly, when the Washington *Post* has with vigor pointed out the mistakes of the New York *Times* or the Los Angeles *Times* or the Podunk *Bugle* the way they point out everything else. It's a fraternity and I guess for a long time I was part of it.

MR. MILLER: Is the *Star* ever going to talk to the *Post*, the New York *Times* ever going to talk to the Los Angeles *Times*, NBC ever talk to CBS or ABC?

3RD EDITOR: Talk about or talk to?

MR. MILLER: Talk about.

1ST EDITOR: We do.

MR. MILLER: Where did you get your sensitivity about those arrest records that we started the afternoon with? Did you get any training?

1ST EDITOR: No.

MR. MILLER: Did somebody tell you about privacy or libel, defamation, the rights of individuals, competing values? Where did you pick those up?

1ST EDITOR: When I started as a reporter nobody gave me a lecture on those things. I started as others did, being told to go out and write something. I just want to say that the Washington *Post* has written columns, run columns, and written editorials that were critical of its own news coverage and that of other papers and it's a little easier to do it about ourselves . . .

JOURNALISM PROF.: Outside yourself, which is sort of examining your navel with great vigor, some outside ones, some examples?

1ST EDITOR: L.A. *Times.*

7TH EDITOR: George Wilson critical of Harrison Salisbury using Communist statistics in his visit to North Vietnam. Page 1 of the Washington *Post.*

1ST EDITOR: L.A. *Times,* in the Manson case and I'm trying to remember exactly.

7TH EDITOR: It was the girl-diary or something.

JOURNALISM PROF.: You have to really test your memories.

MR. MILLER: All right, all right. (Turns to 3rd Editor): You don't want the nose in the tent. You don't want the Harvard *Crimson* to be like the Washington *Post* or the New York or Los Angeles *Times,* right? There is beauty in variety.

3RD EDITOR: It's that I don't want the Harvard *Crimson* imposing standards on me, no more than they want me to impose standards on them. And standards are fashionable.

MR. MILLER: And you don't want to define a floor. You don't even want to define a floor.

3RD EDITOR: Every floor that I've seen defined by the profession is so meaningless in its generalizations that I don't . . .

MR. MILLER: Are you willing to do anything?

3RD EDITOR: Yes.

MR. MILLER: What should your epitaph be? "I didn't want anything done"?

3RD EDITOR: I'm the 2,000-year-old editor.

MR. MILLER: You want to have that nice, clubby 6:00 conference?

3RD EDITOR: No, I want to worry about my newspaper.

MR. MILLER: Period.

3RD EDITOR: Yes, period.

MR. MILLER: You don't want to assume any other burden.

3RD EDITOR: That's right. That's enough of a burden, pal.

MR. MILLER: Well, I can well see that.

(Laughter)

3RD EDITOR: And you leave out one other thing when you talk about training, and that is . . .

MR. MILLER: Why don't you run some seminars for the people at Podunk. Don't set standards for them. Why don't you run some seminars for them? Why don't you send your talent out?

(Simultaneous remarks)

2ND EDITOR: The American Press Institute does that.

MR. MILLER: Have you ever conducted sensitivity training on privacy?

3RD EDITOR: Why do you want us to conduct seminars?

MR. MILLER: I don't know. I'm an academic. I think a seminar's a good thing, particularly if you're paid an honorarium.

(Laughter)

3RD EDITOR: Do you really want us to lecture the rest of the press to say we're going to clone our newspaper throughout the United States? Is that your idea of what the press should be in this country. I mean, I'm thankful for it, and if you want to write it up or run it as a promotion . . .

MR. MILLER: I didn't ask you to go sell Christianity. You know, I didn't ask you to assume what used to be called "the white man's burden." Just disseminate your experience.

3RD EDITOR: We do, in our newspaper as an example.

MR. MILLER: I see. Keep it in house?

3RD EDITOR: No, you can buy it.

7TH EDITOR: Newspaper reporters, editors who go elsewhere.

MR. MILLER: Okay.

(Simultaneous remarks)

8TH EDITOR: There are professional societies that try to promote standards of ethics. The society of professional journalists, used to be Sigma Delta Chi, haggled for two years over codes of ethics. The American Society of Newspaper Editors has had a code of ethics ever since 1923.

2ND REPORTER: To make it more effective then, would be go to them.

8TH EDITOR: Well, I don't know, but I would say that there is a certain sensitivity to the standards of proper performance of journalism.

MR. MILLER: But yet every reporter around this table announced that they went out and did their job without any prior education with regard to many of the things that we've talked about today.

8TH EDITOR: Well, I don't think that's true.

5TH EDITOR: When I went to journalism school 25 or 30 years ago, Harold Cross taught libel. I studied it for a year, and that's all you needed. You didn't need fairness doctrine, right of privacy, prior restraint. What has happened in the last quarter century, particularly in the last ten years, is that we are being surrounded by spiders who are spinning legal nets. We can't handle them. We've got to turn to their legal counsel. If you run a small paper, all the education in the world isn't going to help you. An editor can't go into a court. He can't even stay with half the rulings that are coming in the trade press.

MR. MILLER: I guess the point is to stay out of court in the first place by upgrading the standards so that the lawyer's fees go down. He won't starve. He's got a lot of baby fat that'll keep him going for a while.

1ST TV REPORTER: Professor, just one word before you get to that. I think there's a certain assumption applied that I don't want to let go by, and it is that it's not always true that higher standards will keep you out of court.

VARIOUS VOICES: Right.

MR. MILLER: It may make it easier for the courts to grant summary judgment in some cases.

1ST TV REPORTER: It's not always true. I will not concede that high standards alone will keep you out of court. Somehow I think you . . .

MR. MILLER: I think that's fair.

FORMER GOV'T. OFFICIAL: Aren't you on much stronger grounds, though, arguing to stay out of court if you do have some internal mechanism to set higher standards?

VARIOUS VOICES: No.

MR. MILLER: It certainly has a direct bearing on the question of malice . . . (Calls on 5th Judge): Judge?

5TH JUDGE: Too many people have assumed that what I was talking about was some kind of code which would be promulgated and not observed. I have no particular brief for that kind of code; nor am I sufficiently informed about the British press council to suggest for a moment that what is suitable in Britain is suitable here. I think we generally have to take into account local conditions much more than merely copy something which is used in another nation. But if you take what at least I have gained from this seminar, I do not despair of some form of new attempt at self-discipline within this profession. I have learned a lot, and I hope some others have, from these sessions, and I would imagine that if other newspapers had representatives here, they would have learned something. And it seems to me that as judges have learned that they can teach each other through judicial seminars and have to some extent improved judicial work, I also think the press can do something of that sort. Now I'm far from familiar with any of the detail of this particular profession, but I do not think that because I am unfamiliar it follows that everyone is unfamiliar and unable to be inventive. The question is whether you really care to be your brother's keeper, and there is a reluctance to be your brother's keeper. But this is a charge we bear from high authority, and none of us will escape responsibility if we concern ourselves only about ourselves.

3RD EDITOR: It seems to me that during all this talk about self-discipline, some persons in the room listening to the entire conversation of the press today would come to the conclusion, an appalling conclusion, that the press is far more self-disciplined in what it won't publish than, I think, the impression would have been coming down here. Reporter and editor, one after the other, has said more often than not, I would not publish on these cases, than have said, publish and be damned. And I wonder for whom and at what the call for self-discipline is aimed.

MR. MILLER: Well, as I started out saying this afternoon, one of the difficulties in this seminar is the process of selection of the people here, and that in a real sense, and I mean nothing pejorative by this, absolutely nothing pejorative, that we've got the pinnacle. The difficulty is that often the pinnacle will have to be judged by the performance of the base. I know many of you believe that the three-page case study presents a series of facts and events that you would not participate in, but if you put your collective intelligence together, you would quickly determine that each and every event in this case study is culled from a real case, that is, it really happened. It might not have happened at your papers or broadcast studios, but it happened. And therefore the legal profession may have a skewed view because it's looking at the base, and you're looking, in a sense, over their heads.

3RD EDITOR: Agreed. But I do not want to tell somebody else, "Don't publish that, because I'm not going to publish it."

MR. MILLER: You don't want to have that responsibility. You won't give it to the law.

3RD EDITOR: It's not a question of responsibility. It's a question of my interpretation of the First Amendment.

MR. MILLER: All the rights but none of the obligations . . .

3RD EDITOR: No, there are obligations.

MR. MILLER: . . . to your readers.

3RD EDITOR: What's wrong with that? That's a fine obligation. We also have a deterrent you haven't talked about, which is kind of fun, the by-line.

MR. MILLER: The by-line?

3RD EDITOR: Yes.

7TH EDITOR: We spend more time on the responsibilities and obligations and the exercise of those responsibilities by the press than on any other single subject. How the hell do you get away saying all the privileges and none of the obligations?

MR. MILLER: You may spend a lot of time on it, but we haven't come up with anything but gossamer.

7TH EDITOR: We haven't codified it.

MR. MILLER: Gossamer—no? Far short of codification. We have the fact that there is an absolutist position, at least with regard to some of your brethren and sistern, not all, some. We've got the admission that self-regulation is unacceptable to some of your brethren and sistern. So we're sort of left in limbo. (Turns to 1st Reporter): You are the absolutist. Won't you give a little on anything?

(Laughter)

1ST REPORTER: Nothing, on nothing. You see, I have a problem with the suggestion that if our performance is demonstrably improved, we can trust the courts more. I would like the courts to keep their cotton-picking hands off of *Rolling Stone* and every little snip sheet that is distributed, masquerading as a newspaper. They are no more of the court's responsibility than the Washington *Post* or the Washington *Star* or the Baltimore *Sun* are. It exercised me thoroughly when we were trying to talk about a shield bill in the Congress and they wrote a definition of a newspaper that was confined entirely to the elect, the cultured, the privileged, and the commercially successful. It was just plain garbage, because if there's going to be a shield law—and I personally oppose that under many circumstances—it ought to reach everybody, including the guy who runs the mimeograph machine in his basement and calls it the Third and Madison *News* and runs out on the street and peddles it gratis. The only reason why you have problems with developing standards is because you won't start with simplicity. If you keep the courts out of it and let the press deal with it and let the public either buy or not buy, the thing is very simple.

MR. MILLER (Calls on 3rd Lawyer): Close this out.

3RD LAWYER: About the pinnacle, too, we should remember that we have the pinnacle of the judiciary here today, as well as the pinnacle of the press. The press appears before a lot of gentlemen of the judiciary in state courts around the country, who view them with very considerable hostility and with very little knowledge. I think it is very misleading to suggest that it is the press alone which appears today in its finest garb. The judiciary is here as well in that same garb, and the press appears before members of the judiciary who are often very different from people who are here today. So when we talk about laws and we talk about imposing the state more in these areas, we should at least keep in mind whom we will all be appearing before.

MR. MILLER: Fair comment. I have been outrageous and arrogant and . . .

5TH EDITOR: This is true.

(Laughter)

MR. MILLER: Though, I would say you have not seen the pinnacle of the law teaching profession. I've had a lot of fun, and I hope you understand it's all a role. Thank you.

(Applause)

CASE III:
GRAND JURIES,
CONFIDENTIAL SOURCES,
AND FAIR TRIALS

THE CASE

For the past month, the Gulfport *Daily Sentinel* has published a series of articles on "Oil Rights For Sale," written by prize-winning investigative reporter Ted Harris and calling for the appointment of a special grand jury to investigate allegations of corruption in the award of federal oil leases on land and off-shore, unsavory links between government officials and oil company representatives, and fraudulent appraisals and bids.

In one of his stories, Harris described dramatic incidents in which a close actor friend, at the request of Harris, had successfully taken on two roles. First, he had passed himself off as having great influence with government officials who had power to grant oil leases and had asked for and received cash payments from oil company officials in exchange for giving them a promise of favorable treatment on their bids. Then, he successfully deceived a government official by passing himself off as a "representative" of the oil companies. He offered this official the cash previously obtained in exchange for promises of favorable treatment, and the official took the money. Harris' story of his actor friend's exploits was one of the high points of his series of articles, but the articles were by no means limited to these two incidents or to this one government official. These deeds were arranged by Harris without his editor's knowledge, but once he hit "paydirt," the *Sentinel* carried the story.

On April 15, a grand jury was convened in Gulfport by Federal Judge Bolton to hear evidence gathered by United States Attorney Jackson as a result of the articles. At the first meeting of the grand jury, Judge Bolton advised them in general of their duties and their relations to the United States Attorney. In addition, he said: "I want to emphasize once again that you are bound by the rules of secrecy. Rule 10 of this court makes plain that you may not disclose anything which transpires here unless you are given explicit permission by the court. The same obligation of secrecy is imposed by rule of court on the United States Attorney and his staff, and certain other persons present at the grand jury proceedings, such as stenographers. In this case, it is even more important than usual that secrecy be maintained because of the substantial public interest in this matter. Any publicity may jeopardize the investigation and prejudice the rights of innocent people. I warn you, therefore, that any violation of your obligation will be severely dealt with. I intend to take comparable measures with witnesses before the grand jury, their counsel, and with the news media. Though they are not directly covered by Rule 10, I am exercising my inherent power to protect the court's processes. I shall communicate to them, as I have to you, that they must not make public without leave of court anything which transpires in the grand jury room except, of course, that witnesses may keep their counsel informed. The failure of any of the individuals or entities described to comply with my order will be dealt with firmly by this court, to the full extent of the law."

The judge then sent letters reflecting the above to news media in the area. Reporter Harris was troubled by the court's order because rumors were abroad that the grand jury had been convened only as a sop to public opinion and that U.S. Attorney Jackson would not press matters vigorously. He concluded that he should keep close watch on the grand jury. He found, however, that the judge's order was surprisingly effective, and that he could learn little or nothing about what was happening.

Harris sought out one of the grand jurors, Harold Ripley, Professor of Ethics at State College, reminded him of the grand jury's historic role as a "people's tribunal" which was captive of neither prosecuting attorney nor judge, and persuaded him to cooperate. Harris supplied Ripley with information and leads that had not yet been presented by the U.S. attorney. These were intended to be a test of the U.S. attorney's good faith which would be measured by the degree to which he pursued these materials as they were raised through questions asked by Ripley, at grand jury sessions. There ensued regular meetings between Harris and Ripley in which they discussed in detail what had transpired, what might be presented, and what had been omitted by the U.S. attorney.

Harris concluded that his earliest fears were well founded that U.S. Attorney Jackson had deliberately decided to frustrate the investigation, because it would lead directly to Senator Squire, who had been very largely responsible for the appointments of both Jackson and Judge Bolton. After consulting with his editors, Harris decided to go public on the matter. Reviving his earlier series, he drew on his conversations with Ripley and published a series of articles whose context is reflected in some of the headlines: "Why the Delay in Returning the Indictment?"; "Coverup in Oil Deals?"; "Jackson: U.S. Attorney or Oil Company Lawyer?"; "Judge Bolton's Gag Order and the Coverup"; "Senator Squire— Why Not Answer the Charges?"

Material began to flow to Harris not only from Ripley but from other sources: for example, (1) A handwritten unsigned communication by someone purporting to be a member of the senator's staff, implicating the senator in receipt of bribes, followed by a phone call offering to identify the caller and to supply evidence on receipt of $2,500. "I've been offered that much to appear on a TV program in a mask, but would like to give the story to you." (2) Telephone calls by friends and family of grand jurors reflecting what had, or had not, been presented to the grand jury.

At a cocktail party Harris ran into Judge Carter who was an old friend of his, and who sat in the same district as Judge Bolton. Carter took Harris to one side and said, "Don't ever tell anyone I told you this, but watch yourself. Bolton is mad as hell. He told me that you were unfairly threatening powerful government officials who have helped him, and if you don't cut it out, he'll have your hide."

As Harris' stories increased in number and tempo and in their reliance on material presented to the grand jury, Judge Bolton took several steps. He questioned all the grand jurors, asking if any outsiders had talked to them about the inquiry. All said no. He called Harris into court, at the request of the U.S. attorney, and warned him that he risked serious penalties if he persisted in violating the secrecy order. He also directed Harris to turn over to the court the names of any grand jurors, witnesses, or others who were providing him with information as to what was transpiring before the grand jury. Harris refused to supply the names and, the following day, published a story called "Gagging the Press—What Next in the Coverup?" He referred to a "reliable source" as a basis for reporting Bolton's private threat against Harris.

The next day, Harris and his actor friend were called before the grand jury and asked to testify about the friend's personal dealings with both oil company officials and the one government official, and Harris' involvement. They testified only to the extent of giving what had previously been published in the newspaper.

Three days later, the grand jury returned indictments charging a congressman, a regional administrator, and others with several offenses: among them, bribery, conspiracy to make false statements, the violation of procedural requirements in the award of oil leases, and income tax evasion. In addition, Harris and his friend were indicted for bribery. Senator Squire was not mentioned in any of the indictments.

Judge Bolton also issued an order to show cause why Harris and the newspaper company which employed him should not be held in contempt of court for violating the gag order and refusing to reveal their sources. He also asked the U.S. attorney to convene a grand jury to consider whether Harris, his actor friend, and any other identifiable sources had violated any criminal statute, calling attention especially to the statutes making it a crime to obstruct justice.

The congressman's attorneys moved to dismiss the indictment on the ground that the constant flow of publicity, unrestrained by the court, deprived his client of any possibility of a fair trial. They subpoenaed Harris to obtain his confidential sources.

A prosecutor in Jackson's office resigned from office and confidentially told Harris of occurrences within the grand jury—occurrences that Ripley corroborated. The prosecutor reported that the members of the grand jury had reported informally to Jackson that they had taken a vote among themselves on whether Senator Squire was mixed up in the "mess" and had voted 13 to 9 that he was; that Jackson had urged the grand jurors to exercise "great care and restraint in dealing with the U.S. senator" and not to take action by so close a vote; and that the grand jury had taken no further action as to the senator.

Questions

1. Was it appropriate for Harris to use the actor friend as he did in order to prove at first hand that bribery was taking place? Was it a violation of law, for which he and his friend should be indicted and tried? Should the editor have published the article?

2. Was the judge's order of April 15 a valid order? If not, in what respects was it not? In any case, should Harris have ignored it or sought an appeal before violating it? Is your answer any different if Harris obtained information from Ripley which he thought necessary to publish the next day?

3. Assuming that it was proper for Harris to publish leaks from the grand jury, was it appropriate for him to make the arrangement with Ripley? Was it a violation of law?

4. How should the contempt proceedings be resolved?

5. What should be done by the court in response to the congressman's motion to dismiss the indictment against him?

6. What should the newspaper do with the information obtained from the prosecutor who resigned?

PROCEEDINGS

MR. NESSON: The problem that we deal with this morning I think is an appropriate one to finish the conference. We started out with conflict between the media and the executive branch over national security. We moved then to conflict between the media and individual citizens in the area of privacy. This morning's subject matter deals in a very direct way with conflict between the media and the courts. That is, in the most immediate sense, it is conflict between law and press.

I'm sorry that our reason for dealing with it last was because Al Sachs wasn't able to be here. I feel very badly about that myself. I hope that we will all do his problem justice. I want to make two changes, one slight and one not so slight. First, I would like you to assume that Mr. Harris has not been indicted by the grand jury. Second, I'd like very much to involve the observers here more completely than they were in the first session, that is, I would hope that you would contribute and not feel imposed on if I call on you.

What I'd like to do with the problem, especially since it's not my own, is go right to the basic issues in the problem as I see it; stick with those issues; and bang away at them for as long as we have here. Judge, would you state for us the general proposition which justifies, at least allegedly justifies, imposition of a rule that one must follow an order of a court even though it may in fact be an invalid order.

1ST JUDGE: Ultimately, all civil liberties depend upon a framework of some degree of order. Nobody assumes that in a state which was in real peril of falling, as say England was after the fall of France, any government will respect any liberty that it thinks is at risk. Therefore, I think we start by recognizing that "liberty is the room created by walls." We have to have some degree of structure in order to have any liberty. In an ordinary situation, not a war situation, the degree of order which is requisite is supplied by the judicial system. I don't mean that everything that judges do is necessary to maintain order, but a minimum amount of judicial control is one of the ways in which we maintain the structure within which liberty exists. And therefore the order of a court must be obeyed not because it's necessarily right, and not because in every instance the structure of the nation depends upon *that* order. But it is better on the whole to take a chance that those orders are necessary for the structure. And, therefore, the society requires that the court orders shall be obeyed until an appellate court reverses them.

177

MR. NESSON: If I understand you correctly, what you said basically is that in some situations—in order to preserve order in an overall sense—it's necessary that some rules, even though they may be invalid or illegal, should be followed until they be dealt with in an orderly fashion.

1ST JUDGE: Correct.

MR. NESSON: Now, do you think that that proposition justifies a contempt order against Mr. Harris on the facts of this case?

1ST JUDGE: I would find it very hard to sustain that proposition *ad hoc.*

MR. NESSON: Well, let's take it at a general level. Let's take a gag order imposed by a judge on a member of the press which the member of the press, at least, thinks is an invalid order. Now, compelled by all of the interests of speed and feelings against prior restraint that we've heard articulated here, that reporter says, "To hell with it, I'm going to violate that order." Do you, sitting as a judge, justify the imposition of a contempt sanction on that man, independent of the validity of the order?

1ST JUDGE: Well, ultimately I think that the reporter is morally free to disregard the order on the same principle that Antigone was free to disregard Creon's order. There is a state higher than the state of the law. But the reporter who does it runs the risk that the judge may be as arbitrary as Creon and not in the end see that there was a moral justification and that though there may be a technical right to hold the person it is morally unsound for the person in authority to enforce by a maximum or substantial penalty the order which has been violated.

1ST TV REPORTER: Judge, you're aware that Antigone is still on appeal.

1ST JUDGE: And will be until the end. Only on the final judgment day will we know. But I am betting one way. If you want to bet the other we'll see which one of us lands in hell.

MR. NESSON (Calls on 2nd Judge): How do you come out on it? What I'm putting to you basically is where do you stand on the Dickinson case? [*United States v. Dickinson,* 465 F.2d 496 (5th Cir. 1972) in which the court held that a reporter could be found in contempt for violating an unconstitutional gag order.]

2ND JUDGE: Well, I thought Judge [John R.] Brown wrote a very colorful opinion.

MR. NESSON: No question about that. He didn't want to be outdone by the Judge here if he had the chance.

2ND JUDGE: I'm having a little difficulty. I agree with the Dickinson case but I think we all seem to miss the point that when trial judges go wrong, as they do from time to time, the court of appeals straightens them out. They straighten trial judges out usually in a polite way, as they did in the Dickinson case. Remanded in light of that opinion. I don't think there's any doubt that no judge will tell you that someone has a right to disobey a court order. There is a line of cases in which, if the order is patently frivolous or patently invalid, one has the right or at least can get by with disobeying.

But I have difficulty with this whole problem because I just don't believe in gag orders. I've never had a case—and I'm talking of my own personal experience as a judge—in which I felt it was necessary. But I agree with the opinion.

MR. NESSON (Calls on 3rd Judge): Judge, how about you? Here we have a reporter who violates a court order, which he thinks is invalid. He says to himself, "I'm going to take that judgment on myself. I'm going to act like everyone else, virtually everyone else, faced with some legal edict that I think is invalid. I'm going to take my chances."

3RD JUDGE: Well, of course, I think that in the usual case that he should comply with it. If he doesn't, he runs the risk of winding up in jail. It's a practical thing. The courts are thought to move very slowly, but they need not. I can assure you that my court, in an appropriate case, does not. We have heard and decided on appeal one day after the notice was filed. In a situation like this, judges on a court like mine—if they are asked to—can move very, very swiftly.

MR. NESSON: But, Judge, before you rest on that, what you're really saying is—and this echos discussion yesterday—what you're really saying is yes, we admit this is prior restraint on the press but we'll operate very quickly to make sure that it's just a small restraint. Right?

3RD JUDGE: Well, yes . . .

MR. NESSON: Well, let's just stop with the prior restraint and not worry so much about how long it's on. You recall yesterday we were discussing prior restraint in the context of national security, and the test which we all were coming to, or at least working around, was irreparable injury, direct, immediate irreparable injury to the nation or its people. We were talking big stuff, right? We were talking spy systems, we were talking lives, we were talking all sorts of things like that. Now, where is that standard in this context?

3RD JUDGE: I would suppose it's not there in most cases.

MR. NESSON: So, how would you justify prior restraint?

3RD JUDGE: Well, the only concern about this kind of restraint is a fair trial for somebody.

MR. NESSON: Right.

3RD JUDGE: And this is not a very small thing. To the person under indictment it may be a tremendous thing. It may be his life. But it's not of the moment of what we had on yesterday. I don't like gag orders on the press and certainly they're not common as far as I know in my circuit. We don't get them. I don't like them. I think they're wrong. I think, in most instances, if a district judge issued them my court would vacate them. But their problem is one of tradition. I mean, can you have an ordered society if everyone is free to make up his own mind as to whether or not this order is binding on me and I may or may not obey?

MR. NESSON: I grant you that that's a good question, and that's the question that was framed for us at the beginning—can we have an ordered society if people in the face of judicial orders can take their chances on violating.

3RD JUDGE: So if you assume that the district judge is wrong, should the reporter say well the hell with it or should he apply to an appellate judge to be heard in the morning.

MR. NESSON: That's correct, that is the question. I think that the statement of the question doesn't provide an easy answer.

3RD JUDGE: No, it doesn't.

MR. NESSON (Calls on 4th Judge): Judge, if someone appeared before you seeking prior restraint, an injunction against publication in the news media for some item, and they said to you, "We need this injunction because men's lives are going to be lost, battles are going to be lost, and by the way we may have to sequester a jury in a trial down in New Orleans." Would you wonder what that last little bit was in there for? Would it not seem slightly out of proportion to the magnitude of the interests stated at the beginning?

4TH JUDGE: In a way, two things that you recited don't fit together very well. In the way it's put, of course, you haven't made any case at all for any kind of prior restraint or for the sequestration of a jury yet.

MR. NESSON: In other words you would say I will reverse the district judge who imposed an order restraining the press in that circumstance.

4TH JUDGE: Well, I don't know what fact situation you're assuming, because you've stated it very sketchily. But on the fact situation in Case II I wouldn't have issued gag orders as a district judge, and I would set it aside if it came up on appeal.

MR. NESSON: All right.

4TH JUDGE: As to whether it should be obeyed in the meantime . . .

MR. NESSON: That's the question.

4TH JUDGE: I have the same answer as the other judges.

MR. NESSON: In other words, your answer to the question is that the order which provides the liberty for all of us would crumble if the reporter had to take his chances on obeying that, based on its validity.

4TH JUDGE: Sure. Let's go back a few years. How about Governor Faubus at Little Rock taking the same position that the reporter is here. If Governor Faubus had taken the same attitude toward court orders that the reporter is insisting on, why, we'd have had chaos there. The only way they controlled the situation was by the service of court papers. And they were followed. And *Brown v. Board of Education* might as well not have been written if first the district judges weren't going to adhere to the ruling of the high court and then the people in those districts weren't going to follow those orders of the district judge, whether they agreed with them or not. [*Brown v. Board of Education*, 349 U.S. 294 (1954), in which the Supreme Court held that racial discrimination in public schools was unconstitutional.]

1ST REPORTER: Some of them didn't.

4TH JUDGE: Some of them didn't, and there were contempt citations. We've had 20 years of controversy over it. But the whole system, no matter on which side you are on the substantive issues, depends on court orders being followed until they're set aside by higher authority.

MR. NESSON: Court orders in the area of First Amendment speech, restraining the press?

4TH JUDGE: Court orders, right or wrong, under any amendment or under any problem. If they are wrong they will eventually be set aside either by a high court or by the constitutional process and the Congress, et cetera.

MR. NESSON: And the prior restraint imposed on the press in the meantime is the price we pay for ordered liberty.

4TH JUDGE: I think that is right. I agree that our court has acted and can act and in case of prior restraint would act very fast.

MR. NESSON: Now, Judge, we assigned this homework. How is it that you distinguish the judiciary from the run of rules in all other branches of government?

4TH JUDGE: The same way the high court distinguished the judiciary; in the case of the White House tapes, the high court decided that ultimately the high court had to decide. They were the ones to decide the problem of what the law was, not the executive branch. And whether that's right or wrong, I think that's the way the system has stood for 189 years.

1ST TV REPORTER: But if it's wrong, who's going to say?

4TH JUDGE: Well, the people, through what is admittedly a rather cumbersome amendment process, can change a unanimous decision of the Supreme Court.

MR. NESSON (Calls on 5th Judge): Judge, you're familiar with doctrines of overbreadth, chilling effect, special place of the First Amendment, the notion that a statute if it overreaches imposes, creates a chilling effect, takes special steps to avoid it. How does that line up with this doctrine which amounts to prior restraint, especially for invalid, overbroad judicial orders? How can those two things be squared?

5TH JUDGE: I think it's still the same question, the same problem that you presented to the first judge this morning. You're stating reasons why the judge's order may be invalid, if it's overbroad and chilling beyond a necessity— beyond the stark necessities of civilization and all.

MR. NESSON: But let's be clear. The chill comes not so much from the order but from this rule which all of you are prepared to defend—that even an invalid court order should be backed up by criminal contempt sanctions. That's where the chilling effect comes.

5TH JUDGE: I think that that chill can be moderated in certain respects, but basically chill remains. I think it can be moderated by requiring that any punishment for contempt shall be by a different judge than the one who issued the gag order. That's to some extent been the case now that should be pardoned. To some extent it can be moderated by saying that there shall be no punishment except for someone who had the intention of distorting the trial—I forget now how the American Bar Association worded it, but they put in an element of intent. But in the last analysis it seems to me that the only justification that I can make for it is that the independence of the judiciary, which is not as independent as it should be in some states, is both by tradition and by specific provision of some constitutions different from the wayward passions and the wayward motives of the temporary influences of the other—first, second, and fourth— branches of government. And if it doesn't remain true to these traditions it will be displaced. But while it has those traditions it is likely to have a good batting average on avoiding excessive restraints, and with that the rule provides the cement that holds the society together and is a rule that permits all freedoms to operate.

MR. NESSON (Calls on 2nd Reporter): Do you accept the proposition that society would fall apart if this cement were weakened?

2ND REPORTER: No. I don't think that the rule of law, as practiced at the moment, is so perfect that a challenge, a First Amendment challenge—some-body violating a gag rule, for instance—is going to threaten the republic. And can I just say as a practical matter that gag rules, for instance in trials, are generally violated to some extent. The only general order would be that the lawyers in the case are not allowed to talk to reporters. So what happens is that they will talk to reporters but you won't quote them by name. The republic hasn't fallen, and this goes on at every trial.

MR. NESSON (Calls on 3rd Reporter)

3RD REPORTER: I think you might point out one thing to the judges and that is that in no gag order cases that we've had in the last two and a half years has there ever been an instance where the press was given notice that a gag order was going to be issued; has the press been given a hearing or an opportun-ity to appeal before the gag order went into effect. We can't find any other seg-ment of the population that's repeatedly subjected to *ex-parte* orders which we think should fringe on a fundamental constitutional right. You were talking about the cement that keeps society together. We think that due process and a hearing is one of the cements that keeps society going, and we appear to be the only segment of society which is denied that right.

MR. NESSON: You're really raising a due process issue as independent of the validity of the order. You're saying there should be at least a procedural prerequisite to the issuance of the order, an opportunity to be heard and so forth and so on. All right, I recognize that issue but I'd really like to stay for the moment with the substantive issue. The question I'm asking is what happens if reporters go around violating these orders. What's the worst that happens?

6TH JUDGE (Speaks up): Well, in a specific case the worst that happens is that you get a pollution of a right of every defendant or of any litigant in a civil case to the fair administration of justice.

MR. NESSON: In a specific case.

6TH JUDGE: In a specific case. And speaking more generally I agree, I would say wholeheartedly, with every one of the federal judges who've spoken, that what you have is anarchy. You don't have freedom. The same principle would be involved if the racial bigots, the white mothers in Boston, just decided they weren't going to obey that court order up there having to do with desegregation of the schools and thought that they were free because of their moral and philosophical beliefs to throw stones at the Negro children being brought to those schools, or to dynamite the buses. The same principle is involved if the president of the United States last July had said I'm not going to bother obeying the decree of the Supreme Court of the United States because I know better. That's the principle that's involved here. It's clear to me. I think what would happen is you'd have a breakdown of the political and social structure of a free society.

MR. NESSON: Well, we certainly couldn't have had a clearer statement from more judges of the proposition of that issue, could we? (Recognizes 1st Lawyer)

1ST LAWYER: Well, I think that the remarks that were just made do not distinguish between speech and action. I think if you start off with a premise that the first judge started off with this morning, the conclusion automatically follows from everything that's said around the table. But if you start off from a different premise, to wit that one of the values that society has adopted for a principle of order is that there shan't be prior restraints, it seems to me perhaps you come out at a different end.

MR. NESSON (Recognizes 2nd Lawyer)

2ND LAWYER: It seems to me if you accept the judge's decision then he has some obligation to provide a summary method of having the order reviewed within, say, 24 hours. When the federal judge entered the broad gag order in the Gainesville Eight trial, an immediate appeal was taken to the fifth circuit following Dickinson's suggestion. The court modified the orders related to sketching in the courtroom and sat on the rest of the appeal for a year. Long after the trial was over they then dismissed the appeal on the ground that it was moot. That's the rapid remedy outlined in Dickinson by the Fifth Circuit.

1ST TV REPORTER: There have been analogies drawn with Governor Faubus, President Nixon, what he might have done. Is there any validity to raising the question of the difference between defiance of a court order by an official using responsibilities entrusted to him and abusing those powers, as opposed to an individual who is trying to exercise his own liberties. Is there any distinction there?

1ST JUDGE: Well, you are the fourth branch of government, are you not?

1ST EDITOR: We're not.

MR. NESSON (Recognizes 2nd Editor)

2ND EDITOR: Is there any mechanism in law for a judge to ask a higher court first for permission to institute a gag order and then either receive it or not receive it, rather than turning it around the way it is now?

MR. NESSON: Practically speaking I would say no. It is possible under some circumstances to certify a question but that's not something you're going to get it back in 24 hours. (Asks the conferees): Let me just ask this. Am I completely off base in asking the question that forms itself in my mind as I listen to the discussion? You describe a breakdown of order, true. You describe a break up of school integration in Boston or any place else, or massive violations by the president. You describe, in fact, an ultimate confrontation between the force of law and the force of anarchy. But the question I'm trying to pose is on a much smaller scale, much, much smaller scale. I'm talking about a little reporter down in New Orleans who has a gag order imposed on him which he swears up and down is invalid. And he says to himself, "I know if I'm wrong I risk criminal contempt. I'm not going to oppose law to the point where I'm going to go to war with the system ultimately. If I'm proved wrong in the Fifth Circuit, or in the Supreme Court, I'm going to wind up in the can. But I'm ready to stake my reputation and my judgment and my freedom on the fact that this order is invalid." Now, most of the people around this table are fairly sensible. They're not going to make that judgment, take that chance with their liberty unless they've been advised by their lawyer. They're not going to take that chance without consulting with their editors. They're going to be very conservative about it. And, in fact, in a remarkable number of the gag order cases, just the results we've heard around the table here from judges have proved to be true. On appeal the gag order is thrown out as invalid. To wit, a judgment by the appellate court that yes, we would have all been better off if we didn't have this gag order in the first place so where has order fallen apart if that reporter violates that order.

6TH JUDGE: Well, in the legal system it means once such a gag order has been set aside by the court of appeals for the Fifth Circuit, or the Fourth Circuit, or the Sixth Circuit, or ultimately perhaps for the nation by the Supreme Court it means that that is settled. Then you have a guideline and a district judge won't ever do it again. But the fact that this is a little person doesn't impress me at all. You know as well as I do, Professor, that some of the great principles of law, of constitutional law, have been initiated by the plight or the predicament of little people, be it Clarence Gideon or some of those Jehovah's Witnesses back in the 1930s. Without them we wouldn't have some of those great constitutional principles that we had. Moreover, let me say a word or two, generally. I was amazed and if I may say so I was shocked yesterday to detect—and it didn't take a detective to detect this—the animosity, the hostility, the suspicion, the resentment, the dislike, and indeed the fear of courts among reporters and the publishers here. Where, ladies and gentlemen, do you think these great constitutional rights that you were so vehemently asserting, and in which you were so conspicuously wallowing yesterday, where do you think they came from? The stork didn't bring them. These came from the judges of this country, from these villains here sitting at the table. That's where they came from. They came because at some time or place, when some other agency of government was trying to push the press around or indeed maybe trying to do you in, it was the courts of this country that protected you. And that's where all these constitutional rights came from. You may say, well, we weren't talking about judges like you, we were talking about these state court judges.

1ST TV REPORTER: No, I'm just saying what have you done for us lately?

(Laughter)

6TH JUDGE: Something was done for you last week, and it's not that it was done for you, or that it was done for ourselves. It happened because it's our understanding that that's what the Constitution provides and protects. [*Cox Broadcasting Corp. v. Cohn,* 420 U.S. 469 (1975), in which the Supreme Court held that newspapers have a First Amendment right to publish the identities of rape victims once their names appear on public records.] But, let me point out that the Constitution of the United States is not a self-executing document, and my friend here who's an absolutist—he may be an absolutist but he's not—what was the word the former president used to use—he's not a literalist. Because if you look at the literal language in the First Amendment of the Constitution of the United States it says "Congress shall pass no law abridging the freedom of the press." That's all it says on this subject, absolutely all. It doesn't say a word about what a state can do or can't do. It doesn't say a word about a reporter's privilege before a grand jury. It doesn't say a word about most of the problems that we've been discussing yesterday and this morning. The very fact that these protections are available is attributable to the creative work of the judiciary over the last 190 years. If you say it's self-evident, that this was always clear, let me tell you it wasn't always so clear. If you went back to the original understanding of our ancestors, back in the early years of the nineteenth century, you would find that their understanding of this clause and the Constitution in their judgment allowed them to enact something called the Alien and Sedition law. And if those laws were still on the books Richard Nixon would still be president of the United States, Spiro Agnew would still be vice-president of the United States, and all of you people would probably be in prison.

MR. NESSON (Turns to 1st Editor): What do you think of that?

1ST EDITOR: I've not in my body felt that I represent the hostilities to the whole judiciary system. But besides that, I feel that all the judges together have expressed an absolutist position as to their powers and their status matching the reporter's absolutist position on the First Amendment enunciated yesterday.

I would only say to all you judges, fine, you have all your absolutist powers, why don't you let us have the same sort of absolutism in the area of the press. We can make this very same argument that the vitality of this society is also dependent upon the behavior of a free press, and a press that was jailed by judges, a press that has been intimidated or has been faced with intimidation, with all these forces of the establishment facing them, I think many, many aspects of society contribute to our democracy and I don't think the press is found terribly wanting in that.

MR. NESSON: Well, pardon me if I stay at my mundane level. (Turns back to 6th Judge): Why is it absolutist for a reporter to say, "Jail me if I'm wrong, but please don't enforce your invalid orders against me by criminal contempt sanctions." Why is that absolutist?

6TH JUDGE: It's just as absolute as a person who wanted to shoot and kill his enemy would say, "Send me to prison for the rest of my life if I'm wrong. But I simply don't believe in your law against murder."

MR. NESSON: In other words, you are rejecting across the board Holmes' bad-man theory of the law, the notion that someone should regard the law simply as an operational framework out there that may impose sanctions on him if he gets caught breaking rules, saying I can do whatever I can get away with. And that notion is rejection of the rule of law. That's basically the proposition you're putting.

6TH JUDGE: And you say I'm rejecting that or . . .

MR. NESSON: No, it seems to me you're embracing that.

6TH JUDGE: Well, then, okay.

MR. NESSON: Why don't you put people in jail for violating invalid executive laws?

6TH JUDGE: Such as? I don't understand.

MR. NESSON: Let's suppose that we have a law that says it shall be a felony for three people to gather on the street corner, and a fellow named Shuttlesworth comes walking into town, sees this law, perfectly clear what his notices are, I mean there's no doubt in his mind whatsoever about the law. And he walks out on that street corner and he sits there with three people. The cops come along, they arrest him. Now, we have no doubt that Shuttlesworth shouldn't be put in jail because it's an invalid law. You're not going to say that this statute is unconstitutional, but he knew it was on the books and therefore he should serve his 30 days. You're not going to say that. Now, why isn't that exactly the same situation? [See *Shuttlesworth v. City of Birmingham*, 394 U.S. 147 (1969), in which the Supreme Court held that an individual who demonstrated in violation of an unconstitutional parade ordinance could not be punished.]

6TH JUDGE: Well, there are stays, he would have served his 30 days had he not gotten a stay, and there are all sorts of flexible procedures available. The speeding up of the process, the stays of execution of a law pending its appellate review. There are all sorts of procedures. He should never have been arrested in the first place. That was an invalid law. But it was decided through the orderly procedure of the judicial process and it's something which in my parochial way as a lawyer and a judge I believe with all of the conviction that I have.

MR. NESSON: All right, so here we have two cases. Case number one, Shuttlesworth gets himself arrested, sentenced to 30 days, stay pending appeal. A year later the case reaches the high court, which says the statute is invalid, discharge Shuttlesworth. Case number two, . . .

6TH JUDGE: And let me add that from then on there will be no more Shuttlesworths who are arrested under that law. That law's been declared invalid.

MR. NESSON: We hope. We don't know about that.

6TH JUDGE: We know that, that's our system.

MR. NESSON: That's at least not within the record of this case. Okay, case number two, Dickinson goes to court and he has an order which he has full notice of, which he violates, and he's sentenced for 30 days in jail for criminal contempt for violating that order. Stayed pending appeal. The case goes up to the Supreme Court, let us say, and it says that order is invalid, it was an overbroad gag order imposed by the district judge. But since this was an order of a judge rather than a legislature, Dickinson will serve his 30 days in jail. How do you distinguish those two cases?

6TH JUDGE: Well, the answer's already been given here this morning, and maybe it's a very selfish, arrogant answer. But the fact is that in our system it is the judiciary that has been entrusted with the administration of the law, be it common law, statutory law, or constitutional law. And it was first said by John Marshall [*Marbury v. Madison*, 1 Cranch 137 (1803)], it was more recently said last July quoting John Marshall, Chief Justice Marshall, in an opinion about court in a very important case. [*United States v. Nixon*, 418 U.S. 702 (1974).] And for better or for worse this is our system.

2ND LAWYER: May I ask a question? Suppose you have the Shuttlesworth decision and another exact case comes along, and a district judge, regardless of your decision, puts the guy in jail?

6TH JUDGE: Well, this is a state court conviction.

2ND LAWYER: All right, another one.

6TH JUDGE: And if it's a state court conviction, if the exactly identical case comes along, the only difference is the man this time isn't named Shuttlesworth, it's Thompson. Within an hour he can go to a federal district court and be released under the rule of a Shuttlesworth case.

1ST JUDGE (Addresses 6th Judge): May I quarrel with the premise of the question as you put it? You assumed in the premise that there never is a case in which a person who violates an unconstitutional law may be justly punished. But that is not true. If a law is passed in time of war, which requires that you shall obey an emergency price control order, whether valid or invalid, and you violate that order, you may be punished even though the order is subsequently held to be unconstitutional: *Yakus v. the United States* [321 U.S. 414 (1943)]. The reason is that if the society is imperiled, an order which is invalid must be obeyed, even though the order be unconstitutional.

What is clear enough in war is indeed what exists with respect to the total problem absent of war because a society will be anarchic if there is not somewhere a final authority. Now it may be that the courts ought not to have that final authority, but it has been pointed out that the tradition is that way and if the people of the United States don't want it that way they may amend the Constitution. But unless we do not believe in constitutional liberty, we must preserve the courts until the Constitution is amended.

MR. NESSON: Why?

1ST JUDGE: Because as I said at the beginning, liberty is indefinable except in terms of limits.

MR. NESSON: I have a different question, Judge. Why do you think, as the other judges apparently think, that this problem is such a fundamental challenge to the integrity of the court system? I understand the proposition you make about Yakus. If, in fact, the order of society will somehow crumble, if we have a problem of the dimension of irreparable injury to our nation or its people, something of large dimension, sure, fine. That's the situation that would justify a prior restraint. But why do you and the other judges think that a reporter who says I will go to jail if I'm wrong is as fundamental? He's not challenging the system, he's not challenging your authority to make a judgment. He just wants to take a chance on his proposition that you were wrong, Mr. District Judge, and that the court of appeals will say so. Now, why is that a fundamental challenge to the system?

1ST JUDGE: Well, the reason I think it's fundamental is that under our system if there should be an exception with respect to the press, and I do not say whether there should or not, then the exception could be created legislatively. I quite agree with what was stated earlier that there are many types of restrictions which ought legislatively to be imposed upon the judiciary, with respect to its exercise and power in this class of case. But the appeal by the press should be to the Congress for legislation specifically limiting, defining the authority of the trial judge, or any other judge, with respect to press cases. I would be all in favor of that, and that would be an example of constitutional limiting.

6TH JUDGE: Well, maybe with respect to the contempt power generally.

1ST JUDGE: Yes.

MR. NESSON (Recognizes 2nd TV Reporter)

2ND TV REPORTER: It seems to me that what we're becoming aware of here is how insecure the press is—and how aware we are of the fragility of the First Amendment. And how aware the judiciary is of the fragile nature of their powers. I think there is an inability or unwillingness of a judge to see the difference between throwing rocks at U.S. marshals or school buses and someone printing words when the First Amendment is there already, and I don't think we need legislation. It seems to me that that reflects an awareness, perhaps an over-awareness, by the judiciary that their powers are quite fragile and it depends on habit that you obey judges' orders, a tradition. But I don't think that tradition would be shattered if the judiciary looked at the First Amendment and recognized that there's a difference in words and violence.

MR. NESSON (Recognizes 1st Gov't. Official)

1ST GOV'T. OFFICIAL: I would suggest as a layman who may be out of his depth here that the discussion thus far has missed a central distinction between the case of Shuttlesworth and Dickinson. That is, it's true that they are only words. As my colleague here has said, we're not talking about stones except that the press is able to harm with those words these liberties of the third person. That's a very practical test that Shuttlesworth doesn't raise. And if the press is serious about this responsibility they have as a fourth branch of government, as a party to continuance of liberties, then I should have thought that they'd be aware that there is this kind of distinction that they can be held in a way that Shuttlesworth can't because their words can harm the third parties, the people who are at trial, and so on.

MR. NESSON: Now what harm do you see?

1ST GOV'T. OFFICIAL: The harm that if passions are inflamed or that information which is later proved to be untrue creates a climate of prejudice or otherwise endangers fair trial.

3RD EDITOR: Why should the press be stopped from doing that when government is not stopped, in any sense. Some of the most inflammatory language of the last ten years has been issued by government. I'm thinking of the war in Vietnam.

1ST GOV'T. OFFICIAL: Well, but the press printed it, the media carried it. So the question is . . .

3RD EDITOR: We're talking about what happens if we violate a gag order which all judges here have said is probably invalid in the first place. Why—under what conditions—is a gag order ever justified?

MR. NESSON: Exactly my next question. Would you answer it for me?

3RD EDITOR: Yes, I don't think any. I don't think any. And in the fair trial thing . . .

MR. NESSON: Let's go through . . .

1ST GOV'T. OFFICIAL: Now, does this include grand jury secrecy that you're referring to?

3RD EDITOR: I'll make it that broad if you like.

1ST GOV'T OFFICIAL: Is there that difference?

MR. NESSON: Let's go through it with our problem here. We have a grand jury, and you're a reporter, and the question that you pose yourself and others, is what are the legitimate aspects of secrecy, what are the legitimate possibilities for a gag order. Now, do you have any problem with the gag order on the grand jury themselves? A direction by a judge to the grand jurors that they will not disclose matters which they hear before the grand jury?

3RD EDITOR: There are circumstances under which I have great problems.

MR. NESSON: To wit?

3RD EDITOR: Corruption of the grand jury process, as is suggested in this case.

MR. NESSON: And how would you formulate your instruction to the jurors of that grand jury, were you the judge?

3RD EDITOR: Well, I suspect I might abolish the grand jury system as one way. But failing that I suspect I'd leave the rules of criminal procedure as is. But I would be perfectly willing under the circumstances where there was evidence that the grand jury investigation itself was a fraud, that it had been corruptly perverted, I think under these circumstances at least I would be willing to urge journalists to get into this process.

MR. NESSON: So you say jurists can have a gag order imposed on them, qualification—corruption. How about members of the U.S. attorney's office? Can a judge say to them, "Look you fellows are appearing before this grand jury presenting cases, I don't want a word out of you or anyone in your office and if you do, it's your ass."

3RD EDITOR: As a U.S. attorney, I feel uncomfortable about that. Things don't work out that way. The U.S. attorney is going to tell the press exactly what he wants to tell the press for his own purposes, to get an indictment, to avoid an indictment. Whether or not Judge Sirica or any judge places a gag order, they're going to talk. They may urge the reporter, in fact insist that the reporter not identify them, but there was a gag order throughout the Sirica trial. I'm not sure that it slowed the republic up a hell of a lot but I don't see why it was necessary.

1ST PROSECUTOR: I couldn't disagree more. There's a presumption again here of irregularity that I think governs your approach to what the prosecutor feels he can do and should do. As a prosecutor I will insist as long as I have some breath left that we have no business revealing secrets of grand juries or of making the kinds of admissions to you—background or any other basis . . .

3RD EDITOR: Well that's a purely administrative decision on your part. You don't want the court to force you not to or to . . .

1ST PROSECUTOR: The only way you can have it uniform is if the court has a rule that says you can't do it.

3RD EDITOR: Why, I don't accept that.

MR. NESSON (Asks Prosecutor): If you were to find that one of your assistants had talked to a reporter off the record, what would you do with him?

1ST PROSECUTOR: Fire him.

MR. NESSON: Would you report him to the judge and recommend that he be held in criminal contempt? You're a prosecutor after all.

1ST PROSECUTOR: I think I probably would, I feel so strongly about this.

3RD EDITOR: Then there isn't going to be a prosecution staff left in the country.

1ST PROSECUTOR: The distinction clearly is whether the prosecutor has violated some secret of the grand jury as opposed to saying something innocuous about when the grand jury is going to next meet. But assuming that he does, the prosecutor revealed testimony that was introduced before the grand jury, then that assistant should be fired and he should be cited for contempt.

1ST TV REPORTER: Can I say something, even though it will probably subject me to attack and challenge, yet I feel that it has to be said. We're in a new era today and it's very painful to recognize what that new era is. There are constant references, some of them rather scoffing and derisive references to the press as a fourth branch of government. Whenever that's said somehow it seems to be said sneeringly for some reason, implying that if there are responsibilities involved we should be accepting those responsibilities. But I think it can be stated objectively as one of the phenomena of our times that the importance of the news media today is so great that practically nobody can operate without reference to it one way or another. You cannot get legislation through unless you have public support and even courts and U.S. attorneys are beginning to find that they must somehow try as everyone does to manipulate public opinion through the media. This pristine position of "We have nothing to do with you because we're going through a process of our own," doesn't quite work anymore. You will find Judge Sirica coming out on his lawn and chatting in front of cameras today in a way that judges never used to do. You will find U.S. attorneys, for their own purposes, being willing and sometimes very anxious, on, off, for background or whatever to get a point of view across because the success of their endeavors today will partly depend on public recognition of what they're doing and why they're doing it. Therefore, there has developed a kind of symbiosis today between the news media, which is not formally recognized but has begun to exist. Having said that, let me say that I can understand, using an analogy of our discussion yesterday of S-1, what the courts are trying to do about the court system, about grand juries, yes about prosecutors. If they issue orders to try to maintain their secrets, I can understand it; as long as they don't issue orders that include us. If the government has secrets, the government should try to keep those secrets and maintain its security. When S-1 writes orders that say that once the thing is out that we can be prosecuted because we received it, at that point you have lost me and you have me unalterably against you whereas in the other I'm willing to consider and negotiate with you about your problems. But if the courts say that there are penalities on a grand juror for revealing grand jury secrets, I understand it. I understand the principle of the grand jury system and why it is important to maintain it in a certain way. I would say as a very minimum, you maintain your secrecy by getting your people to keep the secret that you've entrusted them with. When you issue an order against us, you've conceded your failure to maintain your system and you've tried to extend it against us and then I will not accept it.

MR. NESSON: That raises a very interesting question, at least for me. Let me put it to our second reporter. You've talked now to the assistant in the office. The prosecutor has said that he will prosecute that fellow. You know that he has violated the court order. Do you give any consideration to reporting him?

2ND REPORTER: You mean would I consider going and reporting that a prosecutor has spoken to me in violation of a gag ruling?

MR. NESSON: Yes, telling the prosecutor so that this man will be prosecuted so that that order will not be violated?

2ND REPORTER: Certainly not.

MR. NESSON: Absolutely not. Let me put it around the other way. How do you articulate your duties as a citizen and as a reporter so that you don't have an obligation to report a crime which happened in your presence; to wit, criminal contempt of court by the prosecutor's assistant engaged in with you and I would assume unsolicited by you completely?

2ND REPORTER: Well, that's not necessarily a valid assumption. First of all, what's the harm. I don't see that there's been any major violation. The gag order was unnecessary in the first place. I'll get back to my point. As far as a gag order on prosecutors imposed by a judge, it should not be necessary. The prosecutor's duty includes refraining from making any kind of comments which are going to prejudice anybody. The prosecutor should not need a judge to tell him to be quiet and to not . . .

MR. NESSON: You're talking about his duties. I want your duties. Is it your duty to make a judgment yourself as to whether the criminal action you witnessed was really bad or not and if it's really bad, report it? But if it's really not and you think the statute is silly . . .

2ND REPORTER: Are you talking about reported in a news story or reported to him?

MR. NESSON: Reported to him.

2ND REPORTER: Well, I'm not a criminal investigator. I'm not a member of the police or that branch of the government.

MR. NESSON: You are a citizen of the United States are you not, and you see a crime committed. Now you think that because you're a reporter you have no duties to report crimes?

2ND REPORTER: Well, if it were a crime in the sense of the prosecutor just leaking information for his or her own purposes I can see writing a story about that. If I go and ask the question of a prosecutor in an effort to find out information for a story I'm writing, then it would be somewhat hypocritical for me to report it.

MR. NESSON: Let me put a case to you that someone put to me last night which I found very troublesome. Let's take this issue and move it into a context where it's a lot more sympathetic to reporting a crime. Let's suppose you're an investigative reporter and instead of investigating a grand jury situation you're investigating a fellow who you suspect is a pusher of heroin at a local high school, okay? You get your story to a point where you're sure in your own mind that this fellow really is pushing but you haven't got it locked in to the point where you can go with it in print so you're ready to drop it, move on to a new territory. Do you have an obligation to report that to a prosecutor, let him use his subpoena power to see if he can make the case which you couldn't make?

2ND REPORTER: I don't think I would have an obligation, no.

1ST REPORTER: I think you would. I have done this. I think a number of reporters in this room in pursuing things in the Watergate area, in particular, have sometimes gone as far as they could go in trying to investigate a crime. That doesn't need to be there but that's personal experience and a number of them, at the point where they could not break the story, have told the prosecutor's office what they had. The only quid pro quo one hoped for was that if something eventually came of it, we at least wouldn't be second in knowing about it. I've done that without any worry about it.

2ND REPORTER: That's one way of getting your information for your story. You're making a trade.

1ST REPORTER: That operates with the pusher in the high school too, doesn't it.

2ND REPORTER: Yes, but you're not acting because you feel an obligation. You're acting because you want to get the story.

1ST REPORTER: Well, I think I've got a little of the other feeling too.

4TH REPORTER: In the reporting process many times we're doing the same kinds of things that criminal investigators will be doing. Our job is not the same. That is part of what the Caldwell case was all about. [*Branzburg v. Hayes*, 408 U.S. 665 (1972), in which the Supreme Court held that a reporter under subpoena was constitutionally required to appear before a grand jury and testify about criminal conduct he witnessed.] The reporter does not have the obligation to be an extension of the prosecutor's office in his attempt to find a story.

MR. NESSON: That may be what it was about for you.

4TH REPORTER: Okay.

MR. NESSON: I don't think that's what it said.

4TH REPORTER: That's what it was about for us and that's what we took it as.

MR. NESSON: As I recall, you didn't win that case. (Challenges 3rd Reporter): Would you turn that information over to the prosecutor?

3RD REPORTER: The example you posed is a difficult example. I mean it's a difficult example in one way and I don't think you can lay down a general rule for everybody. One reporter may feel one way, another may feel a different way. I think the way most reporters feel is that if they get the information or if they're given access to the information because they're a member of the press that that information belongs to their papers and to themselves as reporters and that they are not under an obligation to turn it over to the law enforcement people.

MR. NESSON: Then we really need to turn the question.

3RD REPORTER: Otherwise, everytime a reporter showed up trying to do an investigative story, the people would say, oh well, you know, we know what's going to happen with this. You're just going to run right down to the local FBI office.

MR. NESSON (Turns to 4th Editor): Our last reporter here says it's up to the editors, property of the paper, you decide.

4TH EDITOR: It's a difficult problem. I think that if you're in the field of information, criminal procedures are anathema to the peoples' right to know and this is a function you're trying to serve. I personally would not let a reporter on my staff violate a gag order. I tend regretfully to side with the judges this morning, largely because I do think—as I talked yesterday on the one side of protracted litigation having a chilling effect—that a widespread abuse or contempt of the law hurts the judiciary beyond the point I'd like to see it hurt. That's the basis for my decision.

MR. NESSON: Well, how about this case of our pusher at the high school? When you find the information of the commission of a crime, and here we're talking about a crime which we can all agree is a heinous one. We're not talking about a gag order in which we all may have some doubts. Is it a reporter's or a paper's obligation to cooperate with the prosecution?

4TH EDITOR: To cooperate or to report it?

MR. NESSON: Turn the information over to the prosecutor or the grand jury?

4TH EDITOR: In the case that you cite I'd say yes, he ought to turn it over.

MR. NESSON (Recognizes 1st Judge)

1ST JUDGE: I think you're starting from an erroneous conception of a citizen's duty and you're going back to old notions of misprision of felony. I do not believe that it is a citizen's duty to report every crime he observes. If I observe adultery surely I am not under any obligation to report it. Moreover, unlike the medieval view, a citizen's duty to report a crime is limited to the most serious crimes, that is, murder. You and I and everyone else observe any number of crimes from traffic crimes on up and it is not our civic duty to report those crimes which are of minor consequence. Each of us exercises independence of judgment with respect to that, whether we admit it or not. It's quite natural that the press, taking into account its view of this particular crime, does not feel a responsibility to report it as a citizen. I don't criticize them for that even though your premise assumes that it is an error on their part.

3RD LAWYER: What about Section 4 of the Criminal Code, at least from the federal standpoint, which codifies the old common law concept of misprision of a felony. [18 U.S.C. sec. 4 provides in part: "whoever, having knowledge of a felony . . . conceals and does not as soon as possible make known the same . . . shall be fined not more than $500 or imprisoned not more than three years, or both."]

1ST JUDGE: I think you haven't read the cases under that section.

3RD LAWYER: Well, there are very few but the statute's on the book, Judge.

1ST JUDGE: You're under no obligation . . .

3RD LAWYER: Well, it talked in terms of actual knowledge of a felony as I recall.

1ST JUDGE: Yes, but it means something more than that under the cases.

MR. NESSON (Calls on 2nd Gov't. Official): Do you have a view?

2ND GOV'T. OFFICIAL: Yes. This is a very serious crime and I'm a little astounded that the press would think that they may ignore the obligation to other people it has since I don't see how it harms the press in any way. If you talk to somebody and he realizes you're going to print if you get the story, then he's already got an inhibition against talking to you. I don't see why he's more inhibited if he realizes if you don't get the story . . .

1ST EDITOR: The example is very easy for the press because we don't use the pejorative phrase, "Turn over the information." When a reporter is stymied and isn't going any further, he would as a matter of his professional responsibility go to the authorities to ask them what they've got about it. When he does that he has, in effect, alerted the authorities to the information he has but he has done this in countenance with his professional responsibilities.

2ND GOV'T. OFFICIAL: Well, we've had that. A couple of times the press has said they don't do things and you begin to examine how it actually works, they in fact do it.

1ST EDITOR: It's not a matter of turning over; stay away from that phrase.

2ND GOV'T. OFFICIAL: But the prosecution gets it.

1ST EDITOR: Right.

MR. NESSON (Recognizes 1st Reporter)

1ST REPORTER: You get a situation where you're not investigating it. You send a reporter out with a president on a trip and he is working for you 12 hours a day and he is somewhere and he observes a purse snatching. Now, if the time situation is such that it isn't going to take him away from covering the president's speech, would you not have him report to the local authorities?

1ST EDITOR: Of course.

1ST REPORTER: You would?

1ST EDITOR: Yes.

1ST REPORTER: Okay, but that's not because he's been stymied in his investigation.

1ST TV REPORTER: That's not the problem.

MR. NESSON: For some people it is.

5TH EDITOR: Well, I was just going to say that we do report things like threats of murders and threats of bombings and things like that routinely that are treated in that kind of serious category of where if we didn't do our citizen's duty and step in, somebody would be harmed. We're back to the difference between harm and no harm again. I was going to ask some of the lawyers how often they observe or have knowledge of felonies that go unreported to the court, as a matter of fact, and they're officers of the court.

3RD EDITOR: It's an interesting point. I'd like to hear an answer to that.

1ST TV REPORTER: It's kind of an evasion of the issue to say that in the course of your investigation, if you require the cooperation of either the prosecutor or some other authority, you may want to share information with him. I think that the issue you raised should be met head on. To go back to the principles that did not prevail when argued in the Caldwell case, the principle sees the press as having a certain function of trying to provide illumination for the public on general problems—social, political. In order to be able to do that they must have access. They must have access to people who will trust that they are giving them information for the purpose of general illumination and not for the purpose of getting individuals into trouble with the law. If that purpose is compromised in any way, it makes the press a lot less effective in being able to shed another kind of a light on some of these problems. That is what was involved in the Caldwell case and it is unfortunate that the courts did not recognize it. Maybe someday that will end up in a book by Alan Barth as one of the historic cases where the court eventually reversed itself. [Alan Barth authored the book *Prophets With Honor.*] Now, I distinguish between myself as a citizen and myself when I am professionally engaged. On a day when I witness a serious crime because I happen to be going down the street, I have no hesitation in reporting that. If I come across evidence of illegality in the course of my journalistic profession and if I think it will compromise my effectiveness as a journalist to report that, then I will not report that. If I do, in the course of trading information, try to find out whether the prosecutor knows more than I do about something and he says thanks for your tip, would you serve as a witness, I will not serve as a witness because I will do as a citizen those things which happen to come to my attention as a citizen, but if it compromises my ability to bring another light to bear for the public, I don't want to compromise that ability and that I think is the issue.

MR. NESSON: So you state a principle that guides your actions. You said for yourself, a principle which says on the one hand you will respect court orders, silence orders, gag orders as long as they don't extend to the press. Let them take care of their own, God bless them, the grand jurors, the U.S.

attorneys, the stenographers but keep off of you, and you say you will respect at least what one official here would conceive your duties as a citizen to be, at least to a point where it doesn't seriously compromise yourself as a reporter. All right, so there's a line that's being drawn there.

1ST TV REPORTER: I'm trying.

MR. NESSON: Okay. Now let me press the line just a little bit. In the course of investigating a story, what actions will you take? Suppose you're Mr. Harris here. What actions would you take to find out what was going on inside this grand jury?

1ST TV REPORTER: Am I speaking under a grant of immunity?

MR. NESSON: Totally, transactional.

1ST TV REPORTER: If I meet a grand juror, I'll ask him, I'll test him.

MR. NESSON: If you meet a grand juror. You're just walking down the street and happen to come across a grand juror.

VOICE: When was the last time you did that?

1ST TV REPORTER: I have not personally been in the position but I know those who have tried to obtain information from grand jurors. To help you make your point, let me say theoretically that if I had opportunity to speak to a grand juror, I would ask him a question designed to elicit the information that I wanted and leave it to him to make his judgment.

MR. NESSON: Would you seek out the opportunity?

1ST TV REPORTER: Yes.

MR. NESSON: Would you call him on the phone?

1ST TV REPORTER: I might, yes.

MR. NESSON: Would you visit him at his house?

1ST TV REPORTER: Yes. This is theoretical because I think your point should be made so I'll answer those questions all yes.

MR. NESSON: So let's make it as concrete as possible. You've just come to my house. I'm a grand juror on this case. I open the door and there you are. I say, "Gee you look familiar. Are you the famous TV reporter?" And you say "yes." Then what do you say?

1ST TV REPORTER: I'm interested in what's going on in this Watergate or whatever the case is. Normally, I would not ask a wide-open question as to what's happening. My habit is to try to have enough background to be a little specific and to say, "I understand that you had so and so forth before you. Did he shed much light on this or is he a target before you or just a witness." I mean, I'd ask him fairly specific questions.

MR. NESSON: All right, well let's take that. Suppose that you have spoken to an assistant in the prosecutor's office and you've got a little information. He says it's off-the-record; quotes those magic words, and his statement is that Mr. Smith has appeared before the grand jury and has implicated Squires. That's what you've heard. Now, how do you use that information?

1ST TV REPORTER: First of all, I'm having it only from one source. I have to worry about whether I'm sure it is true because I don't know the motive of the informant in telling me. I want to be sure it's true so there's an additional reason to try to get it from somebody else, including, if possible, a grand juror.

MR. NESSON: Okay. Now you've just opened the door and that's the information you've got. How do you proceed?

1ST TV REPORTER: I say that I hear that this and this has happened and he says, "Well, I shouldn't be talking to you but do come in. I don't want you standing at the door, that's even worse. All right, if you know that much I guess there's not much harm in telling you, yes that is true, that's the way it happened."

MR. NESSON: So I'm not a great student of this but if the record comes to you off-the-record, that means you can use it but you can't print it, you have to verify it from another source?

1ST TV REPORTER: No, there are all kinds of off-the-record and that is a phrase that has been corrupted in the course of time. It usually means keep me out of it. That is what it is intended to mean. Off-the-record should mean this is information which you can under no circumstance use. It is hardly ever really meant that way anymore. I don't accept information on the whole as being really utterly off-the-record but I'll be very discreet and I will protect you. That usually is enough. Then being in a position to say that I have other sources, I'm in a position to protect the original informant and yes, I go with it.

MR. NESSON: Would you ever think of mentioning this fellow's name, this grand juror . . .

1ST TV REPORTER: No.

MR. NESSON: . . . just as a way of prodding him a little bit?

1ST TV REPORTER: You mean in my story?

MR. NESSON: No, to the grand juror, not your printed story. Would you ever say, George Jones, the prosecutor's assistant, mentioned to me that such and such?

1ST TV REPORTER: No. That creates trouble for him if the grand juror goes and informs the principal U.S. attorney about something. I can't do that. I mean you're talking now about protection of sources.

2ND GOV'T. OFFICIAL: Mr. Nesson, can we find out what the rationale or distinction is. (Addresses TV Reporter): You apparently accept the fact that grand jury information should not get out and, therefore, it's proper for a judge to issue a gag order.

1ST TV REPORTER: I accept the fact that the judge has a right to keep it from getting out if he can.

2ND GOV'T. OFFICIAL: Well, if we think it should not get out, why is it all right . . .

1ST TV REPORTER: You're repeating it in your words again.

2ND GOV'T OFFICIAL: Well, if you think that it's all right for the judge to order the grand jury not to put the information out that must be a judgment of some kind. We think it's best that it not get out. And if that's true then why is it improper to keep it out by giving an order to the press?

1ST TV REPORTER: Because if it is possible by asking the grand juror to get the information then that system isn't working.

2ND GOV'T. OFFICIAL: I know and you're breaking it down and why isn't it possible to plug the leak?

1ST TV REPORTER: It is broken down.

MR. NESSON: It would work better, of course, if you didn't come to the door and ask the question.

1ST TV REPORTER: It wouldn't really be working better. It would only be that the vulnerability of the system is less visible for the moment that's all.

MR. NESSON (Turns to 4th Judge): Judge, what do you think about this reporter's activities?

4TH JUDGE: I want to correct a misapprehension that has been the basis of our discussion for about 25 minutes. I know that Professor Nesson is aware of this and I thought he was going to bring it up. But the prohibition against a juror as distinct from the reporter disclosing grand jury information is not a gag order of any individual judge. The prohibition on the juror and the U.S. attorney who appears in the grand jury room is in Rule 6 of the Rules of Criminal Procedure, which has been in effect for at least 25 years in the present form and had its predecessor for many years before. It plainly says that a juror, an attorney, may disclose matters occurring before the grand jury only when so directed by the court in connection with the judicial proceeding. Then it also goes on, which may have some bearing on gag orders it seems, to state that no obligation of secrecy may be imposed upon any person except in accordance with this rule. So when the juror reveals anything to the reporter, he's violated Rule 6 and he's subject to puninshment for contempt by the judge, if the judge finds out about it. No other order of the court is necessary. [Rule 6(e) of the Federal Rules of Criminal Procedure provides in part: "Disclosure of matters occurring before the grand jury other than its deliberations and the vote of any juror may be made to the attorneys for the government for use in the performance of their duties. Otherwise, a juror [or] attorney . . . may disclose matters occurring before the grand jury only when so directed by the court. . . . No obligation of secrecy may be imposed upon any person except in accordance with this rule."]

3RD EDITOR: Is the reporter guilty of breaking Rule 6?

4TH JUDGE: Which reporter?

3RD EDITOR: The reporter who tries to solicit . . .

4TH JUDGE: The rule in its text does not cover recipient of any information.

3RD EDITOR: We've all examined that but as a conspirator, as an aider and abettor, as an . . .

2ND PROSECUTOR: Accomplice.

VOICE: Are you certain of that?

3RD EDITOR: It's never been tested has it?

5TH REPORTER: Criminal intent, sure.

4TH JUDGE: Well it has never been tested and let's just wait until we test it then. Now the second thing I want to say about this situation is that at least two-thirds of all the problems in this case of the grand jury and secrecy, gag orders, and the whole mess that the court, the prosecutor, and the press got into would have been avoided had this country done what England very sensibly did 40 years ago, and that is eliminate the grand jury. I know it was suggested a few minutes ago and it's an entirely sensible thing. You have a body of 23 persons in the federal system and to expect complete secrecy from 23 people over a period of weeks in an important case with the kind of inquisitive talent that we have in this room is inconceivable. So the English system, as it has been for 40 years, has a director of public prosecutions. He summons witnesses and hears testimony and he has no more problem preserving secrecy than the U.S. attorney has in preserving secrecy when he interviews witnesses in his office. There may be a problem, but it's certainly different from a grand jury problem.

MR. NESSON: Is there a defender of the grand jury in the room?

1ST PROSECUTOR: I want to defend the grand jury because I think the investigative function that it performs traditionally and currently is so vital that it should not be dispensed with. I'm speaking in terms of the inherent tools that the grand jury has that a prosecutor does not have—to subpoena documents, to subpoena witnesses under the threat of charges of perjury if the testimony is not truthful and under charges of contempt of the subpoena if the documents are not produced. Prosecutorial officials and the grand jury simply must have these tools to get at conspiratorial types, white-collar criminal offenses, corruption of political officials.

MR. NESSON: The judge is saying, why do we bother having these 23 dummies sitting around there.

4TH JUDGE: Well, in England that's all vested in the executive authority. You may say that's too much power, but I for one am not afraid of power being placed in hands, if they are responsible and accountable hands, and I think public prosecutors are.

5TH REPORTER: Accountable to the sovereign or accountable to the court?

MR. NESSON: Are what judge, are accountable?

4TH JUDGE: They are accountable and responsible public officials.

MR. NESSON: Is that an assertion of faith or experience or what?

4TH JUDGE: It's an assertion of experience and the function performed by the grand jury. The function performed by the grand jury is only the return of a charge. It's only the charge that's made by the grand jury and in many cases in our system now the defendant in many of these white-collar crime cases waives indictment by the grand jury and accepts criminal information filed by the U.S. attorney. But that's an optional process with the defendant. What I'm suggesting is that the grand jury is only a device for getting information which can be done by skilled investigative agencies. It's only a device for bringing the charge before the trial court and the trial jury--and should be replaced as it has been in England.

MR. NESSON: Judge, I'm just curious—to whom is the prosecutor accountable?

4TH JUDGE: First of all, he is accountable to his superiors in the Justice Department . . .

MR. NESSON: To wit, the attorney general?

4TH JUDGE: . . . and then as an officer of the court, he is accountable to the judge or judges before whom he appears, very definitely. For example, here under Rule 6, the secrecy of grand jury proceedings, boy the U.S. attorney had better pay attention to the attitude of the district judge on that rule.

MR. NESSON (Recognizes 2nd Prosecutor)

2ND PROSECUTOR: With respect to the grand jury, for a moment, let me say this to you. I would disagree with the judge most respectfully. I think an indictment has a devastating effect and we have seen that to be the case in most criminal cases.

MR. NESSON: That is on the proposition that it's only a charge?

2ND PROSECUTOR: That's correct. Indeed in most crimes of corruption or fraud, for all intents and purposes it results in the destruction of the man who is named in that climate case. Indeed, most of the action that a lawyer takes on behalf of a man in that case, that is, a white-collar crime case, is taken before the indictment because the realization comes to pass that once that indictment is returned, for all intents and purposes, an economic, psychological, and socio-logical individual is destroyed. His vitality is destroyed. Now with respect to the prosecutor's comment about the grand jury being necessary: There are many states in the United States that have what are called one-man grand juries. Sub-poena power is available and you don't need 23 people sitting around who act as nothing more than inactive auditors to a process that really, for all intents and purposes, has come under the prosecutor's control. The courts have abrogated their control of the grand jury for all intents and purposes.

MR. NESSON: Abrogated them to whom?

2ND PROSECUTOR: To the prosecutor.

MR. NESSON: Absolutely.

2ND PROSECUTOR: That's correct. Judges do not exercise any control over the grand jury. They don't read the minutes. They don't care what happens in the grand jury. They don't know about the abuses that go on in the grand jury. They're indifferent to those abuses. They're insensitive to them. I was a prosecutor and I know the way the grand jury functions probably better than anybody in this room. I can tell you that, for all intents and purposes, the sub-poena is used as an administrative process; the prosecutors calling people, using the court's process as their process.

MR. NESSON: All right, so now we come back on this occasion to the issue that's at hand; that is we have a statement by a prosecutor that, in fact, the grand jury is subject almost totally to the prosecutor's control. If you want to speak, would you speak to us all.

1ST TV REPORTER: I should quit while I'm behind but I just wanted to underline a point having taken that position, which I am sure shocked some people here of my willingness, although I have never done so, to go and talk to grand jury members, try to elicit information and thereby perhaps undermine the pillars upon which our society rests. What we now arrive at, having started a discussion, is a lot of people find other things wrong with the grand jury system and so perhaps the press serves another function in its constant testing and may perhaps begin to call attention in another way to an atrophied system and may have served some useful purpose in the course of doing that.

MR. NESSON: Indeed one of the things that we've both mentioned is the judge's statement that the prosecutor is indeed subject to control. All he's worried about is the secrecy aspect. As for the prosecutor's statement on the other hand, he's not subject to any real control. The whole thing is totally administrative. There's a large void in here and the question that seems to be before us . . .

4TH JUDGE: I think that what the second prosecutor said supported what I said . . .

2ND PROSECUTOR: That's true.

4TH JUDGE: . . . and having been a U.S. attorney and spent part of that time before some very large, lengthy proceedings before a grand jury, I know something about the problem there and how the process is used. Sure the process is administrative—to get your witness in— and the U.S. attorney one way or another more or less controls and directs the grand jury. That's as a practical matter. Since it is a practical situation, even though the grand jury is the arm of the court and the district court can assert authority if he wants to and is aware of what's going on, why not let the prosecutor do it and let everyone know who is issuing these subpoenas and who's pulling the witnesses in and who's doing the interrogating and it will be done in a much similar way as it is now and you won't have 23 other sources leaking.

MR. NESSON: Well our first TV reporter wants to put the question to you I think, if in fact the prosecutor is running the show is he not seriously accountable, that is, in a practical way . . .

4TH JUDGE: In a practical way he does run it, but indeed, he can be brought up short by his superiors in the department and he can . . .

MR. NESSON: If they find out about it.

4TH JUDGE: . . . be brought up short by the district judge . . .

MR. NESSON: If he finds out about it.

4TH JUDGE: . . . and in an important case such as the District of Columbia has had recently, the district judge stays on top of what's going on in the grand jury or he should, if he's doing his job.

2ND PROSECUTOR: But he doesn't stay on top as a practical matter. He doesn't and he is unaware of what's going on in the grand jury.

MR. NESSON: Hold on. (Recognizes 1st Reporter)

1ST REPORTER: In this particular case we've had one illustration of grand jurors reporting a potentially venal prosecutor. Now, we may not have that very often in the federal system. We have it damn often in the state systems.

4TH JUDGE: You'll find out another way if you've got a venal prosecutor. You'll find out another way and it won't take the grand juror . . .

1ST REPORTER: Well in Indianapolis you found it out by having reporters who were exposing police corruption indicted by a grand jury—by a prosecutor who went through three grand juries until he could find one that was willing to indict. That put that paper, those reporters, through a great deal of expense. The policemen never got indicted. The reporters did. That case got broken essentially because other grand jurors who had heard the evidence the first two times and had refused to indict because they thought it was a fraud went to the papers and told them about it.

4TH JUDGE: Well you'd have witnesses. In most cases and in intensive investigation you'd have a number of witnesses and they would be contacted by the . . .

1ST REPORTER: The witnesses to the corruption of the prosecutor were the grand jurors.

3RD TV REPORTER: The witnesses are not there when the prosecutor makes the recommendation to indict or not indict. I will confess that I have talked to grand jurors and would do it again in similar circumstances. We had a case where the prosecuting attorney was saying one thing publicly then going into the secrecy of the grand jury and recommending something just the opposite and coming out and saying, "My hands are clean. The citizens have acted through the grand jury, there's nothing I can do." Our newspaper wanted to find out what that guy was saying to the grand jury and I was assigned to find out and I did and I talked to grand jurors, I talked to everybody I could and we blew the whistle on the guy. It was a state court, but nevertheless . . .

4TH JUDGE: That's exactly what I mean by accountability. If you didn't have the grand jury the prosecutor would have to make the charge himself and take the responsibility for it and he couldn't lay it off on 23 other people. For goodness sakes, that's what I mean by accountability; what you do.

MR. NESSON (Recognizes 1st Judge): Judge?

1ST JUDGE: With respect to my colleague's views of the grand jury, I'm not sure how I would come out. I think there are a great many considerations to be advanced on the outside. There is, as has already been pointed out, not only the situation of the corrupt prosecutor but also the corrupt executive, and I should think all of us have sufficiently in mind a recent experience so that we know what we're talking about. There is a much earlier case which all of us will remember. Tom Dewey got his first national prominence from being appointed as a result of runaway grand juries in New York which revealed the corruption in

New York to such a point that Governor Lehman had no choice but to name a special prosecutor—Tom Dewey. The grand jury does serve as a very important agency when things are bad enough and if you do not have the grand jury doing this, may I as one who can be criticized for this say that you will have activist judges doing it. It may not be such a good idea to have activist judges whether their names begin with S or W. It may be much better to have grand juries performing the function. There is another consideration and the press, above all, ought to be concerned with this. There are times when the grand jury is still a protector of liberty. There is no one who has forgotten that in spite of the appearance of the great Mitchell, William D. Mitchell, as a special prosecutor before a grand jury in the case of the Chicago *Tribune,* the grand jury would not indict and the press was saved by the grand jury in that particular instance. Andrew Mellon is another person who can say that a grand jury stood athwart a prosecution which I think was at least partly political. Therefore, I am not at all sure that in the American climate of opinion the English model is the best. I'm only doubtful, I'm not sure that I disagree.

MR. NESSON: Judge, if those are your views, would you be in favor of more activist instructions by the presiding federal judge to the grand jury; telling them that they have an independent function and they should not . . .

1ST JUDGE: I'm not only in favor of it, I do it every time.

MR. NESSON (Turns to 4th Judge): Judge, how does that sound to you? That is, you are not the kept pets of the prosecutor, you have an independent function and . . .

4TH JUDGE: Why as U.S. attorney I heard those instructions to the grand jury every time one was convened. Every now and then during the course of their service the district judge would remind them of that and I looked upon the grand jury as a good sounding board. The greatest usefulness that I found with the grand jury was as a testing ground for the witnesses and the evidence. And except in one case in four years—and it was a very minor case but it was part of an epidemic of the type we had—I never pressed for an indictment that the grand jury was reluctant to return because if I couldn't get 12 out of 23 to vote an indictment, I would never get 12 out of 12 in the courtroom when it came to trial.

MR. NESSON (Calls upon 2nd Prosecutor): Do you think that you could write the instructions from the judge to the grand jury in such a way that they would be less subject to your control than they have been in the past?

2ND PROSECUTOR: You could write them so that they would be less subject to control but I think that the instructions would wear off as time passed. The problem here is the fact that in hundreds and hundreds of cases, thousands probably in the federal system, it is very rare and indeed unheard of in my experience for a grand jury to refuse to indict when the prosecutor says we will indict . . .

1ST JUDGE: Oh no.

2ND PROSECUTOR: . . . and indeed most prosecutors talk that way, federal prosecutors and state prosecutors. They say, "We're going to indict you and that's it," and they know they can get the indictment. Now, when you're dealing with common law offenses it may be that the grand jury will exercise some independent discretion, say in certain cases where there are sympathetic potential subjects of investigation of marginal people. But when you're dealing in complex areas of economic crime with very sophisticated principles of accomplice liability and conspiratorial liability where 90 percent of the lawyers involved don't really understand what the principles are and they're constantly shifting and the issues are still open to question, then the juries made up of laymen are inert. They rely on the prosecutor to determine whether they will prosecute or not and indictments are presented in final form to grand juries with the names in there. I have never heard of a situation yet in my experience where a grand jury refused to return that indictment once those counts were set forth and the names were in there.

MR. NESSON (Turns to 3rd Editor): Where do you suspect corruption in the prosecution? What are your guidelines for your reporters as to the extent they can go to in investigating what's going on in the grand jury?

3RD EDITOR: Well, they shift.

5TH REPORTER: Between editions.

3RD EDITOR: I think if the media had never come up against this until the Watergate case I would say that provided there is solid information that information is available that is not being presented, that witnesses are lying in front of the grand jury and no effort is being made to identify those lies, that where witnesses who should be called are not being called, I think the guidelines would be to explore how come and why these facts obtain.

MR. NESSON: Would you write stories in your paper to try to influence the outcome of the grand jury?

3RD EDITOR: I wouldn't write stories to that effect. I might solicit the cooperation of the editorial page to see whether an editorial calling for this would be appropriate.

MR. NESSON (Turns to 6th Editor): Would you write an editorial?

6TH EDITOR: I once did and I have regretted it ever since. The reason that I have so much trouble with all of this is that I think the harder case is not when you suspect there is a venal prosecutor but when you have fairly good reason to believe there is not one. I am thinking of the investigation of Vice-President Agnew. At that time, the press was in fact running stories on secret proceedings in the criminal investigation. We on the editorial page do not believe in the propriety of violating that secrecy. We take the rights of the defendant very seriously and believe in the right of the press to put it all in the paper and I was asked to rationalize all that. I don't want to be too immodest but I do think it was the most sanctimonious editorial that has ever appeared in my newspaper. We heard from Attorney General Richardson, oh I would say about 9:15 that morning, and he and I had a talk and I really found that I could not defend any better our position or rationalize it any more.

MR. NESSON: Tell us what the position was?

6TH EDITOR: The position was that Vice-President Agnew had been complaining like a wild thing and well he might. He is entitled to all of the protections. These are just charges that are being investigated. It is absolutely appalling that he is subjected to the unfairness of having all of this come out. Elliott Richardson and whoever is in charge should certainly take better security precautions to keep us out of it. Mr. Richardson said, and not without reason, "It's all very well for you to argue that. I should lock my drawers at night. I do. You people have 40 reporters crawling all over this thing, putting stuff together, talking to various people. I can't stop this and I can't stop it because of your journalistic enterprise and then I open the paper in the morning and you great civil libertarians on the editorial page are telling me that I am violating Agnew's right." The reason I'm not into this conversation before is that I am no better able to justify all of this now than I was two years ago. I just know better than to write editorials about it.

MR. NESSON (Turns to 5th Reporter): Take the Agnew case for example, an investigation of great public interest, would you take the position that there should be no secrecy with respect to the investigation?

5th REPORTER: I would separate the intentions and the ambitions and the hopes of those who are a part of the criminal justice process from the intentions and the hopes and the aspirations of those of us in the press. I would allow judges and attorneys and grand jurors to go as far as they like to protect their secrecy. By the same token, I would allow us to go as far as we could to breach that secrecy in every fact, every detail, every revelation that is even arguably or even remotely available to us. I do that for two reasons. One reason, most critical, is that I see two communities being served. One is the community of the machinery of criminal justice; that is, the machinery that indicts or fails to indict and where there's an indictment it prosecutes. That is a system closed, run by its own rules, has its own traditions and its own habits. There's a separate community and that is the community of the people of this country who watch how their criminal justice process works. They cannot watch that process through the handouts of the justice department, through the occasional opinions of judges or courts. They have to watch it through the common media—the broadcast media, the daily press, and the periodical press. It is our obligation to that larger community to tell them every damn thing we can tell them that will even remotely suggest to them that their system of criminal justice is or is not working. The rules are no different when the defendant is Spiro Agnew than when the defendant is Tony Russo. Every criminal process that goes forward in this country should be subjected to the robust, eager, if you will, institutionally threatening aggression of a reliable, informed, and eager press.

MR. NESSON (Recognizes 6th Judge)

6TH JUDGE: I think I agree almost precisely with what he has just said so far as the metes and bounds of the substantive law of the First Amendment of the Constitution are concerned. What he said is no more than reflected in somewhat more extreme and absolute terms as what was said earlier by others. But I began by saying I think I do, but where I would stop is in the extreme assertion that anything, any method would be available for him to carry out what he perceives to be, rightly I think, his mission as a reporter. I wouldn't say anything and I wonder if he would include bugging the grand jury room or would he include committing larceny.

MR. NESSON: How about bugging, would you go for that?

5TH REPORTER: Yes.

MR. NESSON: Larceny?

5TH REPORTER: Well again . . .

2ND GOV'T. OFFICIAL: Go all the way. Come on.

5TH REPORTER: No, no. I am prepared to go all the way with larceny if I am forced to make the concession that the theft of ideas and information that is in the possession of the government is theft.

1ST REPORTER: How about kidnapping a grand juror?

2ND EDITOR: What about deliberations of the Supreme Court.

6TH JUDGE: Well, I happen to think in my old-fashioned way that the secrecy of the deliberations of the Supreme Court is quite an important tradition to be observed and preserved but I think it's up to us to preserve it and I think a reporter has an absolute right through any legitimate activities he may wish to pursue, which might include inviting a justice out to lunch and trying to get him drunk, to pierce that and if he gets it, to publish it. To that extent I agree wholeheartedly with him but I don't think you have a right to violate the criminal law by bugging our conference room.

MR. NESSON: Well, let's take substance. We've got a difference on means and we've talked a lot about means here. The substance is really the fundamental issue. In our example, Ted Harris published the nonindictment of Senator Squires. He publishes the story saying that the grand jury considered indictment of Squires but then voted not to. Now how about that kind of a story?

6TH JUDGE: That story is all right if he got it the way he got it.

MR. NESSON: Character assassination by nonindictment?

6TH JUDGE: That story is all right. That's what the First Amendment is all about. It's a matter of substantive constitutional law in my view.

MR. NESSON: How does Squires defend himself from those noncharges?

6TH JUDGE: He's a public figure isn't he. He has access to the press himself, presumably.

MR. NESSON: Now we had an example recently with Erwin Griswold, described in the New York *Times* as having been nearly indicted for perjury. No problem with that as long as it was found out by legitimate means, no problem?

6TH JUDGE: Look now, I agree with what was said yesterday that what the Constitution permits is not necessarily and should not necessarily be the standard of what newspapers do. There are many, many other social forces at work in addition to the lowest level of what the Constitution will tolerate and when I say that the First Amendment permits something or protects something, it doesn't mean that as a matter of ethics or morality or taste or judgment I would say to a newspaper, yes, go ahead and do it and that includes even naming the victim of a rape.

MR. NESSON: Does this judge's proposition gather votes here?

5TH REPORTER: Yes.

MR. NESSON: Is there dissent?

1ST TV REPORTER: It does? I'd like to test it on a couple of things.

MR. NESSON: Is there dissent?

2ND GOV'T. OFFICIAL: Yes, there's a lot of dissent.

4TH LAWYER: I'm getting the impression that the judges think it is all right for a newspaper to turn loose its reporters on the grand jurists. If they talk, they talk. That is a legitimate activity.

6TH JUDGE: It seems to me so.

3RD EDITOR: One judge called it a violation of the law and so has the second prosecutor.

4TH JUDGE: Wait just a minute. It's a violation of the law for the juror. You asked me the question as to whether the reporter was in violation of the law and someone said it hadn't been tested yet and I said wait until it's tested.

3RD EDITOR: Well I thought there was a chorus of aiding and abetting and conspiracy.

4TH JUDGE: That wasn't my voice in the chorus.

3RD EDITOR: I see.

2ND PROSECUTOR: It has been tested.

MR. NESSON: Let me get some of the observers. (Recognizes 2nd Lawyer)

2ND LAWYER: I think many of the dilemmas that we're faced with might be solved short of abolishing the grand jury system by changing the secrecy rules. Maybe secrecy shouldn't be the rule in the grand jury. It ought to be the exception, particularly in cases of investigation of public corruption.

MR. NESSON: The gentleman way in the back of the room. I'm sorry I don't know your name. Yes, you looking around, your views on this.

5TH LAWYER: I'm a little concerned about the press's attitude that they can go unfettered after grand jurors in any respect. I don't agree with the reporter who asserts certainly that he can bug the grand juries. On the other hand, I wonder if the federal judiciary in many instances hasn't gone too far to protect the grand jury system, as it were the grand jurors. I think we've had some rather tough orders issued around the country by federal courts against grand jurors and their contact with reporters. If I were a reporter, I'd still today be very frightened to contact a grand juror and have the prosecutor and the judge find out about it.

MR. NESSON (Recognizes 6th Reporter)

6TH REPORTER: I don't understand the suggestion of eliminating the secrecy of the grand jury. It seems to me you'd have to introduce the rules of evidence into the grand jury proceeding. What would you do to prevent the release of that secrecy? Hearsay is routinely introduced into grand jury proceedings. There are no lawyers present to protect those people who are being questioned. They are completely at the mercy of the prosecutor. I'd be awfully worried about something as basic as that and I can't believe that my reporter colleague really means that in any grand jury investigation he would feel free to go and camp on a juror's door. We're only talking about grand jury proceedings . . .

MR. NESSON: Well that's the usual way he operates. I think that he is asserting that he's our bad man; that is, he's saying, "I will bug him if I can get away with it. I'm going to make a utility calculation as to whether I can get away with it but ethically, morally I am a reporter and I'm going to do it to the maximum I can." As I take it, that's the position he's asserted.

5TH REPORTER: Professor Nesson, I would remind everybody that there is in this country an established press and there is also a vigilante press and the vigilante press is covered by the First Amendment, too. When you're stating arguments here, it seems to me that each one of us is obliged to state the outer limits of the arguments so that people can know how far it might go. If you're talking about matters of larceny, of kidnapping grand jurors, and so on, I think you have to understand that there may well be elements of the press in this country which will do things that are not exactly nice or reasonable. I want it clearly understood that I would hope that the kind of ethical sensitivities which I observe in my reporting and which as an editor I insisted upon my reporters observing are not universally obeyed or observed or even well known. I want to be very clear that I think we do have standards in this profession but just as clear that there are going to be people who do breach those standards and constitutionally, bless them.

MR. NESSON (Recognizes 7th Editor)

7TH EDITOR: The concepts that our enthusiastic reporter has been promoting seem to me equivalent to what the economists do when they construct economic man, who responds absolutely and totally to all the demands of the marketplace, 100 percent. What he has constructed is reportorial man, who has nothing else in life except a duty like a searchlight and we are flesh and blood. We are citizens. We are husbands. We are wives. We are all other things and to say that we would bug, I think this is a construction and a distortion of our function similar to the way the economists have constructed this man that doesn't exist and yet in all the theoretical procedures you run into economic man in all your economics courses. We don't respond this way. We have other duties and other things. During the course of a major, recent investigation we had our sources inside the grand jury like everybody else and I was summoned to a meeting with a prosecutor, a member of the staff. It was a harried, pressured meeting in which I wasn't threatened but what was put to me was a proposition that if we continued, people would go to jail; not only that but this whole important prosecution would go down the tube because it would be all upset, because of leaks. I took it back to the reporters in the office who had security leaks and after consulting with our lawyers I laid it out for the reporters and the answer that came back was, that's an important factor but the most important factor for discontinuing right now is the source is drying up. But it was a factor. We weighed a lot of things. It wasn't simply reportorial men and women at work. There were a lot of things in the decision-making process to cease our contacts with said source.

MR. NESSON: I'd like to move on. I'm sorry we're pressed for time. Let's suppose we have some consensus here of attitudes toward reporters talking to grand jurors. Now let's suppose our TV reporter has spoken to that grand juror and has indeed gotten a good deal of information from him. In a situation where you suspect corruption of the grand jury, just to make it as solid as we can, you're then subpoenaed before a grand jury by this same prosecutor and asked who your source was. How do you respond to that?

1ST TV REPORTER: I can't tell you. If you didn't raise that I would have. It's precisely the problem. You can say we have a deep division now and there seems to be some consensus that you preserve your secrecy, whereas we try to breach the secrecy. Unfortunately, however, you call me in and say, "All right, we don't want to do anything to you but we do want to know which grand juror talked to you because him we've got to get . . ."

MR. NESSON: Exactly.

1ST TV REPORTER: ". . . and you tell me who he is. That's all we're asking. You go scott free but we want him and under a recent Supreme Court dictate if you refuse, you can go to jail."

MR. NESSON: Exactly. Let me ask you this. Would you consider pleading the Fifth Amendment?

1ST TV REPORTER: Would I consider pleading the Fifth Amendment? It would be an improper use, wouldn't it?

MR. NESSON: No, not a bit.

1ST PROSECUTOR: You should because you are possibly criminally involved with that grand juror by reason of your relationship to him.

1ST TV REPORTER: On advice of counsel, I'd plead the Fifth Amendment.

3RD LAWYER: Would he get immunity?

MR. NESSON: Then we plea bargain.

VOICE: And then they give him immunity.

MR. NESSON (Turns to 3rd Editor): As his editor, do you have any problems for your paper in having one of your reporters take the Fifth?

3RD EDITOR: I don't think ultimately if you were really in effect taking the First by citing the Fifth . . .

MR. NESSON: No, he's taking the Fifth.

3RD EDITOR: . . . in this case I would not. There are times when taking the Fifth Amendment by a reporter . . . I mean I can imagine circumstances having nothing to do with the First Amendment where a reporter taking the Fifth Amendment would give me a hell of a lot of problems.

MR. NESSON: What problems?

3RD EDITOR: Well, if he bugged the grand jury, I would urge him to take the Fifth as far as his counsel but his future at my newspaper would be cloudy.

FORMER BROADCASTER: Don't you believe in the Fifth Amendment?

3RD EDITOR: I believe very strongly in it but I don't . . .

FORMER BROADCASTER: But you'd fire the guy.

3RD EDITOR: I didn't say that; cloudy future.

MR. NESSON: Anybody here have a problem with a reporter or editor taking the Fifth Amendment just on the basis of somehow obtaining . . .

8TH EDITOR: Well, I think there's a problem there because most newspapers like to regard themselves as good citizens and a good citizen, theoretically, is law abiding. Therefore, you would have some hesitation about confessing in court that the implication was you had committed a crime and you didn't want to disclose it. There would be that emotional problem. I don't think it's a serious legal problem, probably.

MR. NESSON: That's exactly what my point is about; that is, I don't think there is a serious legal problem but I am curious as to whether your feelings, emotional feelings, given the history and tradition of the Fifth Amendment over the last, say, 30 years really worries the newspapermen in the room.

4TH EDITOR: Given a choice, it seems preferable to take the First rather than the Fifth; the confidentiality of sources. And why go for the Fifth under any circumstances?

MR. NESSON: Suppose your counsel tells you that we've tried that one and that one didn't work.

4TH EDITOR: I'm not sure the battle is finished.

MR. NESSON: What does it take for you? Are you going to set yourself up the way Governor Faubus was pictured and the people in Boston denying the validity of our highest court and bring us to anarchy because you think the . . .

4TH EDITOR: Oh, I think the climate might change in five years.

1ST TV REPORTER: But I'm going to be in jail. (Laughter)

4TH EDITOR (To 1st TV Reporter): I thought it was the mark of an American reporter's integrity to go to jail on that issue.

1ST TV REPORTER: If absolutely necessary but not to seek it.

4TH EDITOR: Well then you would take the Fifth?

1ST TV REPORTER: This is a practical matter to me. I must protect my sources. I will protect my sources.

5TH REPORTER: Absolutely.

1ST TV REPORTER: I don't like the idea of going to jail. My family likes it less. I have legal means hoping to avoid this confrontation and if the Fifth is one of the legal means why should I not avail myself of it?

5TH REPORTER: That's right.

6TH REPORTER: In the end it's not going to do you any good because they're going to give you immunity and say talk.

VOICE: That's right.

1ST TV REPORTER: Well, then, I'll go to jail.

MR. NESSON: Well let's wait a second. (Turns to 1st Judge): Judge, this supposedly corrupt prosecutor comes before you for a grant of immunity, does he not?

1ST JUDGE: Yes.

MR. NESSON: He doesn't issue it on his own. Do you have any discretion as far as granting immunity? Would you listen to . . .

1ST JUDGE: I don't think I have complete discretion. I have to have some basis other than I don't like what's going on.

MR. NESSON: Suppose he makes the argument to you that he's trying to expose a corrupt prosecutor. In fact, the very fellow who's trying to shut up his sources. Would you consider refusing to grant immunity in that case?

1ST JUDGE: I answer honestly by saying I really don't know what I would do.

MR. NESSON (Turns to 2nd Judge): Judge?

2ND JUDGE: I don't have any difficulty with it, Professor, but just give me two minutes if you will . . .

VARIOUS VOICES: Which way?

2ND JUDGE: . . . and I'll tell you that too. I went away from here yesterday intimidated. This morning I've been embarrassed and I refuse to go away frustrated.

MR. NESSON: I apologize for the first two.

2ND JUDGE: That's all right. My contribution to the news media will be to send them copies of *Marbury v. Madison* [Cranch 137 (1803), in which the Supreme Court initially articulated the doctrine of judicial review]. That will be my contribution. The law is the law and reporters have no license to violate it and as to the immunity, in my circuit if the prosecutor has gone through all of the procedural matters I don't think I have any choice but to give the immunity. I might suggest that the next time we have this program the title ought to be changed to Media or the Law because it frightens me when people talk about violating the law. I'm really disturbed that anybody has any hesitancy about agreeing that if you don't like it, change it. But until you change it, you have to obey it. Now in answer to the immunity, I've already given it. I'd give it.

MR. NESSON: You'd give it?

2ND JUDGE: Absolutely.

1ST JUDGE: Since you put the question to me first, I'd like to address the question. That is, how would you react to this proposition: As district judge you might really like to get a ruling from a higher court on this matter and the only way you could get it would be by refusing the prosecutor and thus putting the matter before an appellate court on appeal of abuse of discretion. If you granted it, you couldn't get an effective review.

2ND JUDGE: Well the difficulty is that I may not always agree with what my appellate court says but I try to follow it and I don't think I have any choice but to follow it and I think in my circuit I would have no choice but to give the immunity.

1ST JUDGE: Even in this case which has never arisen?

2ND JUDGE: And the chief of the appellate court will not let me call him on the phone and chat with him before I make rulings and I wouldn't do it. I've wanted to many times like the reporter who took a Supreme Court Justice out to lunch, I'd like to do it but I think I'd be unsuccessful. Really I wouldn't want to do it. It's my responsibility and I'd call it, period. That's what judges are for.

6TH JUDGE: Professor, I wonder if everybody is clear in the room what the judge means when he says he would grant immunity and what the consequences of that would be? I think it's quite important.

2ND JUDGE: The consequences?

6TH JUDGE: Yes, after you've granted immunity then what would happen?

2ND JUDGE: Well, he's got to answer the question. If he doesn't, he goes to jail, period.

6TH JUDGE: Right.

2ND JUDGE: It's as simple as that.

6TH JUDGE: Right.

2ND JUDGE: I would dislike it very much and I would send the reporter cigarettes. I'd utilize the provision to let him turn himself in. I wouldn't even have the marshall take him. I'd just say, "Report to the marshall at 9:00 tomorrow morning," and I think he would and all the children would come by and say goodbye dad.

1ST JUDGE: Don't you think that the question is open enough so that you cannot feel wholly confident of how the Supreme Court of the United States would answer this question regardless of what you think of your circuit?

2ND JUDGE: Well, I think very highly of my circuit.

1ST JUDGE: No, no, but I'm leaving that out. Do you feel confident how the Supreme Court would answer this question?

2ND JUDGE: Yes, yes. I'm one of the lucky district judges, Judge.

1ST JUDGE: You have confidence in the Supreme Court?

2ND JUDGE: Well now, I'm one of the lucky district judges. I'm not always right but I've never made a decision that I thought was wrong and from that point on it's their responsibility and they assume it.

1ST JUDGE: I'm fortunate, too, from a position that I've often made decisions that were wrong, which I knew might be wrong but which I wasn't quite sure about. I thought the best thing to do was to put it before the Supreme Court. I think it's part of my responsibility to get difficult questions over the threshold regardless of whether I get reversed or criticized.

2ND JUDGE: Then you might just as well take a vote of everybody in the courtroom. No, I disagree with you. That's not my way of doing it.

5TH JUDGE: I think a very important question has been raised as to what a utility of this conference might be. It's been raised some times before. In order to prevent the most head-on collision of press or law, part of the process has to be reshaping the rules of action of the courts and make them go faster and make them go more attentively to the needs of the press. A judge mentioned before that appellate courts can meet in one day. I don't know why that shouldn't be the rule when there's a gag order or two days; something a little bit more realistic perhaps, but I think it should be the rule. The rules should be changed to require that in two days after a gag order has appeared it expires unless the appellate court affirms it. It just automatically expires; cannot be enforced unless the appellate court affirms it. I think the very least we have to do is to accommodate ourselves to very serious demands—points the press has put forward for the judges to shape up and do something different from routine. To some extent another judge here does that by suggesting he might take certain action to get an appellate ruling. But there is a great protection in an appellate ruling as contrasted with the trial judge's ruling. There are great difficulties with it, but there is the protection that it is not caught up in the fervor of the instant case and a certain amount of excitement, that it has the advantage of the collegial discussion. I don't know what the implications of it are but I believe that they must be thought through on procedures at every step of the way. As I said yesterday, I cannot tolerate a rule that the press is going to be the judge of its own cause any more than the president can be the judge of his own privilege. But I think that they show a very important reason why their privileges should not be encroached except in case of necessity. I think that necessities have to be limited. I think it has to be reexamined quickly and by a different group than those who impose it. I think that the question of immunity, quite contrary to what my judge-colleague here says, is the assumption that a prosecutor's request is a bona fide request. If the judge has some reason to believe that it's not bona fide, I don't know why he doesn't have a duty to look into the matter rather than to rubber stamp it. I'm not sure that it ought to be that you have to deny the immunity to get an appellate court ruling. It may be that when you grant an immunity and it's a newspaper, that there ought to be an appellate review on the prerogative writ and fast. All of these things are possible with some accommodation of our rules. I think they're possible even without changes of statutes or rules. They're just possible by evolution of appellate doctrine if the courts are sensitive to the problems that this conference raises. I myself will go away from this more sensitized than I was when I arrived Friday and think that there may be rules that do make a difference and that can be set forward. I don't think they require earth-shaking developments. If I felt like my other colleagues maybe I'd say I'd deny it so that it could be tested or maybe if I were in an apellate court I'd accept an invitation to review a grant. In any case, at every step of the line we have to go back to the drawing boards to think of different rules so that the courts don't engage in unnecessary intrusions or one-man intrusions. Now in the particular case of the corrupt prosecutor, I don't know why the courts have to say that if anybody refuses to answer questions and the prosecutor wants them answered that's the end of the matter whether the statute says so or not. I think it's implicit that that grant of immunity is obtainable only by prosecutors acting in good faith. If someone makes a colorable showing that this is not good faith, this is excessive, I believe the district judge has the responsibility to look into the matter.

MR. NESSON: Let me address a question if I may to the press lawyers in the room. I take it you gentlemen have probably looked at the Branzburg decision more carefully than most. Do you take that cáse as a flat elimination of the newspaperman's source of privilege?

4TH LAWYER: No, and indeed there have been decisions subsequent to Branzburg in other circumstances in which the privilege has been upheld—in the civil area, in libel suits, in suits where the press was the third party witness. Moreover, I think Branzburg can be read as a case in which you had three reporters who were witnesses to crimes; one of whom at least refused to even go into the grand jury room; none of whom, incidentally, have ever been called by the jurisdictions that started the case to answer the questions and identify the sources that the court said they could be ordered to identify. Two of those three have walked in and out of the jurisdictions in which those questions were originally raised.

MR. NESSON: But that's irrelevant. You're saying there is a distinction because they witnessed crimes?

4TH LAWYER: I think there are several distinctions.

MR. NESSON: Name another.

4TH LAWYER: That's one of them. I think we do now have some law in the circuit courts which says—well, a reporter wrote a story about blockbusting, if you will, which was an offense under state law as I recall it. Al Balk, the reporter, was called to testify and identify the man about whom he wrote the story and refused. I believe in New York the Second Circuit there said he doesn't have to. He's got a privilege. He can protect that source. There are cases in which sources . . .

MR. NESSON: What rationale?

4TH LAWYER: Their rationale was that his First Amendment rights if you will, his case . . .

MR. NESSON: Then why isn't that clear in Branzburg?

4TH LAWYER: Branzburg, quite frankly, as was previously said, was decided 4½ to 4½.

FORMER BROADCASTER: I stole that from Jim Goodale, who has a piece in the Hastings Law Review and I'm going to send everyone Goodale's piece on 4½ to 4½ because I plagiarized it from him.

MR. NESSON (Calls on 6th Lawyer): I see your hand up.

6TH LAWYER: Some of us had a full day before Judge Richey on the application of the Committee to Re-Elect the President, who had sought to subpoena the press for their sources. We successfully distinguished Branzburg at that time on the civil ground, the blockbuster case referred to, and it really comes down to the balancing case, the balancing problem. We'd have no need for this kind of colloquy if there were the absolute position that has been contended for and that Mr. Justice Black opined but it has never commanded five votes on the Supreme Court of the United States. So we have a balancing test in each of these and the 4½ to 4½ Branzburg case in the grand jury context leaves a great deal of room in the balancing test in other areas.

MR. NESSON: Would you explain to me why it's 4½ to 4½?

6TH LAWYER: The pivotal concurring opinion of Mr. Justice Powell which seeks to put some limitations, not really spelled out, but it's not a clear five to four in all cases every time.

MR. NESSON: What limitations does he suggest?

6TH LAWYER: Well, I did not do all of my homework to reread that page and a half before I came down.

MR. NESSON (Asks someone to help)

1ST LAWYER: Well, let me just say I'm not sure it is 4½ to 4½. I think in some respects you have to look at it as five to four in favor of the press. The reason I say that is once Justice Powell admits there are certain situations in which he would vote with the four dissenters, in those situations there has to be a qualified privilege. So I think what the court really did by counting noses was adopt the qualified privilege in that case.

MR. NESSON: What situations?

1ST LAWYER: Well, first of all not the situation of witnessing a crime. Secondly, in those situations where a test that can be distilled out of the Powell decision and the other four would apply to permit a reporter not to testify. I happen to think that it is in fact Mr. Justice Stewart's test and that Powell's point of view is not that far removed, though I'm not sure that Mr. Powell might characterize his own opinion like that at this moment. It seems to me inevitable if another case goes before the Supreme Court that Mr. Powell will be forced, if he's consistent with the position he took in that case, to so characterize it.

MR. NESSON: Suppose Mr. Harris asserted source privilege in our case here. Where does he fit on your reading?

1ST LAWYER: Well, it seems to me that upon the test that Mr. Justice Stewart announced that there are alternate sources of information for finding out the information that the court wants in that case.

MR. NESSON: In other words, he would have a privilege?

1ST LAWYER: That is correct.

MR. NESSON (Calls on 7th Lawyer)

7TH LAWYER: I'd just like to add that Mr. Justice Powell has spoken again since his concurring opinion in the Branzburg case in his dissenting opinion from Mr. Justice Stewart's majority opinion in the Washington *Post,* Saxbe case, which involved access to prisons. [*Saxbe v. The Washington Post Co.,* 417 U.S. 843 (1974), in which the Supreme Court held that the press has no First Amendment right to interview inmates in federal prisons.] He emphasized again quite how narrowly he intended his opinion to be read. Moreover, we have had within the last year Supreme Court decisions out of two states, Virginia and Vermont, in criminal cases in which a privilege, a qualified First Amendment privilege, was recognized by those Supreme Courts after reading Branzburg and after their understanding of Branzburg, even in criminal cases in circumstances in which there were alternative sources and which the need for the information was not all that essential. So the Branzburg battle is by no means over. Entirely apart from what the vote was on the Supreme Court, there are many issues in this area that remain open even up to the issue of how to phrase generally what the law is in this area. One knows, for example, that there are differences between civil and criminal cases, but one cannot say that indeed these two cases I've just referred to indicate that even in criminal cases, as Judge [Irving R.] Kaufman indicated in the Second Circuit [*Baker v. F & F Investment Co.,* 470 F.2d 778 (1972)], even there there will be cases in which a journalist's privilege, so to speak, is recognized. So you may not have to rely on the Fifth Amendment but I can't tell you that the First Amendment is going to necessarily win for our first TV reporter if he gets to court.

MR. NESSON: So that the Supreme Court might see another case?

7TH LAWYER: Well it might. I'd just like to add a line. I'd just like to respond to some of the judges who have expressed some concern at the attitude of some of the members of the press here because I think this question is at an appropriate time. It seems to me that what must be recognized is that every time a reporter is called to testify, he is on the brink of going to jail. Every single time a reporter goes to court or is subpoenaed in the small cases in little counties around this country, there is a risk of jail because of what the reporters maybe wrongly understand to be their First Amendment rights and their obligations, indeed, under the First Amendment. So it is not paranoia and it is not arrogance that leads reporters and even their lawyers now and then to sound a little bit odd to judges who are used to listening to lawyers talk in different tones of voice. It is that there is an ever-present personal risk for these people on a rather frequent basis.

MR. NESSON (Calls on Columnist): Can I ask you impromptu to speak some benediction on this meeting?

COLUMNIST: Unexpected to say the least. Well I have to tell you that I felt a certain sympathy with the judge's rather dramatic statement, "It frightens me when people talk about violating the law," because it frightens me also. If I may carry the example of the bussing situation in Boston just one step further, I think if the Boston *Globe* were to announce as a principle that it was not going to obey a gag order because it thought the order was wrong, I think the people in South Boston who oppose bussing would quite understandably and rightly say, "Then why can't we disobey the orders of Judge Garrity in the bussing situation?" They wouldn't see this distinction that was attempted to be drawn between throwing stones and writing words; a distinction which, in my opinion, does not exist in terms of the practical effects on the enforcement of law and respect for the law in which this country is not overabundant. I think if the press generally were to adopt the attitude that the law is not for us, it has nothing to do with us, I think it would be terrible for everybody in this country. That's rather an emotional statement. You caught me unawares but I believe it. Now, frankly, I don't think that is the attitude of the press and I think we've seen here a good deal of exaggeration. Perhaps it could be put under the heading of machismo. We're all trying to show how tough we are in the press. We're going to bug the grand jury room. We're going to disobey court orders. Now, in fact, I don't think people feel that way or will in reality act that way. One editor earlier talking about the attitude toward grand juries put it very fairly of what the press will in fact do. It won't as a rule bug grand jury rooms or hound grand jurors or assign people to surround the grand jury room. It will do so only when there is some reason to suspect that the judicial process of law has been corrupted or is not working and I think that's a rule that will be followed and should be followed. I have another point which perhaps is related to this. I think there are questions of priorities and values here and I'm saying all of this from the point of view of the press; that the press has to take account of. First of all, I think the press has to recognize that there are some interests in life other than the First Amendment and the rights of the press, important as those are. One of those interests we talked about yesterday—the ordinary citizen's felt need to make himself whole for a defamation. Another is the right to fair trial. Another is the integrity of the judicial process. I only say that I think we have to at least recognize that some people think those have some value. Finally, not quite finally, I'm sorry, it's a little long, but two more points. In this list of values I think it's important to recognize that the primary role of the press is vis-a-vis the centralized power of government. I think we waste our ammunition if we work ourselves up into a great virago about libel cases from the ordinary Joe Citizen when the real danger that the press is here to fight against is the centralized power of government, especially in the national security area. Let's save ourselves to fight the Pentagon Papers case; let's save ourselves to fight for the right, as I believe it to be, of individuals in the government who see a policy go wrong, their right to print a book about it. Let's fight those big, important issues and not just work ourselves up over less important ones. Just the final point, again coming back to the issue of compliance with law, you asked long ago at the beginning when we were discussing Dickinson, why should there be that special respect for a judicial order? Well, it is a hard question because it looks a little illogical, but any system has to have final authority somewhere. Otherwise we're going to have a kind of politicized system in which the person who can work up the most marchers or the most protest or the most sympathy is going to win. We, as was suggested with Marbury, put our bet on judges. A lot of times they've been wrong. There have been reactionary judges. They've handed down the Dred Scott decision [*Scott v. Sandford,* 19 How. 393 (1856), in which the Court held that slaves were not citizens within the meaning of the Constitution] , did other things I don't like, but if we want our judges to be able to take on presidents and tell Congress when it does something unconstitutional, I think we have to respect them all the time.

MR. NESSON: Thank you all very much.

JOSEPH A. CALIFANO, JR. is an attorney in Washington, D.C., and a writer, with wide government experience. After graduating from the Harvard Law School, where he was an editor of the *Harvard Law Review,* Mr. Califano practiced law in New York City from late 1958 until he joined the Kennedy administration in April 1961. Beginning as one of Secretary McNamara's whiz kids in the Defense Department, he served as Special Assistant to the Secretary of the Army, General Counsel of the Army, and Secretary McNamara's Special Assistant and top troubleshooter. In 1965 he was appointed Special Assistant for Domestic Affairs to President Lyndon B. Johnson.

Since leaving the government in early 1969, Mr. Califano has been practicing law in Washington, D.C. For the past several years, a large part of that practice involved First Amendment issues on behalf of the Washington *Post* and other publications.

Mr. Califano is the author of *The Student Revolution: A Global Confrontation* (New York: W.W. Norton & Co., 1969) and *A Presidential Nation* (New York: W.W. Norton & Co., 1975) and he has written numerous articles that have appeared in the Washington *Post,* the *New Republic,* and the Op-Ed page of the New York *Times.* He was General Counsel to the Democratic party from 1970 to 1972.

HOWARD SIMONS is managing editor of the Washington *Post.* Before taking on his pressure-cooker job in 1971, Simons had spent 10 years at the *Post* as science reporter, assistant managing editor, and deputy managing editor. In 1962 and again in 1964 he won the Westinghouse Award for the best science writing in the United States, from the American Association for the Advancement of Science. In 1966 he won the Raymond Clapper Award for the best Washington reporting.

A graduate of Union College, Mr. Simons was awarded his M.S. from the Columbia University School of Journalism in 1952. From 1954 to 1956 he studied Russian Studies at Georgetown University.

Mr. Simons joined Science Service in Washington in 1954 as a reporter and later became its editor. He was a Nieman Fellow at Harvard University during the 1958-59 academic year. Union College gave him an honorary D. Litt. in 1973, and in 1974 he received an alumni award from Columbia University Graduate School of Journalism.

COMMUNICATIONS TECHNOLOGY AND
DEMOCRATIC PARTICIPATION
Kenneth C. Laudon

*FREEDOM OF THE PRESS VS. PUBLIC ACCESS
Benno C. Schmidt, Jr.

*MASS COMMUNICATION RESEARCH: Major Issues
and Future Directions
edited by
W. Phillips Davison
Frederick T.C. Yu

MUNICIPAL CONTROL OF CABLE COMMUNICATIONS
Robert E. Jacobson

POLITICS IN PUBLIC SERVICE ADVERTISING
ON TELEVISION
David L. Paletz
Robert E. Pearson
Donald L. Willis

PUBLIC BROADCASTING: The Role of the Federal
Government, 1912-76
George H. Gibson

TELEVISION IN THE CORPORATE INTEREST
Richard Bunce

*Also available in paperback as a PSS Student Edition.